A Musician's Guide to TIME

(possible ways to appreciate, discuss, and manipulate time in music)

Rosemary Mountain

All rights reserved.

A MUSICIAN'S GUIDE TO TIME.

First edition February 2022.

Copyright © 2022 Rosemary Mountain.

Cover art and all illustrations by the author.

ISBN: 978-1-7774836-3-0 [paperback]

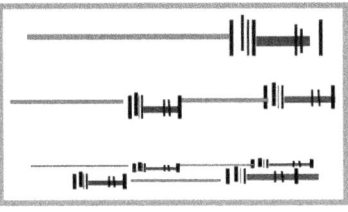

A Musician's Guide to Time

Table of Contents

Preface		iv

I - Introduction

1.	Realities & illusions	2
2.	Challenges to exploring time in music	7
3.	Calendars and calipers	10
4.	An illustrative story	12

II - Typical Perspectives on Time

5.	Time as a continuum: duration *vs.* succession	17
6.	Chronological time: clocks & calendars	20
7.	Cyclic *vs.* linear focus	22
8.	Linear views of time: arrows, rivers & narratives	24
9.	Other models: growth & decay, evolving time	28

III - Human Perception of Time

10.	Psychological / experiential time	33
11.	Movement & change; temporal focus & the "now"	34
12.	Memory & retrieval; parsing; familiarity	37
13.	Heartbeat & drumbeat; body rhythms & internal clocks; entrainment	41
14.	Contemplative time / dream time / art time / timelessness	42
15.	Impact of health, training, personality, culture, clan	44

IV - Interactions of Human and External Time

16. Synchronizing with the community ... 47
17. Human time, historical time ... 47
18. Multiplicities, non-linearity, chaos ... 49
19. Environment and expectations ... 51
20. The role of time in art and literature ... 51

V - Time in Music

21. Time in musical contexts - introduction ... 55
22. Influences of the auditory system ... 65
23. Activity bands and musical functions ... 70
24. General models of time in musical contexts ... 84
25. Influences of the listener's profile ... 98
26. Temporal design & its reception ... 105
27. Creation / perception of illusions in music ... 115
28. Clock time and music performance ... 121
29. Different uses, different concerns ... 124

VI - Concluding thoughts

30. Time theft and our revenge ... 136
31. Gears, mosaics, and waving tendrils ... 138
32. Temporal focus & further speculations ... 145

Appendix A – Sketches for a resource tool ... 151

Appendix B – Topics, perspectives & keywords; temporal measuring ... 154

Appendix C – Some classic & innovative treatments of time in music ... 164

Appendix D – List of figures; notes on illustrations ... 178

Bibliography ... 182

Preface

This book summarizes many years of personal reflections on the subject of time – especially time in music – from both observation and research. It is not designed to be a definitive overview of current research on the subject, but more as a talk to real and imaginary students and colleagues in music and all the cognate areas I have been discovering. My motivation has been simply a fascination with the impact of time on music itself, and wondering how I might learn to design appealing temporal shapes and structures. Increasingly, however, I have realized that much discourse about music (whether aesthetics, analysis, neuroscience, or film soundtracks) would benefit from recognizing the behaviour of time in different contexts. Therefore, I have been emboldened to articulate my own observations and outline some perspectives that have helped me think about the subject. My main objective is to introduce "time" in a practical way, as the main medium in which musicians work. My secondary objective is to stimulate a bit more reflection and conversation on various aspects of time in music and life so that more musicians and other interested parties will feel at ease thinking about and discussing temporal aspects of music as such. As some notable composers in the 20th century chose to think and talk about various intersections of music and time, it also seems that an appreciation of their methods and writings would become heightened if talk about time were more central to teachings in music. Moreover, I believe that musicians can provide significant input into research about our perception of time in general – but that implies that at least some of us need to examine and refine suitable terms and concepts for interdisciplinary discourse.

My own investigations were conducted in a typical artist's manner: I listened to music and played music, and gradually tried to discover and articulate why I found some rhythmic patterns and formal designs so much more exciting than others. It seemed oddly difficult to express these simple aspects, so I beganlistening to, reading, and talking with other composers, performers, artists, and the occasional philosopher and psychologist. In addition, I began reflecting on the human experience of time, and time in other art forms, and what aspects of music might affect it - or be affected by it. (I was also intrigued with both historical issues of the rise and fall of different civilizations, as well as with human memory, and clocks, and calendars, but did not appreciate the connections until much later.) Eventually, as I struggled to find adequate tools for rhythmic analysis, I embarked on a more rigorous investigation within a Ph.D. programme, and immersed myself in music psychology research (especially auditory and temporal perception), along with more extensive readings of composers' and theorists' writings (especially dealing with meter, rhythm, and large-scale form), more conversations with other artists, and a few cursory and erratic forays into philosophical material. I then continued my investigation through continued experiments in my own compositions, playing with different elements that I suspected would influence the listener's perception of time in certain ways.

Therefore, this book is best appreciated as the personal observations of an artist. Although I have worked hard to organize the book in a reasonably logical manner, for the reader's sake, it must be stressed that my perspectives and priorities may well be driven by often-unacknowledged biases and random interests. As I have explained in a companion book, *Conversational Musicology*, such idiosyncratic organization enables non-specialists to discuss topics that are often considered 'off-limits', or to allow specialists to muse out loud before they commit themselves to a particular stance (and in the context of art research, do we really need to commit to one?).

Much of my background research for this book has been presented previously in articles, conferences, or lectures; the current book is designed to present my findings in a more accessible and navigable format and update a few of my terms and concepts. However, in broadening my searches into cognate fields and working to synthesize all I learned, I have inevitably missed out on some of the more obscure and most of the more recent scholarly contributions within the mainstream music world, so I will trust my readers to supplement my observations with others under-represented here. In addition, as I have read or at least scanned many more books and articles than appear in my bibliography, it is beyond the scope of this book to give a detailed critique of them all, so I have retained only those that I remember as being particularly influential on my explorations. Likewise, I have included almost no scores – partly because so many of my influences are in music which is not notated, partly because I would prefer not to exclude researchers who are not sufficiently at ease with complex scores, and mainly because it would require another couple of volumes[1]. However, at the moment I prefer to return to my own creative work, where I hope to be more articulate about the nuances of time-flows that can be represented in sound.

The first part of the book (Sections I to IV) discusses general issues of time: typical perspectives and metaphors; human perception of time, including memory and body time, and the factors that influence them; time in our communities, environments, and forms of cultural expression. The second part of the book (V) deals more specifically with music, especially compositional design and its interpretation and reception, and those factors which may directly or indirectly influence the listener's sense of time during (and after) the musical experience. The intention is to stimulate more reflection on time in music by helping bring these diverse issues into the foreground, suggesting some musical examples - in broad terms - of the more common metaphors about time, and proposing various perspectives from which we musicians interact with time. Without depending too much on a deep grasp of either the philosophical or the scientific nature of time, this book talks about time in a way designed to promote individual reflections about our experience of time in music, and understand something of the various "tricks of the trade" which allow musicians to produce sonic artforms that take the willing listener on unique temporal journeys.

I have included appendices with some personal suggestions of authors, composers, musical terms, and musical works that have particularly interesting manipulations or concepts of time embodied in them, but am quite aware of the inadequacies of those lists to someone wishing a more comprehensive reference. Therefore, Appendix A sketches out what I would like to see as a supplementary (or complementary) set of resources that could point interested researchers to articulate work in the field, and extends a general call for collaboration in setting

---

1   one of which is in the works under the title *Sorting out the Strata*.

up such a resource. It will be noticed by some that my 'chapters' are varied in length, and often very short. This was done for practical reasons, and might be likened to the common discrepancies between the number of pages in a musical score and the time required to play each of them.

Pending a fuller elucidation of the nature of time from some team of scientists, musician-philosophers, or aliens, it seems healthy to have several working models of time in one's head, especially as different uses of time can benefit from different perspectives. Our own mental structures influence the ways in which we understand the temporal aspects of our environments; they can also be studied to discover how we assemble, and tap into, our memories, and how to improve the variable depth of focus and duration that we can control. Musicians are in a particularly rich feedback loop for this, as music's ability to influence the listener's sense of time can be not only studied but also experimented with, and enhanced. I hope that this book will help encourage more articulate reflection on the very rich subject of time in music and life.

Many thanks to all those who gave helped me think about time more clearly – those whom I never met except through their writings or artistic works, as well as those who were willing to spend time in discussion and encouraged me to keep going. In particular, I am grateful to the International Society for the Study of Time, for continuing their founder J.T. Fraser's intent to probe issues of time through multiple perspectives and share findings; additionally, I greatly appreciate the articulate researchers I met through the European Society for the Cognitive Sciences of Music (ESCOM); Electroacoustic Music Studies (EMS); the McGill-based Centre for Interdisciplinary Research in Music Media and Technology (CIRMMT); and other gatherings of passionate explorers. And of course, I am indebted to my life partner Harry Mountain, whose own explorations of time in both artistic and ancient history realms give me considerable and continuous insight, and whose support in all things, from art & research to the most mundane matters, has enabled and stimulated me to keep exploring. My failure in absorbing and integrating all the wisdom collectively expressed will hopefully be offset to some extent if this book encourages others to be more inquisitive about time.

A Musician's Guide to Time

Section I.

Introduction

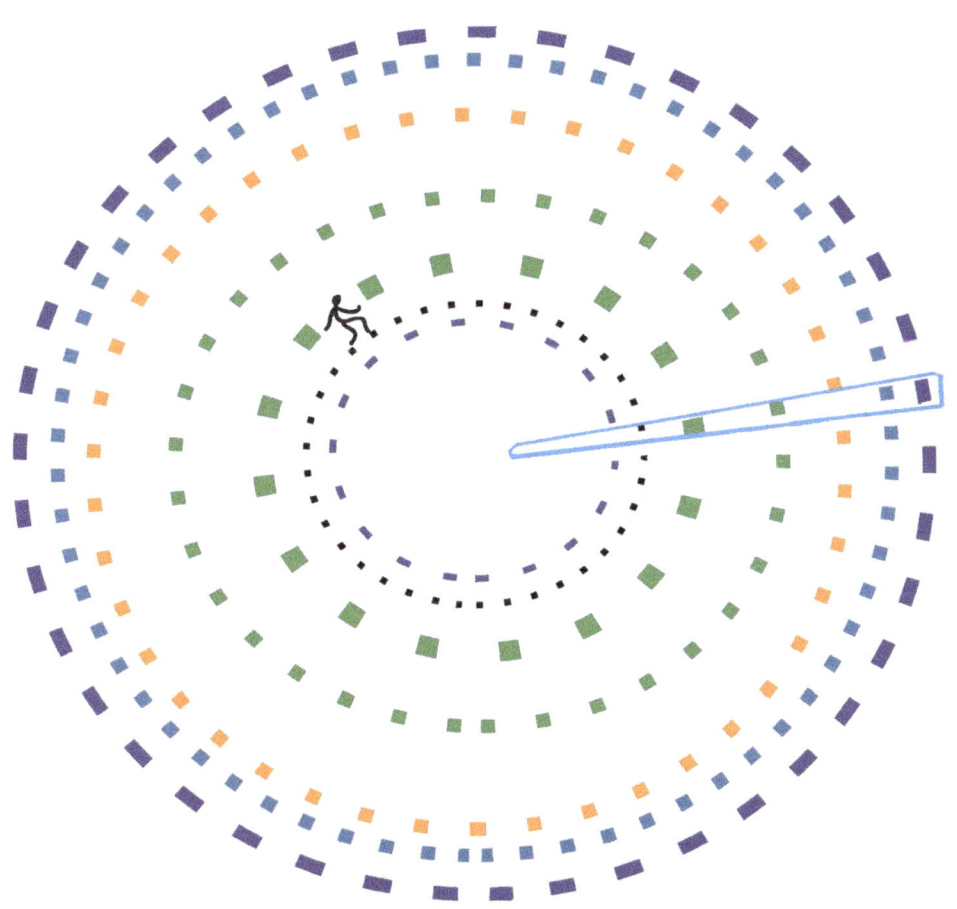

1. Realities & Illusions

There is something we call time, in which we all seem to exist, and which is as fundamental to our existence as the space we move in and the air we breathe. It is not visible as a medium, and it keeps morphing from present into past, and future into present, but it seems to permeate everything in our universe – or at least in our comprehension of the universe and ourselves. Some scientists and philosophers spend their lives trying to figure out what time is, while most others simply accept that it is a basic part of our lives. For example, many of us would feel unqualified to define 'space' to a physicist, but have an intimate knowledge of the spaces in which we live – inside and outside our houses, along the paths we traverse, etc.: not only where things and beings are in them, or how dusty or fragrant they are, but also how we feel within them; we can express that knowledge to friends. It should be similar with time.

A major stumbling block is that our vision of life, our environment, and our universe as a whole is interpreted as operating in time, yet our human perception of time depends on the ways in which we, as humans and as individuals, interact with particular parts of that universe. Therefore, the quest for a meaningful definition that can fit all situations and equations, all disciplines and cultures, seems futile. However, as there are aspects of time which we all find familiar, those of us who see benefits in confronting time may find that collectively we can become much more coherent about the subject.

Our measurement of time has something to do with days and nights, seasons, life cycles and growing old. We keep track of it consciously by clocks and calendars, which in effect substitute for tracking the movement of the sun and moon, the orbits of earth and the rest of our solar system. As everyone on earth can observe these planetary movements, we treat the measurement of their movements as a 'universal' time to which we can all refer, using them to calculate and compare any temporal duration. With a few exceptions that rarely extend past an experiment, we treat this 'universal' time as a constant which has always existed since the beginning of the universe (and maybe a few seconds before that) although there are now some convincing arguments in favour of viewing time as actually evolving (and perhaps speeding up?) in its nature and complexity.² Most of us coordinate our eating, sleeping, work and social schedules, as well as our travel, by using these common references.

But there are other aspects of time, which is how it feels 'close up', 'far away' (as in memories), as a component of our daily experiences, or its behaviour in exceptional circumstances (such as fever). Some hours and minutes, as we all know, seem much longer or shorter than others, and very few actually feel "equal". In analog time-keeping, the ticking of the clock seems in itself generally steady, but its collective nudging of the hour hand from one hour to the next is often felt to be a very poor approximation of how long each hour appears to last. This quality of time (usually called psychological, experiential, or subjective time) is not guaranteed to be shared by others – at least not in any given day by the same amount - and so it seems to be regarded as a bit less 'authentic' – an illusion of time. Unfortunately, the modern Western world has promoted the idea that any sense of time that is not consistent with clock-time measurement is somehow "false". However, this is a major error in thinking about time, in my opinion, and has been responsible for much of the confusion in talking about time in general.

One's personal sense of time is not in fact 'false' or even illusory; it is simply a result of the interface between ourselves and what we are observing, and with what degree of attention, at what scale, from which perspective, and according to which rates of tracking and units of measure. Rather than attending to the clock's measuring, we often focus on the manifestation of change or behaviour in things around us - and that depends entirely on whose or what behaviour is being studied, and by whom.³ A close study of a single thing, for example, might easily cause an impression of time passing that diverges from a mundane event measured in clock time. If the observer need not refer to external markers but simply take notice of the changes, there may be no need to establish precisely how much clock time has elapsed. If, on the other hand, one is studying a complex environment with multiple activities moving at different rates, then an observer may choose to

---

2 See Fraser, J.T. 1982 and various subsequent commentaries on his ideas by other members of the ISST and colleagues.

3 UCT – Universal Clock Time - is in fact an artificial calculation based on the oscillation of caesium (a steady one-second unit) which allows for a structure that can, with the help of occasional leap seconds and leap years, be used as a fairly accurate guide to our planetary cycle for the sake of plotting durations.

use the indifferent structure of an external clock or calendar to track differences between them - although it is just as common to treat the most predictable or familiar activity as a reference for the others. We find parallel phenomena in music. Many composers will think about the number of distinct 'ingredients' in a given passage or movement, each with their respective inner rhythms and pacings, and the contrast between them, as chief ingredients in the design of the piece.

Our knowledge of familiar things and phenomena incorporates their temporal qualities, which might appear as crucial attributes or, at the other extreme, almost irrelevant (compare the speed of an approaching vehicle to the evolutionary rate of decay of a rock). We may or may not have a sense of how those qualities translate into a clock-time duration - who calculates precisely how many seconds will elapse before that car reaches the intersection? - but our bodies and minds will alert us if the temporal qualities appear outside the norm for that particular thing as measured against our memories of previous experience or other predicted behaviour. That in turn means that our memories contain their own embedded time-lines, probably 'hard-wired' to our body clocks, as well as being normally marked as occurring at a certain time of our lives. When the inner temporal aspects of an entity or phenomenon provide important clues to its behaviour, then we try to be alert to the slightest fluctuations in its temporal change. In fact, we seem to "tune" to a series of clues to help inform our image and its changing state. Depending on the rate of change involved, we will consciously or unconsciously try to measure the change against a set of regular or anticipated markers in order to appraise any changes at an optimal level.

These regular markers can be represented by a clock and/or calendar. More commonly, they are measured against our own internal senses of remembered time-scales, learned through years of experience and probably cued to our body clocks for reference. Hence, a small child who can recognize the difference between the sound of walking and running steps and their implication of distance covered (as well as their associations with mood) may still have difficulty in gauging the amount of time needed for a car moving at a certain speed to arrive at the crosswalk. What we learn from experience is the relation between the speed of that car's approach to that of our own body's requirements for moving a particular estimated distance.

When trying to understand 'the nature of time' as it feels or affects our lives, many models and metaphors have been used: the linear forward-moving 'time as an arrow', cyclical views of time, layers like an onion skin, etc. Such metaphors can be extremely thought-provoking, but are often used in common parlance without enough thinking-through. Without much discussion, societies seem to reinforce one perspective or another for time, and it may be difficult to realize that others exist, let alone trying to imagine different ones. One reason for this cornucopia of models is presumably because we need a variety to express its many facets – so, rather than searching for the perfect definition, I prefer to choose a few of the more resonant metaphors we have imagined or could imagine, and exploring each for its aptness in certain circumstances. Then, it can be interesting to reflect on these various metaphors and models with examples of how they may be manifest in musical contexts. Gradually, one can become more aware of and skilled at sliding or flipping from one specific metaphor to another.

It seems clear to me that talking about music, which is created out of temporal elements, can always benefit from more discussion about time. However, mention of time *per se* has a tendency to intimidate many people in the same way that mathematical formulae do. There seems to be a general sense that time is too complex to understand; this is reinforced by the standard investigations into time within the context of philosophical / spiritual worlds (like St. Augustine or Bergson) or the complexities of space-time (like Einstein and his successors). Or perhaps it is simply because we are all taught that time is a constant, signified by the clock and the passing of years, whereas we all know that it's not true: one day is not the same length as another – even in retrospect.

Given that musicians deal with several aspects of time constantly in our art, it seems that we might be able to talk about all the temporal aspects of sound and music with more clarity if we try to think of them as temporal – and even more than that, working within clock-time, body time, and subjective realms. In music, both psychological and clock time play critical roles, along with the body clock timings that form a strong link between them. In the case of improvised music, the clock time aspect may play a very low profile (except for the mundane aspects of coordinating with others for the starting point for performance). But in standard Western musical practice, clock time is much more crucial because it is used as a reference to align the grid on which the composer's directions are overlaid. On the other hand, psychological time is extremely relevant to how we hear a particular piece of music and as such embodies crucial information for a composer who wishes to anticipate and shape how a piece is likely to be received. Many composers design their works to present a specific 'patterning' of time[4] but our Western notation is usually designed to be very literally interpreted by performers, often to an excruciating level of detail, to align it with the clock. This is not a perverse ignoring of psychological time by the composer, but rather a simple way to ensure coordination between performers in an ensemble, and to establish a framework for communicating the composer's temporal structures to the listener. So the musician must, at some level, be conscious of both 'clock' and 'psychological' time and their correlation. However, it seems most common for the performer to practice the correct tempo until it is able to be stored into their personal sense of motor movement, so that the clock functions simply as a calibration guide at the beginning of the learning. The clock-time durations are most commonly interpreted via a mechanical or digital metronome when a teacher, conductor, or recorded performance is not available to indicate the prescribed beat rate. In fact, few musicians will have a precise sense of how many milliseconds any particular note lasts but will be able to reproduce the given lengths aurally on different days to a great level of accuracy, and aurally recognize deviations from those durations in others' performances.[5]

    This interaction is what forms the essence of the issue I think of as the realities (or practicalities) *vs.* the illusions of music. Although there are innumerable ways to express a musician's interaction with time, it is useful to differentiate clearly between the practical aspects of clock time in sound production and performance, and the creation of illusions produced by the interaction of the specific organization of temporal flows and densities on the listener's sense of perceived time. The creation of illusions is itself dependent on some knowledge of human perception of temporal aspects (at a conscious or subconscious level) as explored in Section III. That perception is in fact intricately connected with the realities of our body clocks, but skilled composers and performers may help willing listeners stretch some of those 'hard-wired' links slightly, while stylistic or natural references will provide the tools for the listener to accept a given musical idea as being an exaggerated or miniaturized version of something familiar.

    We have extensive evidence, through writings and interviews, that several

---

4   I adopted this from Doob's 1971 book of the same name.

5   Strictly speaking, the musician will be more accurate in gauging the temporal intervals between successive notes – what the psychologists call the 'inter-onset interval' or IOI – as the duration of the sounding note is susceptible to fade-out or acoustic resonance in many cases.

notable 20th-century composers thought distinctly about time as the medium which was theirs to manipulate.[6] It can thus be useful to reflect on the differences between various practitioners of music in their interaction with time: composers, performers, improvisers, listeners, analysts, teachers, recording engineers, and so on.

2. Challenges to Exploring Time in Music

One of the main difficulties of discussions about time, and temporal things, is precisely that different people perceive time in different ways, even in what appear to be similar environments and circumstances, depending on various factors such as health, mood, aesthetics, environment, experience, training and personality (discussed in Section II) as well as the particular context of what we are observing, and from which perspective. I am beginning to appreciate to what extent different lifestyles and professions are influential on our personal 'default' and 'preferred' views of multiple layers of temporal events, and thus can even shape the ways in which we might appreciate a certain piece of music. A sense of time is also dependent on the duration of an observed event and its internal rate of change.[7] This helps create the illusion of a dichotomy between 'clock time' and 'psychological (or 'experiential) time': the way in which our perception of duration shifts according to personal, subjective factors. Such factors are not necessarily imaginary, or invisible to others, but they are not universal in the same way as our agreement about the regularity of the passing days and years – although the experts know that even such regularity is in constant flux – if only through slow oscillations.

The sense of psychological time (discussed in Ch. 10) is most often produced by several factors, such as the density and predictability of events in an individual's environment, their degree of attention on those events, and their processing skills.

---

6   See Appendix D for a few of these names.

7   For example, listening to a piece of music involves paying attention to how the sounds change from second to second, whereas relaxing at the cottage may be more concerned with appreciating the familiarity of the surroundings year after year.

The personal and subjective nature of psychological time has long been presented as an excuse for our lack of serious investigation into temporal aspects. But as we can identify different conditions that lead to differing impressions of time, we should at the very least begin to discern our own personal sense of time, and speculate on what has contributed to that sense.

We also have varying degrees of awareness, or interest, in thinking about temporal aspects of things. As we usually work on the belief that everything in our physical world (that is, excluding the supernatural, the transcendent, etc.) exists in time, how can we imagine it as a separate entity? However, we may discover that different people's sense of time is greatly influenced by the particular temporal durations which attract their attention: microseconds, or minutes and hours, or days and weeks, or years, in cycles that repeat each day, or month, or decade, or lifetime – or not at all. The scholar who studies ancient civilizations has a markedly different sense of time from the scientist who spends her workdays conducting chemistry experiments or the acrobat practicing her moves - and this probably impacts their respective reactions to a specific piece of music with its intrinsic temporal proportions. Moreover, some people are much more at ease thinking about different time durations simultaneously – aware not only of the current hour in the current week, but how that week fits into the cycle of years, or how the hour or week might have felt for someone else in their surroundings. It seems that such factors may well have an impact on eventual aesthetic choices in music.

Indeed, some people seem to have an exceptional capacity for perceiving certain aspects of time or temporal experience: whether in terms of tracking clock time, or remembering past experiences, or projecting possible futures, or recognizing similar time-sequences, or following multiple 'levels' or 'currents' of activity. Some of these capacities are trainable, as we can discover by studying the top performers from violinists to mrdangam players, who display not only a physically-expressed talent for the intersections of multiple cycles or microscopic adjustments in timing for expression, but also the ability to recognize, remember and reproduce specific temporal patterns over intervals of years.

One difficulty in discussing time is less of a problem for musicians than for our visually-dominated colleagues: time, like sound, is invisible. Its effects are certainly visible, just as sounds are audible, but one cannot point to a visible substance and say "That's time, there." However, as musicians, we have vast experience dealing with the ephemeral. Additionally, we can (and perhaps should) say that time is our medium. We have sounds which evolve in time – but what are sounds themselves other than oscillations of air in time? (Of course, that's a bit simplistic, as one needs a trigger to create the airwave pressure, but all that is needed is a membrane, whether a drum or a speaker, to translate that trigger, and the trigger can be anything from a simple thump to complex digital signal inputs.) We tend to ignore the time-bound aspects of the extraordinarily quick fluctuations in air pressure that create what we call notes: we define 260 Hz as "Middle C on the piano" and 440 Hz (or these days, a few cycles per second faster) as the orchestral 'A' for tuning at the start of a concert.[8] This is because those temporal differences are very easy for musicians to conceptualize in a way that makes their subsequent distribution in time less confusing. Conversely, in many forms of electroacoustic music,[9] the abandonment of the 'notes' designation in favour of the more practical but infinitely broader 'timbre' and its shaping has led to more sophisticated calculations of these microscopic vibrations and their treatment.[10]

The apparent conflict between typical usages of clock and subjective times is responsible for some of the confusion in discussions about music in the classroom and in textbooks (see Appendix B). But there is another even more elusive aspect that could be acknowledged, which is the quality of time as represented by the musical piece itself. Many different models of time are depicted in music: some of these are linked to specific eras, but the diversity of models has increased dramatically in the past century, reflecting the diversity entertained by other artists, scientists, and humanists. Therefore, we can also explore the impact of cultural and historical worldviews on both temporal design and the reception of musical works. In our discussions about music, we also have traces of different models that have become 'unlinked' from their origins. Moreover, in the past century, we encounter the curious impact of recordings and other factors which cause musical works – all with at least some interpretation by performers or diffusioners if not real improvisation - to be 'frozen' in time and 'thawed out' for later consumption.

---

8   In fact, an amusing proof of the fact that we don't actually think time is speeding up or slowing down in the context of a piece is that we don't mistake the vibrations of the leading tone for the slightly faster vibrations of the tonic note at the end of an *accelerando*.

9   By which term I include computer music, musique concrète, mixed music, and other forms incorporating newer sound technologies.

10   These issues are discussed in more detail in Ch. 23.

3. Calendars and Calipers

We measure things against our clocks not only to learn about the particular behaviour of a certain thing or phenomenon, but also to learn what their total durations are: "How long was I in that meeting? Do I have time for a coffee before the bus leaves?" In such cases, the duration as measured by an external clock becomes more important, because the clock acts as a pivotal reference: the meeting and the bus schedule probably have little in common except in one person's chronological planning (although both might be modified by a snowstorm). This is connected to the concepts of duration *vs.* succession, which is explored in Chapters 5 and 24.

The measurement of a duration is easily compatible with clocks and calendars, but the calculation of a phenomenon or animate object's behaviour requires quite a different type of measuring. In those cases, the tracking of change over time is likely to be perceived as the rate at which they move from one identifiable state to another (a 'delta' measurement) - whether a plant beginning to flower, or a cough becoming a cold, or a melody moving from one note to the next. In such cases, we have a sense of how long it *might* take, and then compare it to how long it actually *does* take. In the case of the melody, we are dealing with very small durations, but for the plant or the cold we are dealing with durations that may span several days or weeks.

Such an 'identifiable state' is usually a convenient but abstract concept, as it might not be clear when the flower is declared to be a flower (and not just a bud) or when the cold is actually considered to be present. But one cannot usually spare the time to spend days or weeks doing nothing but watching a plant grow, so we may check it every morning, for example - and then morning and evening, as it becomes ready to open. It seems that this idea of 'checking in' on a semi-predictable behaviour at periodic intervals may be our default way of apprehending change (and therefore, aspects of time), often in conjunction with a mental template (remembered or learned) which suggests the phenomenon's divergence from the 'norm'. That is, we are continually accumulating little snapshots (or, in many cases, soundclips or videoclips) of activity, and arranging them according to a timeline of sorts - often a clock/calendar combination - to plot not only the changes we are tracking, but their likely course. That course may be predicted because one has already seen other flowers bloom, or read a detailed gardening book.

This suggests that we rely on an array of mental 'calipers' to compare the differences in growth between successive days, and between these results and those we remember or expect. Of course, some of us have more tendency than others to want to maintain a chronological order to our memories, even if we might at times prefer a grouping by similarities of quality, for example.

This kind of memory processing is extensively employed while listening to music. Recent psychological and neurological studies suggest that in listening to audio information - which makes up a good percentage of our incoming sensory data - we employ various different parts of the brain and body simultaneously to track the time-flow of audio information.[11] Listening to a series of notes being played on the clarinet, for example, involves one part of the brain which identifies the vibrations of certain antennae in the ear to give information about the pitch and timbre, while another part of the brain checks to calculate their duration, and a third identifies spatial dimensions and motion (if present) through a comparison of left and right ear signals. Other 'trackers' will note the change of the timbre as it evolves from the beginning to the end of each note, as well as throughout an entire phrase, which can convey information we find useful for ascribing 'character' to the imaginary sound-emitter.[12] The brain is thus constantly comparing conclusions from each channel in order to build up a mental image of what is happening. Because there is usually an oversaturation of incoming data (imagine that the melody in the clarinet is accompanied by cello, for example, and that the speakers are distorting) we tend to probe different areas continuously for little chunks of information. I think of this process as involving an array of sampling tools, each taking short samples of audio activity at more or less regular intervals but at different rates and focus, producing continuously-updating mental graphs of the results.

---

11   See for example Phillips 2002.

12   I argue that it is not the clarinet that we imagine as the sound source, but something else represented by it: this is discussed in Ch. 27 under auditory images.

4. An Illustrative Story

Imagine, if you will, the following little story:

» » » » » » »» » « ««« « « « « « «

Two young Celtic warriors went wandering through the woods and across a plain and followed a little brook down to the ocean, where they took turns trying to outdo each other in the art of skipping stones. Then they sat on a log looking over the water, and spent time watching some ants gathering food, and relaxing to the sound of the waves, reminiscing about the changes in the sand dunes from last summer, and wondering what would happen to them in the upcoming winter storms. As if on cue, as the tide turned, the wind came up, and around the headland came a rather large boat that they did not recognize. They turned and fled back to their home camp to warn their elders – but as they ran, one tripped on a root and sprained her ankle. With her friend's help, she managed to hobble on, and they arrived in time to give the warning. Others then raced around to prepare for possible confrontation, while the wounded warrior was led by her friend to the healer's hut, where salve was applied and a curative potion given her to drink, making her sufficiently lethargic that she stopped arguing about missing out on the impending battle.

However, soon afterwards, there was much laughter when it was discovered that the boat carried a long-lost member of the tribe, who had arrived with new friends who had rescued him from danger during his adventures.

In celebration, a feast was prepared and eaten (and drunk!) and afterwards there was dancing, with several of the tribe playing drums and other instruments. Finally, as the energy levels began to subside, the traveller and one of his new friends told the story of their adventure, with much gesturing and appropriate sound effects created by their friends. The bard listened carefully and then managed to compose a few verses that preserved some of the main features of the story. By this time, the young warrior with the sprained ankle was recovering, and her friend, who was always interested in the bardic ways, was emboldened to imitate the style of the recitation, and proceeded to sing a little story outlining their own adventures of the day, while his companion strummed on her little zither. The tribe cheered their effort, and slowly wandered off to talk and sleep. The next morning, several people mentioned how full their dreams were of images and actions from the previous day and its tales.

» » » » » »» » « «« « « « « « «

Now, if we could imagine various different 20-minute segments of this day in the life of the two young warriors, we would have quite an array of different kinds of time and perception:

1. Wandering through the woods and across the plain – no particular hurry, but the passing of time felt intrinsically through the familiar walking pace – which would, however, be different in pace in the different terrains. The brook, with its constant but constantly-shifting babble would also colour this particular sense of time.

2. Skipping stones – the limb movement would not be regular, so there would be little particular tracking of time. Also, the sound of waves is also somewhat periodic, but quite slow compared, for example, to heartbeat, so it can be rather hypnotic.

3. Watching ants involves a concentration on things that move very quickly, in comparison to humans, without moving far, and so it involves a shift of focus to a different sense of time than normal human activities.

4. Viewing a possible hostile boat would completely disrupt the prevailing sense of 'endless' time, as it served to signal the youths that they must jump into action.

5. Running back to camp would be very different from the first wandering because the pace is much faster and the focus is on arriving at a destination as quickly as possible rather than on admiring the surroundings. The heartbeats would be considerable faster as well. The tripping on the root would not only change the rhythm but also increase the anxiety.

6. The preparation in camp for potential battle would be dominated also by a sense of moving quickly, and with several people involved, could be chaotic.

7. Once the wounded youth had drunk the potion, her own sense of time could be significantly altered as body metabolism dealt with the injury and the remedies.

8. The arrival of the long-lost tribal member would greatly alter the sense of time of everyone involved, as the urgency would instantly disappear and links

with the past (e.g. how much he and others had changed during his absence) became primary sources of reflection.

9. Preparing a feast without normal warning would also precipitate considerable activity, but of a different flavour than the previous preparing for battle.

10. The effect of food and drink combined with the excitement of the occasion would alter the sense of time again, partly due to specific effects on metabolism.

11. Dancing, with accompaniment on drums and melodic instruments, would both reflect and contribute to a different sense of time, with repetition and measured phrases.

12. Telling a tale attempts to re-create other times, necessarily greatly compressed, but swelling and fading in sympathy with the essential parts of the story.

13. If well done (which it was!), the summary of the two young warriors' day would likewise encapsulate all the previous time senses mentioned here.

14. Dreams are notorious for their compression of time, and for unnatural temporal events – like jumping suddenly from one point in a narrative to a future one with no apparent connection, or having a body that does not move at the speed expected.

In addition, we can imagine that the sense of time was very possibly 'shared' by the two youths until the time of the accident, and towards the end of the evening may have been converging again into a very similar perspective. And likewise, most of the members of the tribe (though not the traveller) would likely have a similar sense of time at different times of the day as they became involved in the same activities with similar emotions. On the other hand, some of the shifts in the sense of time are quite abrupt whereas others are gradual.

By the imagining or remembering of specific scenarios, we can begin to appreciate the enormous range of human interactions with time. We can see that the sense of time is influenced by external rhythms, body rhythms (walking, running, drumming, dancing, speaking), and the number of perceived events or phenomena. This also brings in the degree of attention (from rapt attention on the ants or skipping stones to almost total disregard of the surroundings when running home) and the breadth or narrowness of focus. Such focus involves not only the pace and complexity of one or many coexisting events, but also on the durational focus. Thus, a sense of time is very different when sitting on a log on the beach reminiscing about other seasons from that of running around in the camp to prepare a feast within two hours, or a battle within 20 minutes.

The reason that I chose to invent a story set in olden times[13] is because I am trying to investigate basic 'primitive' elements in our awareness of time.[14] In a modern world, the amount of chaos might be much higher, but the main elements would be probably very similar. One noticeable difference, perhaps, is that nowadays we may have more difficulty in accepting that we are not all living in the same 'time', as we have instant access to different places and different people worldwide and the "universality" of time is stressed by media. On the other hand, music is generally designed to portray different senses of time, in some kind of pattern – whether a narrative-type structure, an ebb and flow of tension and energy, a multiplicity of events, etc. It is easy to imagine a composer - or various composers - using a story like this as a model for structuring a musical work.

---

13   besides being immersed daily in my husband's extensive research into the ancient Celts - see www.CeltSite.com.

14   taking a cue from Bregman's explanations of his research into auditory scene analysis – see Bregman 1990.

Section II.

Typical Perspectives on Time

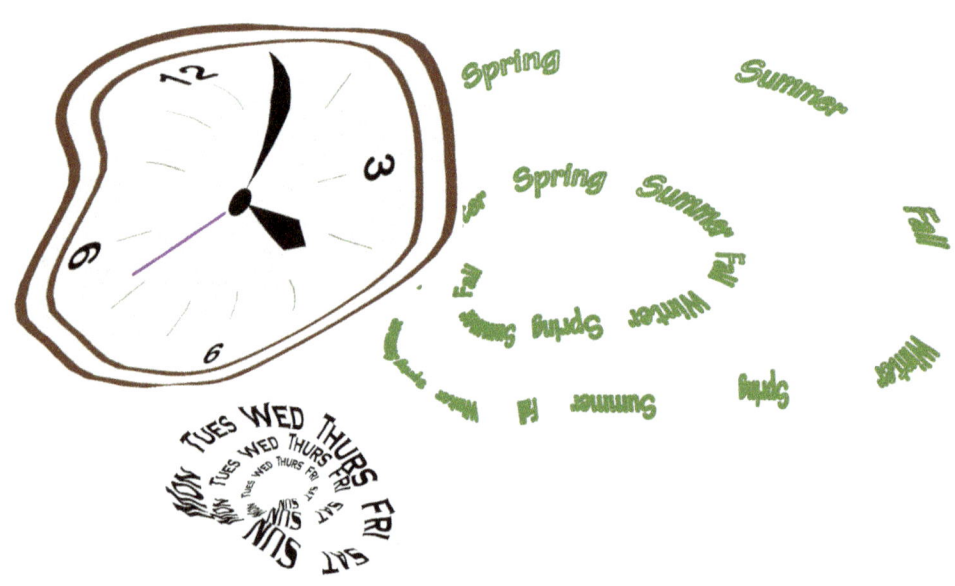

5. Time as a continuum: Duration vs. Succession

A standard way to look at time is as some type of ingredient of our natural world, somewhat analogous to space, or our gravitational field. It has been called 'the fourth dimension' which places it in very significant position alongside the three of space we comprehend (although the implication is then that time is one-dimensional, which is misleading). To many people, time implies something that is measurable, moving at some kind of uniform pace: a continuum in which we exist. After all, we have clocks and calendars, and the Western view of history suggests that time has been present, in its known form, since the beginning of the life of our planet, at least. But these are human constructs – do we measure time's passage *against* the incessant ticking? Movement and change, two aspects that are reflected even in mathematical formulae, seem fundamentally linked to time, as though they are created by the passage of time. Or is our sense of the passage of time simply a mental construct to allow us to grasp movement and change?

The idea of time as a continuum underpins our linear metaphors such as "the river of time" as well as some cyclic models – to be discussed in Chs. 7 to 9. However, we often switch our attention to durations within the flow of time, thereby segmenting it into units that each have a beginning and end, and which can be considered as entities (an evening, a week, a lifetime). Obviously, some of these will be nested (as an evening can always be seen as one part of the day and week, or a [very small] part of a lifetime. In addition, neither of these views entirely accounts for what I believe is a very common perspective: the study of the succession of events within one or more phenomena, viewed simultaneously against a mental grid that places those successions against a continuing constant. In fact, it seems most accurate to acknowledge that most people will have a few 'default' views of time, which will oscillate in their consciousness. To employ a visual analogy: when I am reading a book, my focus is narrow and close, and I read the words and the pages in succession, but I may look up from time to time and glance at the fire burning nearby, or look to a distant corner of the yard, or look at the sunset on the far horizon - or even look at some earlier pages to remind myself of a detail mentioned previously. If I were steering a canoe on a calm lake, I would be likely to focus on broad areas, scanning the horizon, whereas if I turn into a faster-flowing river, I am more likely to be scanning nearby surroundings, with more urgency in the scanning rates. In a somewhat similar way, a performer may focus on making millisecond adjustments in a note while retaining an image of the entire passage of a musical work, whereas a listener may notice the millisecond level only at a subconscious level, while thinking of the entire piece as one segment of the evening's concert. However, the idea of succession will be applied to the way in which the melody evolves - and if there are two simultaneous musical ideas presented, then each one will merit an independent view of their respective sequences of events. This view seems closely modelled on the idea of a 'zoom level' which many people are familiar with in visual technology, and which is in fact used analogously in computer treatment of sounds.

I am increasingly convinced that the listener's normal activities - studying prehistory, involved in a repetitive job in a factory, analyzing almost instantaneous chemical reactions, or puttering in the garden - will influence their tendencies in listening strategies. Additionally, our notion of time includes both past and future. Some people spend considerable time thinking back into the deep past or forward into the far future, whereas others confine themselves to the current days or months. Age is often a crucial factor, as young people have not only a shorter overall duration for comparisons (unless they have a sense of past lives, or assimilate the history of their ancestors), but also are less likely to have the experience of so many different 'pacings' of time, or as strong a sense of the recurrence of phenomena. However, their degree of attention to new experiences might well contribute to a more 'acute' or 'vivid' sense of time perception.

My partner has suggested that, as we can see the past but not usually the future, we might be thought of as going through life 'backwards', guessing where and how we should move into the future based on our past experiences of the path that has led us to where we are now. Extending this metaphor, one can appreciate the seductive means used by some to indicate that the paths from the past they have illuminated to indicate our supposedly shared history can easily be false ones, obscuring the more meandering and diverse paths by which we have all arrived in the present world.

In speaking of temporal duration, we have a semantic source of confusion for musicians, because *every* individual note in a traditional Western-style written score has its own 'duration' indicated by use of symbols (black or white note-head, presence or absence of stem and 'flags') usually in conjunction with an indicated tempo (e.g. ♩ = 60). These symbols have become nick-named 'durations' even though the half-note durations from one section may in fact be quite different in clock-time terms from the half-note durations from another section in the same piece. Likewise, 'durational patterns' as identified by music analysts refer to the particular configuration of long and short notes or gestures of a passage. However, for discussions of time, it is essential to recognize the broader concept of 'duration' and how it is distinguished from the concept of 'succession'.

Duration implies that we are thinking of a single time period, with a more or less identifiable beginning and end, which can be short or long, and everything that happens within it as being somehow coexisting at some level (such as in retrospect – whereby one may remember some of the attractive ingredients in a musical work out of their presented sequence). This perspective is therefore quite different from the linear model discussed in Ch. 8 that emphasizes the move forward from one event to subsequent ones. Of course, most musical events may be viewed from both perspectives, or a mixture, but it seems useful to recognize which is the current view. For example, a composer may conceive of a musical work as composed of distinct broader durations that are designed with certain characteristics: mood, tempo, texture, timbre, etc. This became a strategy [known sometimes as field music] for certain high-profile 20th-century composers such as Xenakis, Stockhausen, and Ligeti, but is also implied in classical music where 'movements' were conceived similarly (see Ch. 26). The ordering of those durations may take place after each part is composed. Or, a specific kind of texture can be composed and then its overall length and tempo adjusted to fit a particular [clock-time] duration that gives a better proportion to the overall work.[15]

---

15   Cowell used the term "elastic music" to refer to a technique he employed while writing music for Martha Graham's dance when he was working at a distance. In order to accommodate slight changes in the choreography or preferred tempo, he composed certain parts of passages as small units that could be repeated *ad lib.* (rather like the 'vamp' of rock) to fit the required duration - see L. Miller 2000.

6. Chronological time: Clocks & Calendars

The clock is one of the most common and clearest metaphors for time – especially when coupled with the calendar. It refers to both linear and cyclic aspects of time as we perceive it in the world around us. Both together function as a modern person's short-cut reference to the natural markers of the sun, moon, and rotation of the earth – defining the day, month, and year respectively.[16] As we can usually tell when it is daytime and when it is night,[17] when it is summer and when it is winter, the clock and calendar simply provide a more precise coordination between people. In fact, the clock and calendar do have the tendency to distort time for us because they present themselves as reliable constants, although spring does not always start in mid-May in the same town in Canada every year, let alone in different places in the northern hemisphere, and not every quarter-year has exactly the same number of minutes. Einstein's discovery of space-time was exciting because it suggested an even greater elasticity in the previously-regarded constant of 'clock' time, but it did not seem to have immediate relevance for those living on earth, beyond its conceptual level (which in itself had resonance for several 20th-century composers).

The clock and calendar therefore represent the commonality of temporal existence. If we say that a person lived for fifty years or that a flower lived for 10 days, we all have an idea what that is. The calendar indicates the years and days; the clock indicates the hours and minutes. We have the impression that these are finite and fixed entities, as we tend to assume that in a basic sense, all minutes

---

[16] The moon's association with the night is common, but only based on its increased visibility; the sun defines both day and night by its presence and absence. Attempts to reconcile the moon's cycle with the sun's have plagued calendar-makers since early times, and have been successful only when their coinciding is admitted to being a cycle of many years – 52 years is only a rough calculation and will eventually slip out of sync. The Persian calendar used in Iran is the most noted of all common currently-used calendars for its accuracy.

[17] Although less easily in some contemporary urban situations where the outside natural environment is treated as a distraction or irrelevant.

are equal in length. (Although at a very fine glance, it turns out that they aren't .... see below.) However, we know equally well that not all minutes or days feel equal in length. This is due mainly to what is called 'psychological time' but also involves what might be considered the density or texture of the duration.[18] When old friends reminisce about shared experiences, there is often an ingredient of how time felt during those experiences, and even how similarly or differently the intervening time was felt; the memories thus contain a sense of shared knowledge about the nature of time itself.

✺ The Risk of Inaccurate Measurements

It can be important to understand that the principle of significant figures should be applied to time measurement as well. Durations like a fortnight are perfectly suitable for some calculations, and would be inaccurately portrayed as being 1,209,600 seconds long.[19] In fact, our days are not all exactly the same length, and so compromises are made in our clocks and calendars.[20] But the duration of a fortnight has been used as a unit of calculation since ancient times, and doubtless is based on the moon cycle, a duration that can be easily calculated. It does not imply any more precision than the specific number of day-night cycles (precision can be added by other instructions: one fortnight from now, at sunset). In addition, given that the moon and sun present a lovely polyrhythm, clocks that are calculated to reflect the sun cycle are liable to be misleading in measuring the moon cycle - although some ancient civilizations did accurately plot their dance. Western society in particular seems peppered with those who become fixated on the microscopic subdivisions of time without recognizing that innate roughness,

---

18   I like the term 'mundane time' for 'clock time' in artistic contexts. "Mundane" refers to the world, and as such encompasses the universality of the 'clock time' references. But 'mundane' also implies the everyday, unexciting sense of time that contrasts with time in art and in more exciting lifestyles.

19   14 nights x 24 hours x 60 minutes x 60 seconds. It is interesting to compare languages: 'fortnight' is a contraction meaning 'a duration of 14 nights' whereas in Portuguese, for example, the translation (quinzena) signifies 'a duration of 15 days'.

20   This can be seen through an examination of the two types of solar time and sidereal time, which use the slightly fluctuating cycles of earth's turning as their basis, plotted against the sun or stars respectively, and appreciating that oscillating clocks can be constructed to maintain a stable measurement, with reference to the universal time unit of caesium oscillations, which are exactly one second long.

precisely because they prefer to pretend that time does not have such fluctuations. The move in some Canadian schools to neglect teaching children how to tell time by looking at an analog clock seems to some of us as quite irresponsible: the division of time into hour-long chunks represented by a circle which can be easily visually subdivided into 2, 4, 6, or 12 units gives us a common reference for useful chunks of duration, whereas the currently-preferred digital unit requires computation to arrive at calculations of 'a half-hour from now' while pretending that the minute is a significant measurement and not simply a component of its artificial subdivisions. In fact, the whole issue reminds me of the classic explanation about the length of the British coast: if one looks at a map to scale and measures the outline of the island, the answer to the length is drastically shorter than if one went on one's hands and knees with a 6" ruler at the water's edge and measured – at low tide. I wonder to what extent this might apply to time as well: when we examine each second, will our lives appear longer than if we plan it in weekly chunks?

7. Cyclic vs. Linear Focus

Linear aspects of clock/calendar time are clear in the numbering: 2 o'clock follows 1 o'clock, March comes after February, March 5 is one day after March 4. The cyclic aspect is nonetheless just as strong: 2 o'clock will recur every day (or twice a day, for those not using the 24-hour clock), March 5 comes every year, and the earth passes through the Leonids meteor path every November (although our respective trajectories are slowly shifting over the millennia – just as the ancient horoscope designations are now out of alignment).

Clocks and calendars are often thought of as indicators of the linear quality of time unfolding steadily ahead of us or destroying it relentlessly behind us. However, some cultures and ages encourage an emphasis on their cyclic aspects, and it is often pointed out that the Western world tends to emphasize the linearity and the Eastern world the cyclic. As the linear view seems increasingly compelling when a human reflects on his or her own life expectancy, a religious or philosophical view that stresses long-term cycles can counteract that sense – whether in a general view of life ever repeating itself or a more specific one of reincarnation. The biannual celebrations of solstice and equinox, which played a major role in the life of many ancient cultures – such as Celtic and Persian –, served to emphasize the larger cycles of the solar year and its effect on the earth, animal and plant behaviour. Beyond a simple marking of the passing time, it compelled the community to enter into rituals and festivities that were repeated from year to year, which would emphasize the aspect of repetition that is essential to cyclic events. Although a participant might be sensitive to the variations from one repetition to another (for example, the difference caused by aging, or a new tribal leader), such individual reflection was probably quite subservient to the celebration of the solar cycle's stability.[21]

The urban Western world has been moving increasingly into a fairly undifferentiated year, living in environments as isolated as possible from outside variation, buying food out of the local season, growing plants in artificial environments, and keeping wild animals at a great distance (although those of us in cold climates cannot easily escape the obvious differences between winter and summer). Both cultural and personal circumstances can influence one's perception of whether linear or cyclic aspects are more prominent. Someone feeling trapped in a boring but secure '9-to-5' job with two weeks of summer vacation annually will have a different appreciation of the year from someone else who is self-employed and free to travel to different climates while subject to unpredictable ebbs & flows of income. Many jobs try to deny all seasonal changes, as well as personal energy levels and needs, stressing instead the daily and weekly patterns. Others, such as the gaming or film industry, will impose a series of client- or budget-directed deadlines that may take months of predictable stages of work intensity, but similarly ignore both the seasons and the workers' cycles. Likewise the market-gardener will share a high awareness of cycles with the commodities broker, but those of the market gardener are earth-bound and seasonal, with perhaps some sense of year-over-year trends, while the broker's is frustratingly unpredictable because the length of each cycle and sub-cycle are unknown.

Both cyclic and linear aspects are easily portrayed or emphasized in music, and typical manifestations will be discussed in Section III. Cyclic form in particular is quite dependent on the listener's memory, which is discussed in Section II. In addition, music provides examples of repetition involving cyclic scans that are

---

21 These astronomical time-marking festivals are still observed in some cultures, such as Iranian; a similar but more distorted noting of a year-long cycle is caused by the celebrations of monotheistic religions which were carefully displaced a few days from that of the forbidden pagan celebrations of the natural events.

linked not so much to our sense of passing time but our sense of stasis, as we confirm that patterns remain predictable through multiple scans similar to our visual strategies.

8. Linear views of time: Arrows, Rivers, and Narratives

❋ Arrows

The "arrow of time" is a familiar metaphor to many. It embodies one of the most fundamental aspects that most of us believe about time: it is forward-moving only. Most of us think that 'going back' in time happens only in a metaphorical way, through memory – or in a time machine in a science-fiction movie. This is not to say that at a sub-particle level, time may not exist free of this uni-directional flow, or that we might discover more details about 'quantum foam' in space-time – but that is hard for most people to reconcile with a practical interaction with time, and seems hardly relevant for musicians except as potentially stimulating conceptual inspiration for a composer.

Oddly enough, the idea of going around and around can still imply linearity – so this may help explain why societies and cultures differ on the emphasis: if one is totally within or riding the arrow, it may seem uni-directional but from 'outside' it seems cyclic. The sense of spiral can be formalized to imagine an ever-climbing cyclic pattern, for example – but then, as proponents of string theory will point out, anything that climbs will probably subsequently descend, and then climb again....

❋ Rivers

The "River of Time" is one of the easiest metaphors for some of us to grasp. Not only does it imply a continuum of a single substance that moves at a more or less steady rate, but it also implies a single direction of flow, which conveys the uni-directional quality of time which most of us consider one of its most basic attributes. The concept of never being able to step in the same river twice is also part of the metaphor for some, as it suggests that the constant flow embodies constant change. However, in trying to visualize this metaphor of time as a river more clearly, I began to wonder: do we imagine that we are all swimming in the river? or can we stand on the bank? can we dive in and climb out again? walk on a trail alongside, watching? Perhaps we are sitting on a boat; if so, is it a sailboat, a power boat, a canoe? and can we control its speed?

Reflecting on the river metaphor has led me to elaborate on it in my own mind. I often think of time as a kind of viscous liquid (one which, miraculously, does not impede breathing!), flowing in one direction, in which we and our contemporaries and our surroundings are situated. But it appears that this liquid

varies in density and texture: it has thick parts that move sluggishly, and thin parts that are very pure; little rivulets and bigger currents. We and everything we know are in this liquid, but some of us are in the faster-moving parts and some in the slower-moving; some move from one rivulet into another by accident, others deliberately. There are eddies – just as in rivers – and that is where one's sense of time can seem quite different from those nearby, even though one is at roughly the same point. One might further imagine that in some places the river has very murky waters, obscuring long-distance views. Recently (2020) I expanded this analogy into imagining humans as similar to various types of sea-creatures with arrays of tentacles for determining the temporal character of the things around us.

The river metaphor generally ignores the questions of source and destination, although many humans do imagine that there was a beginning of time and will be an end. Perhaps that is another appealing aspect of this metaphor – that it conveys a feeling shared by many that we are being carried along by a force much too great to resist.

❈ Narratives

A basic aspect of the river metaphor is its linear flow that implies a fixed sequence – a leaf thrown onto a brook can be watched as it moves downstream. This aspect is more easily revealed in the idea of narrative structure: a storyline that purports to tell events in the order in which they happen (i.e. tracing the path of the leaf). This metaphor is fundamental not only to the majority of Western novels and films, but is frequently employed in Western classical music, and is discussed in Section V. It can be interesting to study the dominance of narrative form in film, for example, where despite wonderfully imaginative early experiments by artists such as Man Ray and José Val del Omar who made full use of the ability of film to disrupt linear flow, films made for mass consumption usually do little more than jump ahead in the time-frame of a story – flashbacks remained an 'arty' concept until the last few decades,[22] just as Virginia Woolf's writings such

---

[22] The popular 1970s TV series Kung Fu incorporated flashbacks regularly – within the context of the story of a half-Chinese man trained in Eastern religion, thus justifying the break in narrative structure by alluding to an Eastern sense of time. One of the first examples I remember noticing was in the "spaghetti Western" *For A Few Dollars More* where the music of the pocket watch helps the audience pick up the transitions. (Leone's movies were unusually rich due to the musical contributions of Ennio Morricone.)

as *To the Lighthouse* were startling, as in the very realistic tracing of a woman's thoughts jumping from one thing to another in apparent randomness, or Proust's wonderfully detailed descriptions of remembered moments.

❇ PATHWAYS

This is not a common metaphor *per se* but one that shares enough attributes with the river model and narrative models that I find it can help expand them. My own take on this is to imagine different speeds and means of travel, much like the riverboats & swimming variations – one can imagine a complexity of highways and byways, bicycle lanes, 'moving sidewalks' and rough paths, with the occasional slide or cliff ascent.

The metaphor also embodies the notion of changing speed more easily (by simply changing lanes, for example), while implying an ever-forward direction; it can also explain what happens when we are confronted with various musical ideas presented at the same time – as investigated further in Ch. 27. To improve on this metaphor, it would probably be best to imagine not only a complex meander of (sometimes intersecting) paths, over different territories, with different views (fields, sky, water, human constructions) and borders (hedges, stone walls, highrises, electronic billboards) but also filled with flocks of birds, insects, and / or drones, for example, whose presence in one lane and not in another would easily influence the traveller's experience.

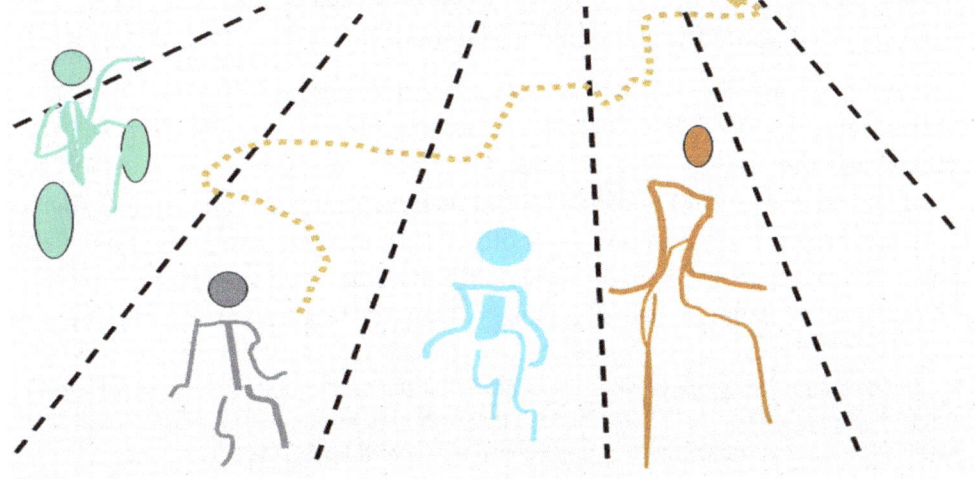

9. Other Models: Growth & Decay, Evolving Time

A crucial aspect relating to our perception of temporal behaviour is incorporated into the "growth & decay" model. It is closely related to "ebb & flow" and is an important ingredient to my own version of the 'populated river' metaphor. Every animate thing we know has a life-span. This can be characterized by an embryo-type state, birth, infancy, childhood, adolescence, maturity, old age, death. The temporal duration of any animate being's lifespan is within a certain range, but we have a huge variety of life-span durations within the animal-vegetable kingdom. Yew trees can live for over two millennia; some insects live for a day. Average human life expectancy has lengthened over the last few centuries, but is still generally under 100 years – less than the African Grey parrot, for example.[23]

In a broader sense of the concept, short events also have average durations that can help us measure time. Waves that crash on a beach may be slower or faster in their rate depending on weather conditions, tides, and the particular characteristics of the shoreline. But if we went to an unknown beach and found that the waves were rolling in at a speed of once every 3 seconds, or once every 25 seconds, we would think that something has gone wrong, or that we are on a different planet. Likewise, we expect a fluttering of wings from a small bird and a slow flap from much larger ones and would be puzzled at the reverse, which involves a basic grasp of the principle of feathered wings and air currents more than a specific knowledge of the bird in question.

Although activities do appear to move at different rates (from each other) in a global sense, each of those events are usually themselves a conglomeration of sub-activities manifest at different rates of motion or change. A raven in flight will flap wings up and down at a rate that seems quite different from, if fundamental to, its movement from one tree to another. A rainstorm may have identifiable phases of heavy rain and light drizzle within a general duration of an afternoon. A group of youths playing a ball game may convey the impression of a considerable

---

23   My partner Harry Mountain has discovered that the extraordinary life-spans of a few notable mythological characters –such as Methuselah - are not quite so fantastic when treated as being counted in 'moon-years' [months] rather than 'sun-years'.

energy of movement in a roughly constant speed, but that movement is in fact distributed between them, and any given individual's movement might be much more irregular. Experience teaches us that there are standard ranges for events of all sorts: a raven will never fly under nor over a certain speed; youth likewise have upper and lower limits to their running range. For each familiar thing or event that we witness, therefore, we have a sense of the 'clock time' duration or periodicity which its behaviour or lifespan implies. Some of these innate rates are so familiar that we will be very sensitive to any discrepancy with our expectations. By the same means, our sense of 'slow' and 'fast' in music with a beat tends to arise from the amount of deviation between the beat-grouping level and our perception of a 'normal' walking pace.

To be aware of the growth and decay cycle of different things simultaneously while imagining that each one has its own rate of evolution leads easily to a sense of concurrent but differently-moving elements or phenomena. Even though all are often imagined as moving in the same direction, they appear to do so at different rates, and with rather different trajectories. I believe that it is exactly this sense that is characteristic of much 20th-century music. In preceding centuries, many societies were accustomed to focussing on their own society's stories – usually linked by the propagandists with the images of progress and evolution - and this stance was mirrored in much of the music where one idea would be presented at a time. An increasing awareness and fascination with other perspectives and cultures naturally led some composers (see Appendix C) to create musical representations of concurrent but unsynchronized events which can provoke a sense of instability and unease for those who prefer their art to suggest a more ordered universe.[24]

Patterns of storms and other weather phenomena present attractive analogies for the behaviour of time – especially given easy access to animated maps of world weather trends (though I would prefer to see a full holographic projection). We know that winds will rise and subside, that they often follow very similar patterns across the earth, affected by seasons and geographical features, that they may be characterized by gusts or appear slow-moving, that they

---

24 Alternatives to viewing music history as a linear connection in favour of drawing them for stylistic and other reasons is an attractive idea; I have made my own charts for years, and discuss it in (a very brief) Ch. 3 in my 2021 book, noticed a part of an exposition at the Liverpool Tate around 2014 drawing similar non-linear links artists, and have just come across a reference to a 2015 book on what appears to be the same subject (which I have not read, but added to the bibliography) by J. Johnson.

may carry changes in temperature and precipitation – and yet they still remain unpredictable in their specific timing and intensity. It seems therefore reasonable to imagine that time (which is of course a coefficient of weather) could itself share some of these characteristics. Like the river metaphor, one can reflect that we might be riding the wind or ocean currents, or standing in one place feeling their effects. Some psychologists have found it useful for mental health assessment to distinguish between those who feel that they are 'riding' time and those who feel 'buffeted' by it.

A fairly recent development in science is String Theory – superficially attractive to many musicians as it uses the analogy of a vibrating string as a model for various aspects of the universe. This seems to be an evolution of the idea that the Big Bang is perhaps followed, eventually, by a Big Crunch and then repeated in an organic way (sometimes referred to as the Big Bounce theory). I will not attempt to summarize its essence here, but merely point out that the idea of life being based on the idea of vibrations is quite attractive for those of us who had to study acoustics and who rely on vibrating strings and air columns to produce our art. On the other hand, the Big Bang theory is linked with some fascinating ideas about time which are rich for speculation (and possibly imitation in art), such as J.T. Fraser's investigation of the emergence of time with its nested hierarchies. While I cannot claim to have fully grasped his proposals, it seems that his thoughts about evolving time incorporate the idea that the behaviour of time itself is growing in complexity. Depending on the degree of human adaptability, our own perceptions of time thus need to adapt. The potential impact on this for music and musicians makes another fascinating topic for reflection. Should we advocate looking for evidence for an Orchestral Theory, for example, where String Theory operates in a variety of ways – harmonically, polyphonically, or in unison, perhaps – with Brass, Wind, and Percussion Theory, forming a multitude of behaviour types of time?

As artists involved with time, we are always intrigued by different ways in which time might be imagined. My partner recently suggested that time might be beneficially regarded at times as more like a globular mass of points rather than a familiar linear connection, for example. This rather delightful image slightly shocked me because I realized that I do find such an analogy more remote to my thinking although it is in fact much closer to that of the "big bang" origin of time, which is usually conceived of as relating to our spatial images of the solar system. Is this tendency to linearity because of my excessively long association of music linked with its written linear-temporal arrangement, which I learned to read soon after learning to climb onto the piano stool? There is certainly some influence, but soon after learning to read music from classical or pop repertoires, one encounters the 'repeat sign' which requires backing up and repeating a part of the music over again, so the local linearity is thwarted when extended beyond a few passages. Even before reading music, the young child in a musical environment is likely to be aware of nursery rhymes or lullabies, for example, where the same tune is repeated numerous times in sequence, or two tunes in alternation as verse + chorus. Only slightly more complicated are simple rounds, where even small children can learn that the resulting sounds are produced by staggered entries of identical parts.

I find it stimulating to imagine other models for time as well, to help tease out what seem the most important aspects to encapsulate. For example, time as represented by the growth of a tree seems plausible at first glance – they embody qualities of organic life and growth and share features with the river. But, like most analogies, this one instantly begs a series of questions: if the trunk represents the earliest times, are we at the tips of the branches by now – and what is its life expectancy? Or do we revert to the other analogy of 'family trees' – and then extend it to each culture forming its own trees, with the occasional hybrids, and we are collectively creating a forest? In order to echo the feeling of 'permanent motion' which the river analogy contributes, we would have to be tiny insects feeding on the tree whose lifetimes are far shorter than that of the tree they are on. But as any geologist will tell you, rivers also dry up and disappear….

SECTION III.
HUMAN PERCEPTION OF TIME

10. Psychological / experiential time

'Psychological time' is the term generally used to refer to our sense of how time seems to be passing – not only 'slow' or 'fast' but also how aware we are of it. This is often referred to as the "experiencing" of time (hence the alternative adjective 'experiential'), as psychological time refers to our differing sense of how long an hour (or a day, or decade) is in different situations. Psychological time is generally imagined as being *in opposition to* clock time – in that everyone's impression of the length of an hour or day will be different. Moreover, it is often regarded as an aberration of perception, and therefore may be discarded by some as irrelevant. As a result, we don't seem to have much of a common vocabulary for discussing the different 'paces' and 'textures' of temporal duration, beyond references to time 'dragging' or 'racing by'. This is despite the fact that most of us could imagine quite easily the various senses of time sketched out in the "Illustrative Story" in Ch. 4, or contemporary examples like the difference between an hour waiting in a doctor's office from one spent strolling along a park trail with a friend, or working with inferior software on a project.

Psychological time seems most often the product of several factors such as the density and predictability of events in an individual's environment and their degree of attention on those events; therefore, it may be radically different for two adjacent people, but if they are similar in interests, have been through the same or similar experiences in the very recent past, and are able to process the same kind of information, two people may feel an almost identical sense of a particular duration. Friendships doubtless develop in part because of an ability to recognize, empathize with, and perhaps even synchronize with each other's fluctuating sense of durations.

11. Movement & change; temporal focus & the "now"; permanence; scale

✵ Movement & change

Time is very often perceived through an awareness of change, as all change by definition involves time. This is manifest at very different levels of consciousness, including vague long-term spans ("I was much more agile a decade ago – I'm obviously getting older") or over the course of a couple of minutes ("the supper is burnt – I must have miscalculated how long I spent talking on the phone"). Movement is likewise measured in terms of time – a quick sweep of an arm takes less time than a slow one – so by noticing that something is quick we are at one level talking about the time elapsed being less than it might have been. In other words, the mind will attempt to categorize incoming data suggesting movement into a folder of similar motion trajectories that contain a 'default' range of differentiation from a basic model. This kind of categorization and modelling plays a part in music where we deal in illusions (discussed in Ch. 27).

Based on experience and personality among other factors, different people have different perceptions of, appreciation of, and tolerances for change. For example, someone who has lived for most of their life in a quiet town around familiar people will usually find a day in a busy urban environment full of movement and change, whereas someone who works downtown daily might find the same day and environment particularly restful, because the traffic is a bit less heavy and the road repair is finished. In this case, the change is measured against expectations more than against an imagined scene with no change. Conversely, the urbanite who spends a week in the country may be bored from the lack of activity, while a local of the area might be conscious of the precipitous actions of specific familiar birds and minute changes in growth of the vegetation as indicating that spring is advancing more quickly than expected.

✵ Temporal focus & the "now"

A critical issue in time perception involves the 'window of time'. This refers to the span of time that the perceiver considers to be the present. In scientific research, this term is used generally to refer to very short durations of time, and is thought to hover around 2-3 seconds in length, lengthening perhaps upwards to 10-12 seconds. In strict psychological terms, this temporal duration allows the individual time to grasp everything around them and consider them to be happening 'at once'. Things outside this time frame are considered to be in the past or the future. Of course, this window on the present is constantly shifting as time passes (or as we go forward into time, depending on how one views things). This 'now' is vital for information theory, which is a useful framework for understanding our processing of data in the world around us (see below), but has some different relevance for listening to music, as it can then serve as a useful metaphor for a particular listening strategy if we loosen the boundary markers. It has been argued that through meditation, for example, this sense of 'now' can be expanded beyond the 'normal' human range, and it seems very likely that a similar case can be argued in many musical contexts, where people deliberately suspend their analytical calculations to enable a coexistence of sound events over long durations.

In a parallel way, different people may look at very different durations of time as their own 'present'. One advantage of being a full-time college student, for example, is that students can, and often do, feel a sense of being insulated from the outside world while they are studying. Some may extend this only to a single term or academic year, especially if they do something quite contrasting in the summer or are unsure about their own completion of the programme, while others may feel that they don't have to think about the time passing until they graduate. Therefore, they may not be as sensitive to change in themselves or their friends, for example, as they are considering the entire duration of the study time as 'now', to be followed by the unknown 'later'. On the other hand, if one is starting a new job where one has no security or confidence that it will last more than a few months, each day or week may seem like the full extent of the present, as tomorrow is already the (unknown) future.

In talking about the broader, metaphorical sense of presence, it might be useful as thinking of a sliding scale from microscopic to macroscopic, where the microscopic is at or below the millisecond level (a sharp stab of pain, for example, can focus one's attention on a second-by-second progression in time) and the macroscopic is that of the swami who feels that this lifetime is all in the present. It seems likely that the ability to shift smoothly along this microscopic / macroscopic scale would be a generally useful talent, and probably a healthy one.

The so-called "early stages of perception" fall well within this 'now' and deserve special attention because they have extreme relevance for music perception. This band includes the realm of *onset asynchrony*, which refers to the degree of simultaneity between stimuli, or the temporal distance that elapses between them. In broad terms, things that happen exactly at the same time are considered to be probably part of the same phenomenon, whereas a delay will suggest that they may come from different phenomena. However, we also have a vast repertoire of models that include the particular relationships of component particles and their expected behaviour, which will be discussed further in Section V.

❋ SCALE

Our appreciation of 'scale' of a sculpture has to do with its physical dimensions, especially as compared with our own human bodies, the level of detail, and the proportion of the representation with its model in the physical world (if applicable). Thus, a human-looking figure that is 6 meters high may look considerably more imposing than a 10-meter-high structure that appears to be a castle in miniature. Once we have grasped the general scale of the object, we appreciate the detail in relationship to it. With performing arts, one may not know in advance exactly how long a piece is going to last (although there are community / social norms, as well as contextual norms - to the extent that extreme variations are often advertised as such). Then, the opening few seconds and minutes can become essential as guides for the overall scale of what is expected, as musicologist Lewis Rowell recognized and clearly articulated (Rowell 1981). The sense of 'proportion' within a musical work - which is often used to discuss the different temporal durations of contrasting sections - is an integral part of the overall 'scale' of the work.

❋ PERMANENCE

Permanence is likewise a perceived attribute that depends in part on the perceiver and their personal window of time. To most of us, for example, a rock is considered a permanent element in a landscape. To a geologist, however, it might be obvious that (a) it was carried there from another site by a glacier, and (b) that it will probably disintegrate within another hundred (or thousand) years, given its composition and susceptibility to erosion. Thus, permanence means 'something which I don't expect to change within the (my) (immediate / calculable) future'. A sense of permanence is easily established in musical contexts by sustaining or reiterating sonic configurations in an otherwise actively-changing context, as the scale of comparison is shrunk, and the duration of a section of music is considered the background against which events are understood.[25] Persistence, durability, and stability all refer to this same concept with similar degrees of variability depending on the perceiver - even eternity is generally considered 'beyond time' but the fact that it is used frequently in hyperbole ("we spent an eternity waiting for her to arrive") indicates that many use it to refer to the extreme end of progressively longer durations.

These concepts of change and permanence are also applied to much shorter durations of time, to describe the character of a phenomenon. "It rained all summer" implies a large-scale unchanging condition, even though most people would understand that the rain was in fact not constant throughout each hour of each day. Thus, we find that descriptions of temporal states can differ depending on the duration under discussion. Even more interesting, if confusing at first glance, is that a state of constant variability, or change, may be appreciated as static even though the characteristic is apparently the opposite. This becomes crucial in music.

12. Memory & retrieval; parsing; familiarity

Naturally, our sense of 'times past' relies on our memory or knowledge of them. This applies not only to our remembering of yesterday, last year, and childhood, but also what happened five minutes ago. In music, memory is an essential ingredient in the appreciation of a work, and this depends on the health of the listener's memory and on their ability (and determination) to notice, codify and arrange relevant details to facilitate later retrieval. The repetitious nature of a cycle – for example, the seasons of the year – usually depends on some memory of previous cycles to understand that there is a repetition. In some cases, memory can be substituted by historical records, whether oral traditions or meticulous data collection. The linear quality can be emphasized by remembering where one was at a previous point in the cycle: "Was it just last spring when I first learned how

---

25 See the discussion under ostinato, Ch. 22.

to play that piece?" Memory plays an enormous part in our perception of time, because it is through remembering how something was that we know it is now different, and therefore that time has elapsed. This is equally true in music, and the difficulty many people have with avant-garde 20th-century works, or music from foreign cultures, is precisely because they cannot easily grasp, codify, store, and retrieve the information the way in which the original design was planned or expected to be received.

Memory is generally separated into short-, medium-, and long-term – but these terms are not intuitively obvious; as 'short-term' for psychologists refers to a mere few seconds, it is more appropriately called 'working memory'.[26] This span of time corresponds to the 'present' mentioned above, where everything is perceived as more or less happening 'now'. During this time, the brain is obliged to pick out the important things that are happening from the plethora of information retrieved, and store them in some appropriate way into longer-term memory for later retrieval (which may be a mere few seconds later). A key limit on this time span is that we are constrained by a very small maximum number of things (or 'chunks') which we can hold in this sorting state without overloading.[27]

This issue, generally studied under the guise of information theory,[28] contributes useful analogies to the elusive question of time perception. It seems that our sense of subjective time fluctuates in relation to clock time according to the amount of information we receive (and pay attention to) per second. The upper limit of bits of information that can be processed by a human seems to be around 15-20 bits/second. Information (measured in bits) refers to those parts of the message that are so significant that the meaning would be to some extent incomprehensible without knowing them. The analogy that I find most useful

---

26   Strictly speaking, 'short-term' describes the storage space and 'working' incorporates the mental processing.

27   This number has often been summarized as 'the magical number 7 plus or minus 2' (i.e. 5-9) after a prominent publication in 1956 (See G. A. Miller 1956). However, although current research agrees that we are constrained by a small upper limit, there are now a variety of proposals.

28   Information theory was introduced into the music research world by Abraham Moles through his widely-read book *Théorie de l'information et perception esthétique* (Paris, Denoël, 1973), and reached many more through the work of Meyer (1967), but was originally evolved to study the problems of electronic signal transmission.

- for those of us who are old enough to remember - is that of the old-fashioned telegram, which is written with the highest information level possible, and the least redundancy, due to the cost per word. ("Arrive Thurs Boat Stop Flowers in Hand Stop Impatient Stop A). There is an obvious loss of nuance in most telegrams, and grammar and natural flow are sacrificed, and at first glance, the meaning might even seem impenetrable – especially if the sender uses 'codes' such as allusions to more lengthy literary references the receiver is expected to recognize. But the informed receiver of the telegram will be able to reconstruct the message sufficiently, *given enough time* to read, re-read, and decode. In much well-proportioned music, on the contrary, the message unfolds slowly enough, or is sufficiently familiar in many aspects, that the receiver has a chance to absorb the most significant features of one part before the next instalment arrives. Nevertheless, some contemporary composers assume that as their work will be available for re-listening in some digital form, they can write denser pieces that *do* rely on repeated listenings (and even analysis) for their structures to be discerned.

The difference between a highly trained listener and a casual listener who has little musical experience with the genre of music in question is that 'things' or 'chunks' can mean very different amounts of data. For example, a quickly-ascending scale played by cellos followed by a slowly-descending scale on violins might be considered a vast amount of information by someone who hears each note as a separate event, and each instrument as a different voice, whereas someone familiar with the musical context can hear the passage as a single event of "a rising-falling gesture in the strings, with a tempo & timbre shift for the second part". In addition, deciding which information is irrelevant also depends on familiarity with the style: for example, in the context of an avant-garde piece, someone coughing in the front row might be initially mistaken for yet another unfamiliar timbre from the percussion.

This kind of sorting and identification requires a bit of time and brainpower (only in minute quantities of time, but continually) and therefore in constantly complex situations the brain will tire and begin to be 'muddled'. In both speech and music, there are usually mixes of complexity and simplicity to alleviate this problem. Redundancy – a word that has positive rather than negative attributes in information theory – refers to the repetition of familiar or predictable events that can effectively reduce the overall density of information in a given period of time. Parsing, a term used mainly in linguistics but also useful in musical contexts, refers to the way in which different sections of a phrase, sentence, or longer passage are recognized in the listener's mind. In language, we learn to expect certain forms of sentence structure, syntax, tense, etc. depending on the context. Therefore, when we hear a sentence, we have some idea where we are in it – where we might expect to hear a noun, a verb, an adverb, a prepositional phrase, etc. Likewise, in most classical and popular music, we have a sense that a phrase will not exceed a certain length, or change tonality in mid-phrase; that one part is a melody and another is a (less important) accompaniment; that it will have some kind of cadence or slowing of movement at the end; etc.

For those of us long immersed in more avant-garde musics and/or music from different cultures and styles, we will have a wider set of expectations but with a correspondingly vaster amount of time listening to them all, so that we will have a similar sense of what might be coming based on what we recognize of what has just happened. However, someone who lacks such experience may quickly drown under the apparently chaotic inclusion of sounds that seem to defy contextualization. And if one is listening to a piece of music which seems not to make sense, then it may be impossible to perceive any return to previous material later in the work, so the situation becomes compounded. A listener who becomes frustrated at an overload of information during what was anticipated as a pleasant aesthetic experience will doubtless end up with a different sense of the time elapsed during the work than the listener with a highly-developed ear and mind for a particular style who enjoys the challenge of quick decoding.[29]

It is clear from reflecting on this issue of memory and cognitive processing that being tired or being in a noisy environment will also have a negative impact on one's ability to make sense of what is going on.

---

29   These situations arise frequently when a public believe they have paid for accessible entertainment while the artists have interpreted their payment as license to charm their close circle of friends with imagined futures of their métier.

13. Heartbeat & Drumbeat; Body Rhythms & Internal Clocks; Entrainment

Referring to the 'beat' in music has often been thought of as a kind of heartbeat, but this is rather misleading. There is an apparent correspondence in that exciting music usually has a faster beat, just as being excited may cause the heart to beat faster. But the correspondence deteriorates under scrutiny, as the heart is unlikely to fluctuate as quickly and as dramatically as a musical beat in many types of music. On the other hand, if one thinks about drumbeats, the body correspondence gives an excellent fit, as it then refers to limb movement, motor movement, or body movement in general. Although most of us are not drummers, many people do have a tendency to tap a finger or a toe to certain musical styles, and dance is all about moving one's body in synchronization to the beat.

A fascinating research compared the curves of the speeding up and slowing down of professional runners' footsteps, and found that they corresponded perfectly in contour to the preferred *accelerandi* and *ritardandi* of certain performances of classical music.[30]

One reason why music was used traditionally in the function of 'work songs' (rowing boats, waulking wool, marching, etc.), as well as in processional music for rituals, is tied to this strong correspondence between limb movement and pace of beats. The phenomenon, which operates on several levels, is now studied under the topic of 'entrainment', wherein the body can become more efficient – and can more effectively coordinate with others in the same activity

---

30   See for example Friberg & Sundberg 1999, also Honing 2004.

– by adjusting internal clocks to match a perceived rhythm.[31]   These 'clocks' operate a bit like gears, multiple ones in sync with each other at different rates. We depend on them for all our movements – such as picking up a teacup and lifting it to our mouth, where fingers, hand, and arm are all involved in slightly different movements but coordinated (usually) to complete the gesture smoothly. Moreover, body movements of others in one's close community can be recognized as expressing a variety of energy levels and emotional states, and the nuances of those movements are easily conveyed through sound especially when they are part of an ultra-familiar and rhythmic activity like walking. Although for many years it was assumed that humans each have a "master clock" which regulates all the motor movements, oscillations, pulse, etc., that is now being discarded in favour of a model of multiple, independent clocks[32] – which corresponds very nicely to my own investigations. The implications of body clocks in general for our perception of music are vast, and discussed in some detail in Chs. 22 and 23.

14. Contemplative Time / Dream Time / Art Time / Timelessness

Timelessness is often associated with the metaphysical: the eternal world of the Gods from which our world was created, or the realm of ideas and absolutes where change is not present. In some music, the absence of a noticeable beat seems designed to avoid reference to body movements and other familiar periodic events of the environment, therefore provoking reflection on the eternal by moving the (willing) listener away from the time-passage of the external physical world. Examples of this sort abound in the Eastern musical traditions, such as the Buddhist shakuhachi repertoire of Japan and the Chinese scholar-priest's music for the ch'in, and also underline earlier Western traditions of liturgical chant and its traces in subsequent works such as those of Palestrina.

---

31   London (2004) gives a thorough explanation of entrainment and its relevance for metric music - although I have expressed my reservations with one detail of his explanation (Mountain 2007).

32   See for example Buhusi and Meck 2009; Phillips 2002.

❋ Art Time

There is a phenomenon in the life of many artists which psychologists have called 'the Flow' (see for example Csikszentmihalyi 1975). This is where an artist, often after weeks, months, or years of preparation, will throw her/himself into a creative mode so fully that the sense of clock time disappears, along with a self-critical sense. Such a state allows the artist to work unimpeded by the usual accompanying rational decision-making, allowing indulgence of subconscious urges. As these urges are, in the best cases, the result of considerable reflection on the work and years of skill in expression within a particular medium or context, they are not as random as might be expected, and may allow the artist to produce solutions to a creative problem that would in more normal situations be considered too wild or inappropriate. In such a state, the artist may well forego eating and sleeping, even though the state might last a day or two.

Such states are fairly rare in modern society outside of the artists' world, and seem disapproved of by many, as they demonstrate a rejection of the clock-time organization that keeps urban society working in some kind of coherence. Oddly enough, though, these states must be similar to those experienced by those in rituals such as marked different passages in life of ancient cultures – rituals where drugs and chosen environments (such as particularly resonant caves) were calculated to enhance the experience. In those cases, although the participant may have momentarily lost a sense of clock time, the rituals themselves accented the life cycle, in a way in which modern life often ignores.

A fascinating aspect of time within the context of a temporal art experience – whether music, dance, film, or even the experience of walking around a sculpture – is that the entire chunk of time forms an impression, if not a directly-retrievable memory, which can be 'replayed' either in the imagination or on a renewed contact (such as another performance of the same piece). The most memorable of those impressions often contain enough detail that they 'encapsulate' a certain sense of time which can become a welcome environment for ducking out of one's current pace of life. Thus, artworks can become 'time capsules' even more compactly and precisely than those of Andy Warhol. Rather like a walk through a favourite part of the countryside, where we can enjoy lingering to admire the forest flowers while knowing that soon we will reach that look-off with a grand view off to the sea, we can listen to each series of sounds and know that each time we will be able to hear more connections and intricacies, while aware that the upcoming section will be satisfying in its proportions and development.

❊ Dream Time

Those of us who dream frequently (and remember them) will be familiar with the odd behaviour of time in our dreams. For one thing, the 'plot' often seems to involve hours or days of activity, although the dream itself usually lasts only a few minutes. But even more odd is the behaviour of things in time – we may be suddenly transported from one place to another with no intervening time to arrive, or we try to move quickly and find that our body responds excruciatingly slowly.

It seems that this experience of time is often very close to what we may experience in a musical work. A sense of time may be clearly established, and then suddenly be replaced with a slower or faster pace; a musical element such as a melody or gesture will suddenly reappear in what seems a different and unexpected context, as though viewed through a very different lens.

15. Impact of health, training, personality, culture, clan

Internal clocks are very susceptible to derailment or at least temporal shifts in pace from chemical changes in the body. Common causes are caffeine, alcohol, and drugs (prescription and 'recreational') but can also be triggered by fatigue, stress or disease.[33] Aging also impacts perception of time – not only because motor movements may slow and memory weakens, but also, and perhaps more importantly, older people have a differing 'default' sense of scale – e.g. against a backdrop of decades rather than mere years of personal experience. Having more past can give a person more familiarity with the possible varieties of temporal

---

33 For this reason, I urged my composition students to check the tempo markings of their compositions over the course of a week, at different times of day, so that they would not find that a tempo indication chosen after 2 cups of coffee felt 'wrong' in concert after the listeners had consumed a glass of wine with dinner.

experience and better frameworks against which to view a myriad of events. Additionally, some of us are intrigued by the changes in historical perspectives, and may find some young people 'stranded' in the present-day without having sufficient temporal perspective. Conversely, as the pace of modern life increases dramatically, older people may feel bewildered at the speed of change.

Training can certainly impact one's temporal acuity at different levels: acrobats and gymnasts, for example, have to master a precision of executing movements to the level of the millisecond, just as musical performers in metric music and ensemble playing usually have to coordinate at very fine levels - even though such levels will be related to body clocks more than wall clocks. Electroacoustic musicologists have noted that those involved with electronics and computer music, where sounds can be 'sculpted' to an almost infinitesimal degree, become used to thinking about such microscopic levels while planning their compositional design.[34] Although most people will notice tiny shifts in a sound's frequency components, amplitude, and general behaviour, the effect will normally be 'felt' rather than consciously recognized, as those characteristics are often absorbed into a global sense of the sound. Electroacoustic music aficionados, however, are often excited by the challenge of identifying these individual temporal characteristics, and become increasingly skilled in consciously perceiving the various components.

Just as some people may be drawn to such a focus on the microscopic, there are many who like to track the slower rates of temporal phenomena, whether it be the sense of how long one clock-hour lasts, in any context, or an appreciation of the recurring seasons of the year. Friends and/or society norms may also reinforce the importance of one kind of time-tracking or another: a tendency to bask in memories of earlier times, or conversely to refuse to contemplate the past in favour of a relentless focus on an upcoming project. Such tendencies doubtless impact a listener's reaction to music that patterns time in one way or another.

---

34 See for example Rossetti, Antunes & Manzolli (2020).

Section IV.

Interactions of Human & External Time

16. Synchronizing with the Community

Our days since ancient times have been punctuated at the very least with meals and rest. The necessity of sunlight (or dawn or dusk) for most activities, along with a need for periodic nourishment, provided the model we still use most frequently, which segregates day from evening and night. Increasingly, we have been organizing ourselves by often stricter time-frames for working, commuting, and daily tasks.

In such cases, we are frequently tracking time in the background, and many operate with 'one eye on the clock'. The ability to track it extremely well is often admired in certain professions and positions: 'Very business-like; always punctual'. Others realize that being free of the 'tyranny' of the clock can be healthy and liberating in some circumstances – such as when making art (although it may interfere with preparing food at appropriate times, for example, or showing up in time to hear - or perform in – a concert). Although generally a learned skill, some people seem to possess innate capacity for estimating temporal durations at certain time-scales, while others seem quite inept. However, such awareness of the clock is often deliberately suspended while listening to music.

17. Human Time, Historical Time

Although we may think of time as unrolling at a constant speed, as indicated by the steady cycles of the sun and moon, we also collectively contribute to a sense of the evolutionary speed of our own culture. In this sense, it is very difficult for most Westerners to conceive of an ancient civilization such as Egypt's, where it appears that society changed very little over a few thousand years. Language, customs, dress, and technology appear to our findings to have remained quite similar there from one century to another– although critical study begins to reveal changes caused by invaders, for example. Now, however, drastic changes are easily apparent within a single lifetime, at least in much of the world. Many of us still easily remember life before computers, to say nothing of internet and e-mail, and our parents and grandparents remembered life before any widespread use of cars and airplanes (which both 'shrink' the traditional time duration required to traverse a particular distance). However, it is also interesting to remark on the constancy of such change. In a region where life has continued with little change for a few centuries, one cataclysmic event – an invasion or earthquake, for example – might have more impact than in today's environment, where many people are in a kind of permanent state of anticipating catastrophes. On the other hand, the recent Covid-19 pandemic has made many people realize that their expectations of the onset speed of any potential change were too conservative.

The sense of how quickly 'things' are changing doubtless affects a community's sense of time. Even with the computers and other technological developments, some people involved with nature – whether studying brains or growing food – will still find it useful to assume that things are as they have been for millennia: food still tends to grow at the same rate,[35] and brains (we imagine) operate in very similar ways. The strength of a community's cultural traditions is also a major factor: both musicians and audience celebrating performances of music in India, for example, can directly tap into centuries of musical traditions.

Again, it is partly a question of perspective and focus – what are we using primarily to gauge the passing of time? The portrayal of our history is a good example of this, and explains some differences between North American and European attitudes, for example. Many Europeans have lived in regions close to if not identical to ones where their direct ancestors have lived for at least a millennium, whereas most North Americans have not (with the obvious exception of some Indigenous peoples, although others of that 'group' have traded in a more nomadic life for a settled one also distant from their ancestors' stomping grounds). A few decades ago, we remarked that our Canadian friends and colleagues seemed much more likely than our American ones to think of themselves as still belonging to a family or clan group coming from another place (even though it might have been 200-300 years ago), whereas many we met from the United States preferred to emphasize their New World status. Likewise, "history" as presented in high school, for example, is always quite subjective although it often purports to be an objective result, and the different styles of portraying the historical timeline influences a culture's thinking and actions. It may appear that modern scholars

---

35   The current experiments in making food grow faster through GMO, for example, will hopefully be more closely monitored as it becomes clearer how the taste and nutrients are usually diluted as a result, and/or the plant's overall lifetime becomes shortened.

(and media) are working hard to correct these subjective histories, but in fact there has been an unfortunate blurring of the issues, with simplifications, exaggerations, and lies being called into the service of providing a politically-corrected narrative.

This kind of manipulation of information is critical to society, as the number of tangible and intangible artefacts of past inhabitants of a region will have a clear impact on one's own sense of historical time, whether they are remnants of a previous time when one's own culture was dominant, or show the remains of a previous culture dominated by one's own or someone else's, or simply appear 'foreign'. Until recently, history traced one's own culture's rate of 'progress' through time, and gave an indication of the preferred time-scale of focus. What can be interesting to those who study other peoples' histories, without preconditioning, is that one begins to see both the community's tendency to certain ways of operating and the dependence on propaganda or tradition to shape the future: 'we lost that region four hundred years ago, but we'll get it back' or 'our people have always been moving to different lands'. These attitudes will often influence the community member's tendency to focus on the present, past, or future, and whether these are thought of as being broad or confined: decades or millennia.

18. Multiplicities, non-linearity, chaos

Chaos refers to the appearance of total disorder: random events, with no apparent causality linking them. However, as Arnheim (1971) pointed out, what seems chaotic may be simply the result of an inability to recognize multiple coexisting orders. Of course, it can also be simply randomness, although our current knowledge of the natural world shows little true randomness except at a certain microscopic level, which can be interpreted as its own [stable or slowly-evolving] state of fluctuation – like the Brownian movement of gas particles in air (a fundamental element in Xenakis's design of his musical work *Pithoprakta*).

An increasing interest in plurality and diversity was clearly reflected in much of the 'art music' of the European-North American 20th century. Composers like Ives, Stravinsky, Varèse, Mosolov, Messiaen, Cage, and Stockhausen were particularly noted for their portraying of multiple events or phenomena simultaneously within musical forms – in a kind of larger-scale counterpoint of musical textures and layers. Electroacoustic music is particularly rich in such designs, due in part to the ease of assembling coexisting sounds, through splicing and particularly multi-tracking, even in early analog studios. Many listeners have developed the expertise to enjoy following such multiple streams, while contact with models of temporal design in other cultures' art forms can also contribute to the development of such appreciation – the slightly-out-of-sync passages of Steve Reich's phase pieces and Jon Hassell's work are both given acknowledgement to African traditional styles, and my early awareness of their work may have helped my appreciation of the same phenomena in both Tuareg and Afghan styles, in which I sometimes find myself imagining the shifting movements of individual camels in a camel train.

The listener's sense of time experienced while listening to such complex music seems much more vulnerable to distortion from clock time - which may in itself be one of the attractions of this type of entertainment. The nature of the distortions are more unpredictable for the composer to design, however, because they depend not only on the listener's reaction to each different stratum of musical information, but also to their ability and/or interest in distinguishing them all. Some people enjoy this kind of complexity far more than others, and will therefore develop the skills that make the deciphering of apparent chaos a rich reward. The way in which this works can be best explained, in my opinion, by recourse to the fields of psychology and especially auditory scene analysis;[36] I have developed an analytical tool based on these principles that is expounded elsewhere.[37]

This kind of formal design of musical works seems closer to a different metaphor of time than that of the single flowing river of many earlier musical works - perhaps closer to one of viewing various rivers from a helicopter.

---

36   See for example Bregman 1990.

37   Mountain 2009; pending further elaboration in a forthcoming book called *Sorting out the Strata*.

19. Environment and expectations

For those who have been accustomed to thinking of time as a linear unfolding of events in some type of sequential form (Ch. 8), the increasing awareness of other cultures and their respective historical records may present quite a different perspective. Depending on the individual, that perspective may provoke unease, as it threatens their own knowledge of history. But of course, this is only when one feels the need to reconcile it all into one line. In fact, most cultures and sub-cultures evolve within their own spheres, and it is only recently that many of us have realized that those evolutions seem to happen at different rates. This was always more evident to those who travelled extensively or at least to faraway places; the other place not only had its own history, but had a world-view often unaffected by that of the traveller's own culture. Although much of the Western media is working to give a sense that we are all now aware of events in every part of the world, the extremely selective accounts they provide, with a lack of context and tendency to generalizations and over-simplifications, only confound the picture.

20. The role of time in art and literature

Time is an essential ingredient of all arts, and also fundamental in storytelling and literature. Not only do these artforms need time to be presented or absorbed, but they often consciously (if obliquely) refer to the passing of time.

In painting, for example, the main composition may be able to be grasped more or less immediately, although one might well want to savour the image as one might savour an apparently still view from a mountain lookoff. However, many paintings need time from the spectator to absorb the various details, and some - ancient Egyptian friezes, Indian cave carvings, Indonesian tapestries - relate stories in order to preserve historical or mythological sequences of events. Others, such as the Dutch and Flemish painters of the Renaissance such as Avercamp, portrayed different concurrent events in small images of fine detail (the so-called genre paintings) which cannot be easily grasped without narrowing one's focus to a subset of the entire canvas - and even requiring that the viewer alter their body position in order to see other parts at the same level of detail. Such images are in themselves comments on the different but apparently concurrent experiences of time of their subjects.

Sculpture also demands time from the spectator who needs to move and change perspective before being able to grasp the whole - although in some cases, as with paintings, the overall image is so familiar that one can anticipate to some extent what the unseen parts will look like before confirming. The 'capturing' of a moment in time - especially when a body is in mid-stride or mid-strike - allows an appreciation of a temporally-bound action outside its normal ephemeral state. The ability to portray the concept of motion through the evocation of a suspended movement, especially in a static material such as marble, has long been an indicator of quality, from Michelangelo's *Captives* [or *Prisoners*] to Boccioni's *Unique Forms of Continuity in Space*. In the mid-20th century, easier access to technology and often a good dose of whimsy enabled some fascinating kinetic sculptures sometimes reminiscent of ancient clock mechanisms and other mechanical devices, while some proponents of the concurrent earth art movement led to a much more profound reflection on human appreciation of time by drawing our attention to different natural time-scales and human constructs - from Smithson's *Spiral Jetty* to Heizer's *Double Negative* and Oppenheim's *Time Line*.[38]

Novels in particular are generally quite clear about the timeline in the story, although sometimes there are ambiguities that may play an important part in their appreciation. Many stories have a simple forward-moving narrative, although the 'action' may jump unevenly, with detailed descriptions of conversations and then a skip forward to a month or year later. Therefore, the pace of the story shifts between semi-realistic portrayals of the progression of minutes (as in the explicit description of a dialogue), more encapsulated pockets of longer durations ("the evening was characterized by a general frivolity / the summer was full of lazy days"), and 'fast-forward' gaps which are often encapsulated by descriptions of the evidence of time having passed ("the gardens were now in full bloom / her hair was beginning to show grey / the tensions between the two countries seemed to be subsiding").

In dance, the pacing of time can be considerably more abstract. Familiar

---

38 See for example H. Mountain 1980.

actions - walking, running, jumping - will normally occupy a similar number of seconds as the same actions in the course of everyday activities, although they may be subject to small adjustments in order to exaggerate the movement; however, the length of the repetitions involved may differ markedly, with truncated strolls or concatenated gestures. Likewise, the movements of traditional dances may be referred to in direct or oblique ways within modern contexts, with a similar impression of the time required to move in step around a circle, for example. But the combination of elements is often unrelated to mundane activities, and may focus on cyclic patterns that go against the Western trend to think of everyday life as moving in a forward, linear way. [39]

Music has extreme freedom from the confinements of everyday motion. While narrative structures are common in certain styles, much music is full of different textures and apparent motion. The physical limitations of moving fingers and arms to produce sound on instruments will provide some audible boundaries of tempo in solo music, but even two or three performers in combination can produce extremely complex patternings. The world of electroacoustics has expanded this almost into infinity, as the various approaches to composition revealed such richness of the microscopic detail of our sonic environments and our perception of them that composers and listeners were drawn to their exploration. (Indeed, the linking of perceptual issues to music seemed more frequent among early pioneers in electroacoustics than with other composers.) Therefore, there is a practically limitless range of temporal densities and pacings available to the composer, and in the 20th century, these were fully explored. Nevertheless, each style has its own sense not only of the variety 'allowed' but also the overall duration of a piece, which remains very conservative for the majority of audiences.

---

39   The fact of an entire dance occurring in the same space, despite using limb movements usually associated with changing location, is doubtless a strong factor.

Section V.

Time in Music

21. Time in musical contexts:
INTRODUCTION

The act of listening to music incorporates and reproduces many of the normal aspects of human interaction with time. It needs to deal with some potential differences, however, such as compressed and expanded time-scales that can draw the attention to very quick events normally confined to subconscious interpretations, or cause one to suspend time-tracking for unusually long time-periods. In addition, the listener's attention will almost always be dragged from one 'event' or 'environment' to another more frequently than in the mundane world. An analytically-leaning listener may well enjoy trying to identify different music components with their respective features – including their temporal behaviour – and build an abstract image of the overall proportions and design. However, the listener's ears are so inundated with audio information that some crucial choices of how to organize all the sounds into something 'meaningful' have to be conducted at extremely fast levels.

By 'meaningful' organization, I mean simply a structure that makes sense to the listener - similar to the way in which we might grasp the nature of a poem in a language we know. There, although the logic of prose may be absent, and the actual sounds arising from the combination of consonants and vowels may have been chosen for their sonic impact more than would happen in normal speech, the words do suggest certain concepts, ideas, or characters. In traditional music, the 'meaning' may be limited to recognizing the melody *as* a melody, and the accompanying texture *as* accompaniment - but this is already a major step in continuing on, and possibly recognizing a fragment of the same melody later on in the piece, even if it is transformed in some features (timbre, range, mode, etc.) With some complex 20th- and 21st-century works, the listener may identify things 'wrongly' according to the composer's original concept, or the music analyst's suggestion - but it might still provide an interesting grouping of the available sounds and provide an aesthetic experience. (The advantage of following an analyst's recommendations should be that the analyst has considered various options, and omitted some plausible groupings as less likely because, when studying the whole work, those groupings don't exhibit the same coherence with other features in the piece, at the same or higher hierarchical levels, as the recommended ones. However, there are plenty of analysts whose aesthetic preferences are sufficiently different that they will seem to 'miss the point' of some pieces another person may enjoy – if for example the listener is fascinated by timbres and tunings, while the analyst places more value on complex harmonic structures.)

It is important to understand that the role of memory in music involves memories from months and years ago as well as those of sonic events of a few seconds earlier. Likewise, "past experiences" include not only fleeting memories of events which the musical mood has conjured up, but a large framework of musical and auditory experiences which inform the listener of probabilities. Without such clues, the piece may be absorbed on a purely sensory level of listening to various frequencies without any sense of shape or form. Certain minimal pieces and other styles can indeed be enjoyed that way - and are likely to invoke a sense of timelessness because there is no awareness of inherent succession.

At the level of microseconds to half-minutes, our appreciation of the musical activity is closely linked to our knowledge of our environment as received on aural channels. The aural signatures of physical actions, speech and vocal utterances, and the movement and behaviour of other phenomena, are just one part of their character while the visual trace is often tagged as presenting corroboration. For example, the sound of footsteps getting louder is linked to the idea of a human or other animal moving towards the hearer - a phenomenon that has been perceived often enough that the listener is more likely to think about the meaning of the movement than about its particular sonic attributes. Nonetheless, long association will allow the listener to link footsteps with speed and mood, and in many cases, even with a specific person. Similarly, we often recognize the sound of someone talking even if we are too far away to understand the actual words (for instance, in a nearby room), but we are likely to understand the emotions underlying the speech, due to the particular amplitude contours, rhythmic patterns, and timbral configuration; we may be able to recognize the specific speaker if their voice is already familiar to us.

However, in music, aural signals are usually presented in a kind of isolation from their usual source. The fact that the listener may be watching performers playing instruments to produce the sounds is actually a potential distractor from the idea of the imaginary source, just as a film or multimedia piece may present images that contrast with the soundtrack. Traditionally, composers would use timbre as a unifying factor in describing a certain configuration - such as a melody or gesture. The fact that instruments have often been used to imitate the voice can make this clearer: if we hear one voice speaking, we tend to think of it as one character and the various words as part of a narrative or at least as parts of a single phrase. If and when that voice changes to another voice, then one might expect (unless it seems like an echo) that the other voice is saying something different - whether complementary or contrasting. Many composers throughout the centuries have designed musical passages with the same kind of model, so that when a flute plays some notes and then a cello plays some notes, the flute notes appear to form one unit (or stream) and the cello notes form another. This is equally true when the timbres result from a grouping of instruments: brass + percussion contrasting with strings + woodwinds, for example. Therefore, a second level of hierarchical organization can be established when the aforementioned contrast between flute and cello become subsumed into a larger section where they represent a common texture in contrast with the brass + percussion.

In other words, musical activity is often reminiscent of familiar non-music activities, and although the resemblance may be noticed or felt at a subliminal level only, it may determine how we initially try to parse the musical content, and colour our appreciation of it. We can recognize a walk or a hand gesture (such as a wave hello or goodbye) as fast, average, or slow, and interpret the different speeds as potentially expressive of different moods. We can likewise recognize certain types of musical configuration as fast or slow gestures, or hear the beats as delineating walking or running paces. Imitation of vocal expression is so intertwined with instrumental music that, even without training in rhetorical devices, we are likely to make connections between certain patterns of rising or falling gestures and mood. However, if the sonic representation is at a rate or speed too far from its original model we may well not recognize the original as its origin.

Such actions are measurable and expressible in terms of clock time, and easily grasped through their relationship with our body clocks.[40] The correlation to external clocks might seem elusive (as the link is often not mentioned in musical contexts) but is plainly visible on careful scrutiny in notated scores where durations are calculated with reference to beats per minute (metronome markings). It can be rendered more clearly if the notation is translated into a graphic representation where the units of time are uniform, as that is how we are more accustomed to

---

40 As discussed in Ch. 24.

reading scientific data delineated against clock-time.[41] On the other hand, some elements of the musical form are perceived less directly, and sensed at a much slower level - spans of minutes and even half-hours in some cases. In such cases, memory, attention, training, and experience become much more relevant to one's appreciation of the nature of the time passed. The sense of duration will then be felt on a much more subjective level, and thus approximate our general personal experience of time, not always in sync with clock time (as discussed in Ch. 10).

We *expect* to sense time experientially in music, though - just as we expect to be led into a contemplative state by much art - and it is thus open to other 'surface' features[42] designed to produce a psychological impact and modulate the established pace of (clock) time. Such impacts can be heightened by sharp contrast of musical material, or other unexpected configurations, where the listener who has been tracking the time at a certain pace will suddenly become distracted from that task.

In general terms, our perception of the passage of time in music, as in life, depends to a large extent on the densities of information. That in turn depends on the listener's tolerance for information density in general, and their ease with processing the information in the music. As 'information' includes aspects like the predictability of any given pitch set, rhythmic configuration, timbral diversity, etc., the individual listener's experience, interest, aesthetics, and mental processing speed (itself susceptible to temporary conditions such as coffee or fatigue) will become paramount. A third aspect is the listener's interest in listening to different hierarchical levels of the musical structure, by simultaneously tracking large-, medium, and small-scale features – such as listening to the details of the foreground patterning while being aware that it belongs to the accompaniment of the third theme and will probably evolve in a similar way to its first and second iterations. Such tracking (which is simultaneous only when considered in the large scale, as it will generally exist more as an alternation between attention distances in the short

---

41 The first examples I saw of that type were in Cogan & Escot 1976; I subsequently found it quite informative to draw my own visual graphs of certain passages in compositions I was studying for insight into temporal organization, with the x-axis representing time and the y-axis the frequency, in a stricter version of the traditional Western notation designed to be read left-to-right with higher notes of the staff being located upwards – e.g. Figs. 18 & 19.

42 By surface, I mean the rhythmic level of the individual notes or other short sonic components.

term) is closely linked to the information density issue, as it is also subject to the varying densities of the respective time-scales; the hierarchical relationships may themselves exhibit simplicity or complexity; and the listener may or may not be interested or skilled in retaining a multi-level view.

❋ Time Compression – uses & limitations

A crucial difference between the sense of personal experience of time in music and that in one's personal or community's lifetime is that the music experience is extremely compressed - just as the action of a play which might follow its characters and their changing relationships and moods through several seasons of their lives is telescoped into a few hours. Nevertheless, the local details of tempo must remain at their own realistic pace in order to maintain the illusions, just as the rate of delivering the lines in a play are governed by standard speech rates in order to be comprehensible.[43]

When there is a noticeable beat in the music, it can function as the ticking of an imaginary clock; this is a familiar analogy among musicians and rhythmic theorists. However, the beat is such a common aspect of music designed for physical activity - whether working, walking, or dancing - that the 'clock' thus represented lies somewhere between the external clock and the body clock. In both cases, the beat can operate as a powerful indicator of regularity, measurability and forward progression (although if nothing much seems to be happening except for the reiteration of a beat, the sense of forward movement may be traded for a sense of static permanence[44]). The beat establishes a reference which then emphasizes the irregularities of any other material, such as melodic contour, gestural interjections, or a 'pregnant pause': I often think of it as a basic unit of the temporal graph paper on which the music is designed. In Figure 1, I sketch my impression of the graph paper with various adjustments to demonstrate its distortions in a usual piece.

---

43 It might be noted by some that the delivery of lines in a theatre are in fact usually a bit slower than in everyday contexts - to help comprehension and compensate for the atypical acoustic environment of the performance - and similar factors apply to music as well, although the beat itself is felt internally, so it needs to be closer to the original model for successful comprehension.

44 This is not surprising on reflection: if a beat suggests something like a footstep, then one expects it to change in amplitude - moving towards or away - and if it doesn't, it resembles something more mechanical.

A Musician's Guide to Time

The addition of logarithmic shading to the graph comes from a hypothesis of mine that, as our perception of pitch and loudness are logarithmic, and pitch discrimination accurate in a certain range (around that of the human voice) that our perception of rhythm might well have a similar logarithmic oscillation as well as a natural tendency to the most finely-tuned clock-time perception centering around the beat-meter range. After all, we are rhythmic and oscillating beings, with built-in compression-decompression cycles - lifting a foot up and putting it down again; waking / sleeping; inhaling / exhaling. Composition students learn that information density must be carefully controlled in order to allow the salient features of our designs to be appreciated. If this is all true, then we should follow the research of those who study micro-rubato: instead of looking at any performer's deviation from the clock-time version of a given piece of music, we need to deduce the 'base' fluctuation and plot any performance 'deviations' from it.

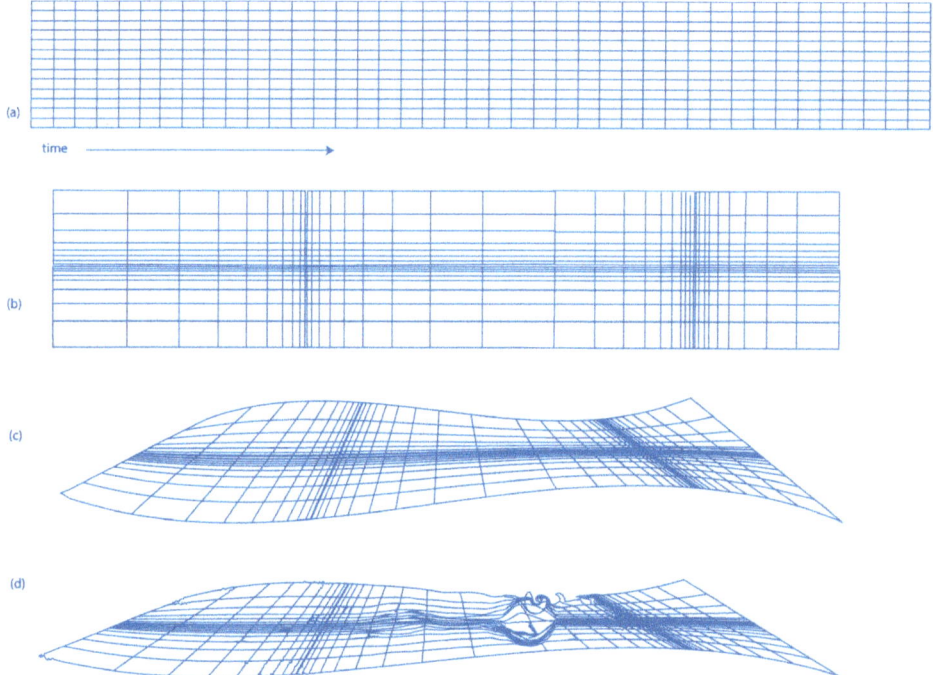

Figure 1. Time axis of music represented by graph paper: (a) clock-time; (b) logarithmic adjustment; (c) effect of musical illusions; (d) listener's focus.

The second 'distortion' in my illustration represents the way in which the music shifts the sense of clock time by various means (the given example representing a fairly simple rhythmic form), and the third represents the listener's additional twisting of linear time by focussing on certain components and reflecting on them for a few seconds after they have 'disappeared'.

In most Western concert music, the beat is rarely emphasized audibly at each occurrence in a musical passage; rather, it is suggested and subsequently internalized by the listener to 'track' the rest of the activity (referred to as 'entrainment', which places it correctly within our physical action systems). Most frequently, the beats are organized into higher-level groups (meter) and typically, every third or fourth beat may have some accenting feature, to enable tracking without slippage. This 'bar-level' periodicity (which I call the 'super-pulse' so it can be used even in the absence of notated meter) is a typical choice for aligning the mental calipers we use to measure the temporal proportions. Composers often depend on beats and bars to establish and then subsequently subvert the "clock time" of music through devices such as rubato, irregular beats, irregular phrase lengths, tempo changes, a disturbed flow, or suspended tempi.

At a slightly more abstract level, but one which is arguably related to human motion as well, we may hear the motion implied within a musical gesture (for example, rising in pitch at an increasing rate, or quickly reiterating a single chord), as gentle, foreboding, or frantic depending on the specific rates of the main notes, the amplitude (which will often share the same or similar curve), and the specific timbres and harmonies. When spatial distribution is involved – a device heard easily in electroacoustic music, where a sound can be 'panned' from one speaker to another – the sense of motion is even more emphatic, as our basic senses are used to interpreting the speed of motion in our environment through auditory cues in space.[45]

Thus, within a given time-frame, a human listener will experience the various temporal events of the music in different ways, depending on those events'

---

45 John Chowning's early computer music piece *Turenas* (1972) was remarkable in its sense of motion as it incorporated techniques to simulate the Doppler effect, so that the illusion would be even stronger. These 'pan' effects are extremely affected by the distance between the speakers, however, which is why they aren't easily transmitted by CD to an indeterminate home system.

character, density, rate of change, familiarity, etc. Likewise, all the participants (composer, conductor, performer, sound engineer, listener, analyst, critic, teacher, historian, etc.) have their own characters, experiences, moods, and trajectories, which will influence how they interact with any given temporal design.

Several terms have been used by musicologists and composers to refer to temporal aspects of musical structures: rhythm, pace, form, beat, meter, spectromorphology, etc. (see Appendix B). Most of these have some overlap, and some are much more specific about their range of applications and pertinent duration levels than others. 'Pace' is one of the more loosely defined terms, but one that proves useful in describing the unfolding rate of 'information' which determines to a large extent our perception of a musical work's temporal profile.

A special point in the difference between time in music and time in our everyday lives is that, as with all temporal artforms, there is a notable added layer: the artwork or music itself is designed to present its own temporal patterns *as an aesthetic experience*. In everyday life, many people will not think about the ways in which various adjacent temporal durations interacted with each other, nor will they file their memories away by category of temporal denseness/sparsity or their degree of alignment with the clock and calendar - although such characteristics may be recalled on demand. And although we may have a natural tendency to relax after a busy day or month, we don't always calculate our lives according to the establishment of pleasing proportions of durations - and if we do, it often has more to do with the energy and activity involved rather than a measuring of the specific length in hours or days.

Temporal arts, however, often incorporate allusions to extra-musical states (such as being hectic or calm, aggressive or subtle) and can present balanced and/or exaggerated contrasts between simultaneous or juxtaposed sections that rarely occur outside of an art environment in any coherent manner. The listener is often encouraged to pay attention to very minute details of temporal activity and changes, at an exceptional level compared with our normal awareness of time's duration and experience.[46] Likewise, the musical context provides a 'safe place' to experience chaotic bursts of activity of a nature, which would be

---

46 We do pay attention to minute details of our sonic environment, such as extracting expression from speech utterances, but as this is more efficiently absorbed into the longer temporal unit of the word and sentence, it does not usually hit a conscious level.

unlikely if the sounds actually represented their imaginary physical counterparts. This constantly-shifting but often close-up focus on different levels of the flow of time can produce the impression of compressed experience or microcosms of larger-scale occurrences. Nonetheless, the specific clock-time rates of the various musical elements are pivotal to our perception, as they correspond to our body's internal clocks and normal movements. These influence our perception of speech, motion, and general appreciation of our sonic environment at a subliminal level. Thus, the perception of time within a musical experience is dependent on many aspects: some that directly parallel our everyday perceptions of time but others that are quite unique.

❋ Timelines of Music

At a broader level - which is not simply conceptual, but actually temporal in itself - each piece of music has its own timeline, which we could break into the following:

History - from the earliest roots of its tradition through the composer's own development, and including the compressions (and distortions) from accidental or deliberate editing, a shifting view of essential *vs.* gratuitous features, and the general quality of memory storage & retrieval;

Creative conception - the imagining of sonic images, textures, gestures, melodies, motives, etc. and organizational structures for their arrangement;

Transmission - the codification of compositional ideas into sonic information, usually set down in some type of score and subsequently decodified by performers;[47] or, in the case of improvisation, the more direct transmission by the creator(s)/performer(s) through sound-producing instruments;

Reception - the listener's attempts to organize the sequences of sounds into a set of coherent aural images, whether live or from a delayed (and decayed) reproduction on their mobile device;

---

47 Including diffusers - the ones working at the console in electroacoustic music who are able to influence the details of individual speaker volume thus affecting the perception of fundamental aspects of representations of movement and energy.

> ECHOES - the aural echoes of the work in the listener's mind hours or years later; analytical attention by later musicologists; inclusion into categories of cultural heritage; etc.

The 'transmission path' includes all of these - except perhaps the echoes. It can be understood as extending from point A to point Z, through a number of intervening points. In such an analogy, Point A would be somewhere between the mind(s) of the composer(s) and the roots of the cumulative tradition of sound art in the composer's community. Point Z is the listener's mind, where the sounds are decoded into a series of designs and images which may or may not accurately reflect the original idea (in itself dependent to some extent on their familiarity with the tradition involved).

Intervening points may include:

- the composer's ability to adequately notate the sonic designs and images into a notation which can be suitably decoded by a good performer, and/or the composer's or technician's ability to create the desired sounds in an electronic studio, computer programme, etc.;

- the characteristics of the performer(s) [48] - who may or may not have the necessary level of technique, sympathy with the composer's intentions, skill and maturity to transmit the more ephemeral aspects of the music (such as emotion), and, if applicable, to mesh their own part successfully within the ensemble;

- the characteristics of the musical instrument(s) and/or recording studio to allow for reproduction of the sounds as imagined;

- the characteristics of the performance context (including architecture & acoustics, ambient sounds, and visual aspects of the presentation which may or may not enhance or obscure the performance);

- the characteristics of the recording engineer, studio, & playback systems which may capture the performance and displace it to a different physical environment with varying degrees of accuracy or appropriate enhancement;

---

48 By 'performers' I also include vocalists and conductors, if any, as well as the diffusers in an electroacoustic concert when they adopt a performance role.

- the listener's ability & willingness to suspend normal time-tracking;

- the listener's capacities & predisposition for various temporal experiences;

- the specific temporal designs as exhibited in the musical structure, correlated more or less directly to clock time;[49] and

- the representation or illusions of specific temporal experiences presented in the music.

(These last points are discussed in detail in Chs. 25-27.)

22. INFLUENCES OF THE AUDITORY SYSTEM

Perception of music involves most or all of the normal mechanisms of human auditory processing, as well as factors that depend on other attributes of the listener's unique position as influenced by experience, mood, character, aural acuity, listening environment, aesthetics, etc. As our normal auditory processing involves many decisions based on extremely fast sorting of data, much of it is relegated to subconscious decisions. Such low-level processing does depend on the physical state of the listener in terms of basic hearing limitations, metabolism and fatigue, as well as on their experience in terms of familiarity of the sounds and structures (which will allow for more rapid parsing decisions). But it is grounded in our ability to sort all of the audio data received by our brains into appropriate streams, with or without the corroboration of visual and other senses, in order to provide the necessary information to navigate and function in our environments. Our skills in this area have been greatly under-recognized, partly due to the ephemerality of both the audio and the mental processing, but recent research has benefitted from technological advances – from signal analysis to brain monitoring – to provide increasingly detailed information. For the purposes of understanding music and time perception, it is useful to understand that at these fast rates, different receptors are optimized for receiving different types and combinations of

---

49 For ex. through notation indicated with reference to a tempo marking of beats per minute.

data, with expectations being triggered when certain patterns occur, and trackers are adjusted to anticipate their continuation. Even the perception of regularly-recurring patterns is quite dependent on the specific rate of the periodicity involved.

Our brains are constantly 'scanning' the audio environment to identify what is going on - how to match data coming in on different channels to produce plausible identification of sound sources. Based on the assumption that our receptors were already highly developed in ancient times for reasons of survival, we can map more modern acoustic phenomena onto their resemblance to basic sonic ingredients from our collective past. These might be grouped according to the following categories:

- speech and other vocal utterances for communication or expression;
- bird, insect, & animal sounds;
- other natural phenomena such as fire, flowing water (streams and rivers), falling water (rain), ocean water (waves), avalanche, cracking ice, wind in trees or crevices;
- naturally-produced sounds from human activity, including tools and machines (footsteps, handclaps, flint-knapping, blacksmith's hammering, scythes, grain mills, chariot-wheels, potter's wheel, etc.)
- music for dance, work, or ritual processions (where coordination of limb movement between people is important);
- songs for expression of feelings and for ritual;
- sounds of (simple) instruments.[50]

In addition, we rely on our body clocks to inform all our physical movements - from walking to picking up a cup of coffee. In fact, we are oscillating, rhythmic beings: even when we are not walking or grinding grain or rowing a boat or climbing a tree or swimming or drumming or texting, our hearts are beating and our lungs are breathing air in and out in entirely familiar rates. Fluctuations in heart and

---

50 Instruments are in some ways a subset, as they were probably developed mainly to imitate one of the preceding categories, such as song or birds, or to provide the rhythm for ritual music, but sometimes they were doubtless invented for playful reasons, and occasionally, as is argued in the case of the monochord, for mathematical calculations and demonstrations.

breath rate are closely connected to mood or energy: more excitement and more energy usually translate directly into faster (and often louder), while relaxation corresponds to slowing and dying away of energy and sound. Music - whether dance, song, ritual, or art music - has depended for millennia on these connections for purposes of expression, communication, and inducing a desired state of mind (or mood) in the listener. In modern contexts - especially within the last century - some musicians have chosen to play with these links themselves, presenting rhythms in their familiar guises and then stretching, shrinking, interrupting, or superposing them on other elements. Others have chosen to avoid regularities on all levels, presenting more chaotic configurations that demand new ways of interpretation. When we compose and listen to 'art' music, therefore, we can take advantage of all of our auditory processes and our motor control coordinators to decode what is presented in the musical context, and transfer the identification of sonic information into a freer identification of musical images, patterns, textures, gestures, and lines.[51]

In the everyday world, as soon as the brain has identified something that sounds like speech, for example, certain receptors will focus on various components of the audio signal listening for confirmation and further detail. Those components will include attention to the main pitch-band of the speaking voice(s), the audible overtones and their respective amplitudes, the formants or resonant areas created by the specific vocal tract(s), the length of vowels and sounds of consonants, the length of phrases, etc. They also involve, concurrently, the more cerebral process(es) of decoding the verbal information being transmitted. Such receptors have to cover quite a range of channels: even confining ourselves to the recognition of a few words, it involves sorting and coordinating multiple streams of data from various receptors in the 20-16,000+ Hz. range, as well as the slightly slower range involved in the careful assessment of onset (a)synchrony, durations, temporal proportions of vowels, consonances, and silences.[52]

On another array of channels - those which search in the range of around 400 to 5000 ms. - if we identify that a sonic event repeats (or is re-initiated) every

---

51 It should be noted that the identification of the actual sound source(s) may be somewhat incidental, as composers often try to 'fuse' the sounds from different instruments into a single imaginary sound source, with a particular character and behaviour.

52 See Appendix B for translations of milliseconds (ms.) to Hz., tempo markings, etc.

second or so, we tend to relate it intuitively to our repertory of limb movements. The way in which we hear music with a beat has been clearly linked with our tendency to track these beats and beat-grouping rhythms with our own bodies, in the process called 'entrainment'. This is what happens when we dance, and as dance and music doubtless share origins, the feedback between this limb movement and music has been reinforced for millennia, with most of us continuing the reinforcement during our lives (although these days, over-dependence on digital media as well as other automated machines from cars to blenders means that the link between limb and action has become significantly less direct for many younger people). Additionally, pre-technological work methods often involved coordination not only of one's own body, but of several bodies in a team (rowing, pulling, scything, chopping, etc.), and entraining to regularities at these levels was both natural and encouraged, as it makes the work more efficient and less tiring.

Not only is it easy to entrain to music with a beat (even for infants), but it is difficult not to; only those of us who aim to become more versatile composers or admirers of complex polyrhythms will enjoy the challenges of moving out of step (asynchronously) with a simple audible beat in that range.

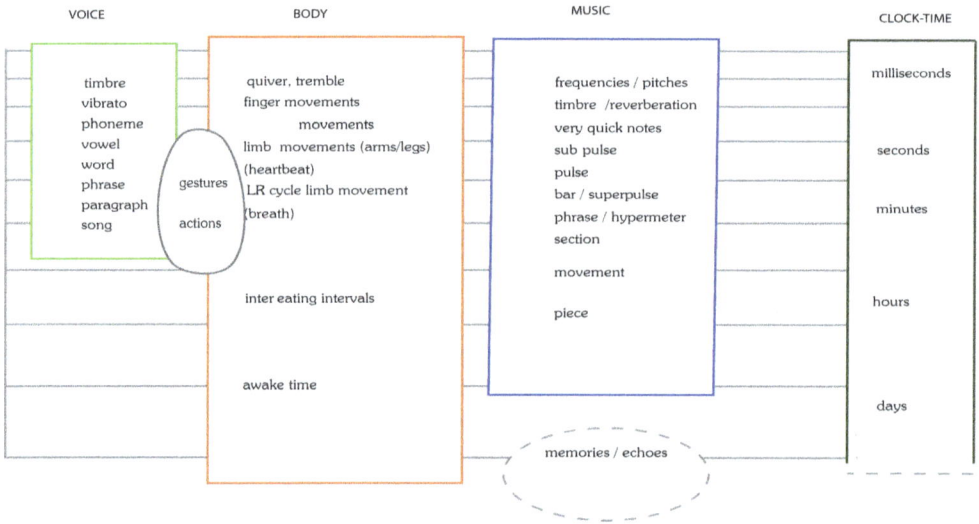

Figure 2. Body rhythms, musical functions, clock time[53]

---

53 See Fig. 3, next chapter, for more clock-time detail.

The central pulse rate of music in fact corresponds very neatly with the range of human footsteps (more than with the heartbeat, notwithstanding its similar name); the bar-level grouping of pulse, or those events that happen every 1-6 seconds (a band which I denote as 'super-pulse') corresponds perfectly to a full cycle of left-right limb movement, as in a drumming pattern or walking gait. In fact, this super-pulse level can also track variations on an uneven walking gait, such as those which incorporate a limp, a hop, or a waltz step; the super-pulse is normally much more stable than the pulse, as we seem to expect some degree of inner fluctuations but expect the full cycle to be steadier.[54]

Even if one senses that the sonic material with an audible beat is not directly linked with limb movement, our innate familiarity with that range of durations allows for very accurate gauging of differences in the length of musical phrases, for example, allowing an easy tracking of larger-scale irregularities (e.g. series of equally-spaced beats in irregular-length [higher-level] groups).

Other categories of our audio reception strategies which do not exhibit particularly harmonic or recognizably periodic components may still evoke familiar natural models: a sound that seems relatively constant over a longer duration but with considerable rapidity of slight changes in pitch and timbre might suggest something like babbling water or a chatter of birds; a persistent sound that manifests a steady-state form might be a human-invented machine; another with a certain noise profile incorporating a logarithmic increase in attack densities and amplitude will suggest a more energetic event. Shorter-duration sonic images with a particularly quick but fluid change in pitch, timbre, and/or amplitude will likely convey a sense of 'gesture', for which we have a number of stored templates based on embodied experience - they may relate naturally to the energy trajectories of physical actions or vocal utterances (see for ex. Godøy's research). Given these tendencies, one can reflect that the portrayal of fairly static textural passages would normally not suggest a potentially hostile threat, whereas increasing amplitude, density of pulses, or quick changes in any notable parameter might provoke an 'alert' mode. We may assume that remnants of such primitive reactions are quite

---

54   My invention of the term 'super-pulse' was to facilitate discussion of this important rate when it happens not to coincide with the notated meter. This is quite common in 20th and 21st century Western music as well as many other forms where a metric approach is not fundamental; it is also invaluable for discussions of works that contain two or more contrasting 'strata'. It can exist with a metric-type subdivision of beat and optional sub-pulse, with irregular subdivisions, or no clear subdivisions at all.

A MUSICIAN'S GUIDE TO TIME

likely still embedded (and rightly so!) in such unconscious processing.

Of course, all of these different categories of sounds - speech, water, machines, birds, footsteps - can be present in an environment simultaneously, in which case it is even more urgent to sort all the various data into their respective 'streams' so that we can build up a correct picture, with constantly-refreshed data tracing their independent behaviours over time. How we actually manage this is the crux of the auditory scene analysis research area.

23. ACTIVITY BANDS & MUSICAL FUNCTIONS

Music exhibits many different levels of frequency of activity – at the level of the note, the phrase, the section, the piece, etc. As the human system uses different strategies for appreciating the various levels, it can be helpful to identify them as 'bands' of activity. There are various suggestions how this can be done – see for ex. Bielawski (1981) and Roads (2002) – but I have found that a fairly simple framework can serve for a general examination of music across genres. These are roughly sketched in Figure 3 and can be viewed as the pitch band, the timbre-ornamental-textural band, the meter band, the phrase band, the section band, and the form band – with an outer atmosphere of memory, repertoire, and cultural heritage. The meter band is usefully subdivided further into the sub-pulse, pulse, and super-pulse (bar) bands. Those that do not incorporate traditional metric schema (like much 20th-century repertoire) or even omit pitch-based organization (like much electroacoustic music) are still constrained by the associations involved. We are more or less 'hard-wired' to the fastest of these bands, whereas the slowest ones of the level of the piece can be almost entirely at an abstract cognitive level depending on a vast array of factors. Different functions in music are thus naturally relegated to different rates of sonic activity, and as we shall see, the functions emerge naturally from our manner of processing things at different rates of activity.

A rough guide to the zones of these bands is as follows:

AUDIBLE SONIC FREQUENCIES: 20 Hz. to 20k Hz – although most humans lose the upper range with age or over-exposure to noise;

PITCH: subset of frequencies, commonly limited in music to about 40 Hz. to

4000 Hz., or the range of a piano, which can be identified with highest accuracy when the prominent focus is within the range of human speech and song of approx. 80 Hz – 1000 Hz.;

TIMBRE: closely intertwined with our perception of pitch, but dependent on a noticeable amount of time passing (e.g. over 50 ms.) to be thought of as such, as it relates to the evolution of the pitch components in time;

ORNAMENT: slightly slower than the faster end of timbre, as we have to notice it more consciously in order to identify it *as* ornament;

TEXTURE: establishment of a texture implies that there is a sense of stability of a particular sonic pattern, so therefore often dependent on the quick oscillations in timbre or ornament to establish its presence, but also on a longer duration of minimal change to maintain its identity;

SUB-PULSE: in metric-based music, a sub-pulse is a subdivision of a pulse, and rarely more than 5 times the speed of a pulse, as otherwise it would blur into the textural level.

PULSE: the tracking beat of much music, corresponding to a step in a dance form or march, for example. Very rarely exceeds the range of 40 – 120 beats per minute, or the range of walking/running; faster 'beats' are usually sub-pulses and slower are usually super-pulses.

SUPER-PULSE: any regularity at a level around 1500-6000 ms. (1.6667 Hz – 0.66667 Hz) and usually a grouping level of pulses, such as the bar level of regular metric music. The number of pulses within a super-pulse is usually 2-5.

PHRASE LEVEL: much more variable – and may be subdivided into sub-phrases. In Western music (classical, pop, blues, jazz, etc.) the phrase or sub-phrase will often be about 2-6 super-pulses long; if there are sub-phrases, then the phrase may be able to be audibly extended to a much longer duration.

SECTION LEVEL: much more variable and partly dependent on overall piece length.

PIECE LEVEL: rarely under 8 minutes or over 60 minutes in Western classical traditions but sometimes *much* longer in experimental, rock, and many non-Western traditions.

A Musician's Guide to Time

FREQUENCY BANDS BY FUNCTION	RELATED BODY RHYTHMS	ESTIMATE OF CLOCK-TIME DURATION *
pitch / notes noise	vocal sounds eye blink shivers / tremors	> 50 ms
ornamental/textural	vocal formants, vibrato, tapping, fast finger mvts..	25-100 ms
sub-pulse	tapping, finger movement	100-500 ms
pulse	leg / limb mvt. /[heartbeat]	500-1500 ms (0.5" - 1.5")
super-pulse (pulse-grouping level)	left-right limb cycle / gait	1.5 sec. - 4.5 [6] sec.
meta-pulse (super-pulse-grouping level, phrase)	breath	> 3 - 30 sec??
passage / section	expression of full thoughts / depicted action	> 30 sec
temporal design / form	conversation / activity / event	> [1 -2 min.] 4 min.

(Annotations on figure: "timbre" bracket spans pitch/notes–ornamental rows; "gestures" bracket spans sub-pulse–super-pulse rows; "meter" brackets sub-pulse through super-pulse; "hypermeter" encompasses the broader range.)

* estimates only, derived from various sources; note that new evidence might lead to re-calculations

Figure 3. Activity bands and musical functions.

❋ Pitch, timbre, temperament, tuning

The area of pitch may not seem so clearly related with our perception of musical time, as we tend to regard notes as 'things' which we place into a temporal design, but it is very misleading to leave them out of consideration for several reasons.

Firstly: the perception of 'pitch' is normally a strategy for appreciating that several almost simultaneously-sounding frequencies belong to the same sound source but are collectively distinct from others. Several factors are involved: not only the specific frequencies of the component harmonics, inharmonics, and noise but their relative ratios, onset (a)synchrony, and the millisecond shifts in frequency and amplitude will be taken as indicating relevant information regarding the source (voice, instrument, wind, bell, etc.) and its location (through spatial cues and the recognition of certain sounds as being echoes or reverberation of the main source in the particular environment). Though the term 'onset asynchrony' is foreign to most musicians, it is a salient feature of music and often critical to making decisions about groupings such as in distinguishing a figure (melody) from a ground (accompaniment texture). When a single beginner pianist or a group of amateur instrumentalists play together, chords which are meant to fuse together into one sonic unit may be so staggered in their entries that the mind needs to work harder at making those decisions; conversely, a skilled pianist knows intuitively that when a melody loses its privileged place in the upper register of sounds, it may become necessary to play the melodic notes fractionally 'early' in order to retain the clarity of line. The measurement of onset asynchrony can be significant in mental processing even at 30-40 ms. [milliseconds] but is dependent on factors such as the listener's expectations and familiarity with the material (speech, timbre, chord, etc.), and differs when possibly-associated visual or tactile information is also present.

Secondly: the division between pitch and rhythm is a blurry region perceptually; psychologists generally estimate 20 Hz. as the frequency 'divider' above which we hear 'notes' and below which we hear 'rhythm': that is, information appreciated for its temporal character. Individual notes that follow each other at extremely fast rates, especially within a narrow register, will tend to fuse into a sonic line or shape, in which the particular pitches will contribute a 'flavour' from their combination but their order will be appreciated only in the sense of an overall direction or character. In addition, some simple patterns can be sped up and slowed down again 'across the boundary' without completely losing their identity. The realm overlaps with the area known in computer music as 'microsound', as the technology allows for new ways of conceptualizing and controlling sonic design at that level.[55]

Similar temporal durations are involved with the tracking of the sound's timbral evolution, or spectromorphology, as the conjunction of frequencies will typically have its own 'envelope' or onset times and amplitude profiles: it was shown as early as the late 19th century[56] that cutting off the first milliseconds of a recorded note significantly reduced the listener's ability to recognize the source instrument, while subsequent studies have identified the frequency bands which provide a key to the perception of emotion in a human's voice, doubtless related to the physiological effect of the emotion on parts of the vocal tract, and its realistic

---

55 See for example Thomson 2004 for an introduction to 'microsound'; a term popularized by Roads' 2002 book of the same name.

56 Strumpf 1883-1890, reported by Winckel (1960/1967), p. 34.

portrayal by actors (performers) when evoking the same.[57]

The area of pitch discrimination is also involved in the perception of temperament: not only the different combinations of pitches chosen for a certain piece (C minor, whole-tone scale, etc.) but in the actual frequency ratios, or intervals between elements, which characterize that mode. Many of us pay keen attention to the particular relationships between the different fundamental frequencies of sounds identified as single notes or pitches, but an increasing majority of Western listeners will tend to ignore the nuances at this level. Such a trend is clearly due to the slippage of Western tuning into the equal-tempered keyboard arrangement which eventually predominated even in ensembles where such alterations are not 'hardwired' into the instrument, and now many pop singers use software which automatically 'corrects' deviations from the equal-tempered divisions from a recorded source. As such, the natural and easily-replicated octave relationship is quantized into a maximum of 12 intervals, each 100 cents distance from the next (but no such logical ratio in the logarithmic frequency zone which produces the referent octave), whereas all other tuning systems have either specified or variable distances which imply a more precise measurement.

The advantages of equal-tempered systems are that they allow easy moves from one 'mode' to another, although all such modes are necessarily a compromise to stay within the quantized system. On the other hand, non-tempered tunings are much more suitable to invoking association with human speech and other natural sounds; they provide flexibility of expression; and certain intervals – whether played together in harmony or in sequence melodically – will have clearer implications of 'consonance' or 'dissonance' according to their nature which can be sensed (as well as expressed mathematically) as being in more simple or complex relationships (the purity of the 2:1 octave or 3:2 perfect fifth as contrasted with the 16:15 minor second). Many performers will naturally adjust notes in a given passage to produce clearer harmonic relationships, for example, but their success will depend on the flexibility of the instrument and the acuteness of the performer's (and listener's) judgements of pitch.

---

57 There is also research on the sensual effect of a voice singing very close to a microphone, as it implies that the singer is inside the private physical space of the listener, brushing the ear with their breath.

Western notation is traditionally very sketchy on the specific tuning of a note, along with its timbral shaping, and the performer relies on the nature of the instrument and their own oral / aural training to interpret it. As a result, the majority of clear examples of nuances in tuning and timbre are found in the repertoire of specific performers: examples abound in blues, jazz, and more experimental rock styles as well as performers in 'early music' and improvisers in the non-Western traditions such as Indian, Persian, Chinese, Indonesian, etc. In Western vocal music, it is difficult for a composer to urge classically-trained singers to abandon the narrow repertoire of church choir / art music / operatic 'voices' in favour of learning new notational codes or to risk ridicule by experimenting with other styles: exceptions like Berio's score for *Circles* turn out to have been dependent in part on the composer's close association with a wonderfully flexible singer (Cathy Berberian) just as the famous vocalise in Villa-Lobos's *Bachianas Brasilieras* also depended in part on the initial demonstrations by his acquaintance with the talented Salli Terri. The strength of oral tradition and home-made instruments allowed blues music to become known in its non-tempered state, and the fixed tuning of bagpipes helped maintain the non-tempered playing of many fiddlers throughout the 20th century (while many highly-trained classical violinists cannot suppress their suspicion that it is 'out of tune' and try to 'correct' it when attempting to demonstrate their own genre versatility). Jazz singers were liberated in part by the technique of 'scat singing' in which the vocalist imitates instruments; this leads easily to a challenge to learn a much wider range of vocal sounds, such as championed by Maria João.

Since Western classical string instruments allow any nuance according to fingering, performers on those instruments can easily learn to adjust to mean-tone, just, or other more natural tunings when playing in ensemble, as the clarity of consonant overtones can become faintly audible to alert participants, and the ready reference to open strings and natural harmonics can help reinforce it. This can be furthered strengthened when strings are playing alongside clarinets, horns, trombones, euphoniums, etc. which are designed to produce their sounds through access to natural overtones which exhibit simple harmonic relationships. Although the increasing inclusion of instruments like the equal-tempered harmonium, accordion, and electronic keyboard, along with fixed frets on guitars, has set up blocks to such discrimination, the advent of recording technology was able to capture some valuable evidence from less contaminated sources before the same technology spread equal temperament music more widely around the world. Meanwhile, artists became interested in exploring the sonic attributes of natural and human-made sounds, including those resulting from early electronic instruments (and subsequently, electronic controllers, amplifiers, etc.), from simple time manipulation of recorded sounds, and the challenges of trying to synthesize the human voice. Freer movement of people across the planet also resulted in many traditional instruments from various countries becoming integrated into new contexts, whereby the standard Western orchestra gradually broadened its percussion section from timpani and triangle to vast cornucopias including brake drum, thunder sheet, and even the repurposing of traditional instruments like tapping on the cello body or plucking the prepared piano strings. The full spectrum of sound became a region of focus, and the boundaries that had been found useful for conceptualizing music dissolved.

❈ Ornamentation

I have labelled the region of activity with events recurring at levels around 50 to 150 ms. as the 'ornamental/textural band'. At the lowest end of the frequency band - around 20-16 cycles per second - we begin to lose the ability to hear a 'pitch' and instead begin to discern the note's individual oscillations, which can appear as quick pulsations. (This threshold is not only the pitch/rhythm divide, but also coincides with the boundary of the fastest rates of digit movement, and therefore corresponds nicely to the top speeds of playing on any instrument with keys or finger-holes.) Musicians can often identify the various sonorities in a series of notes played very rapidly but are significantly less confident at identifying their relative temporal position in the sequence. Additionally, when a single note is reiterated at that speed, it tends towards fusion and is likely to be interpreted as a sustained sound – just as a fast succession of pictures can appear to represent fluid movement when the frame rate begins to exceed 16 fps. At the adjacent levels, between 16 Hz and approx. 5 Hz (close to the lower boundary of the sub-pulse range), there lies an area usually reserved in music for ornaments and 'surface features' like trills, mordents, grace notes, tremolo, vibrato, and quick glissandi or runs which can provide considerable character - resembling for example a quivering from nervousness or excitement. In fact, that resemblance might help explain why we do not generally expect a harmonic link between such periodicities and those of the pulse and super-pulse level - since a body trembles more from involuntary neurological sources and is thus unrelated to deliberate motor movement that is normally controlled by more regular 'clocks'. I believe that some of the stars of improvised music – whether Archie Shepp or Sharam Nazeri – gain their status in part because of their mastery of this 'ornamental' layer, controlling vibrato and tremolo to an exceptionally high degree, and thus shaping longer phrases by a control of emphasis on the fine details.

Vibrato provides a good example of the 'boundary' area between pitch and rhythm: it is often thought of as an exaggeration of a natural feature of the vocal timbre; whereas a trill, which is in many ways the same feature of an oscillation between two 'adjacent' pitches, is already considered an aspect of ornamentation and is often more audibly 'quantized' in pitch. Therefore, a trill can be audibly shrunken or stretched in time so that it emerges from vibrato to become a slower alternation between two pitches in the sub-pulse level or *vice versa*.

Figure 4. Vibrato slowing to alternating notes.

Tremolo, which is basically a very fast repetition of a single pitch, is similar: a very fast tremolo, especially when compounded by individual iterations of a string section in the orchestra, will cause a blurring into a continuous sound with a certain grain, whereas a slowing down of the same figure can result in the perception of increasingly-distinct repeated notes. (The Persian *tahrir* is a vocal technique resembling a tremolo that likewise hovers between timbre and audible rhythmic shaping.)

Similar effects include short grace note figures like mordents and acciaccaturas, which abound in 16th-18th-century music as a way of specifying the precise placement of embellishments which improvising performers used. These identifying terms are thus partly an attribute of notation; the Indian musical systems (which traditionally did not rely on notation) include similar figures (gamakas) on certain pitches within a specific raga, but they are not considered separate entities as much as a particular 'character' attributed temporarily (for that raga) to a certain pitch /frequency group. Likewise, blues traditionally depends on more or less accurate reproduction of 'blue notes' but also on the 'bending' of certain pitches – which takes it into a more clearly timbral shaping region, as it incorporates the identification of a gradual pitch shift from one fundamental frequency to another.

In the electroacoustic world, the area traditionally reserved for timbre and ornamentation has become prominent as composers grew fascinated with the ability to delve into what was typically the realm of the performer in shaping each second of sound, and with the ability to take any known sound and stretch it into lengths where it would become transformed into something quite different – or not. Increasingly sophisticated software allows for extracting features of one sound to apply to another, or modifying familiar sounds with unusual means such as granulation. I have realized that the avoidance of a beat, which alienates many listeners from such music without suitable preparation, is most likely an intuitive or even deliberate avoidance of cluttering up the neighbouring activity band to ensure proper appreciation of the faster activity, just as the most significantly ornamented passages in Baroque music will happen in the slowest movements.

❋ Beats, subdivisions, & groupings – pulse, sub-pulse, super-pulse

The regularity and predictability of a repeated beat may seem tedious to adventurous musicians, but it is greatly appreciated by our auditory processing systems. For one thing, it seems that some of our trackers operate like little "time samplers", so that once a periodicity is suspected, we anticipate it, and turn our attention to that stream of data periodically to note whatever change might have occurred since the last iteration. (I have imagined this like an array of little gears of various sizes whose gear teeth pick up data at each revolution, with an option for locking them together into synchronous sampling.) This strategy allows the brain to reduce the tracking time for that stream to a fraction of its evolution – in a way parallel to compressing the resolution on a digital image. Moreover, such periodicities often occur in nested hierarchies in simple ratios of 1:2 or 1:3, so the brain will often set other trackers on those levels in anticipation. Once a periodicity in these central ranges (approx. 200-4500 ms.) is established, the brain (or the body, at least) will not easily discard it, despite several missing iterations, unless it is clearly contradicted by a different or steadily-fluctuating pulse. With a nested set of periodicities (as in meter); this effect seems intensified. It seems that by assigning these regularities to tracking by our motor systems, we effectively free up the very limited resources of our short-term memory, which often depends on repetition to keep items within the accessible time-frame.

It is worth clarifying the importance of these simple ratios. Even though the 'beat' seems the most prominent of these levels in music, I have concluded that the 'super-pulse', or beat-grouping level, is actually the main reference in any music where it is strongly iterated (e.g. metrically-organized), as it corresponds to a full limb movement of left-right in any oscillation such as walking or drumming, and is much more likely to exhibit regularity than the beat itself – in music and in locomotion. Epstein noted how older Baroque ensembles appear to have maintained strict tempo in the rhythm-establishing members of an ensemble while the rubato was exercised by the others independently.[58]

The idea of a binary sub-division of the super-pulse or bar is clearly indicated by any steady marching, drumming, or similar activity - and thus easy to grasp in a musical allusion. However, a triple division is also common, and although this is well-reinforced by the number of triple-meter dance steps (such as the waltz) it is more accurately imagined as simply a more relaxed swing (on either the pulse or the sub-pulse level) which can result not only from a carefree lilt in a walking gait, but also from the motion of a rocker or swing, for example, as well as a from a set of familiar gestures. In the English language as well as many others, many words fall naturally into triple patterns, which leads to strong poetic influences even in nursery rhymes.

In attempting to explain our perception of musical rhythms, Zuckerkandl (1956: 170*ff*.) proposed a 'wave' model which illustrates how the oscillations between two downbeats - or their equivalent on a higher structural level - may exhibit irregularities of speed on an internal level (i.e. between the wave crests) but predictably so; Clynes and Walker (1982: 190) expanded this by pointing to the natural rhythm which results when we try to describe a circle in the air with our arm at a moderate rate. In that case, gravity increases the speed as the arm moves downward, and provides more energy to reach up to the top again, but with a (predictable) slowing.[59] This gesture seems more aptly described by a triple meter than duple, and doubtless promotes some primitive association of triple and duple with looseness and regimentation respectively. One can imagine that in the past, the triple or swing motion would be exceptionally familiar to infants, from being rocked in the arms or carried on a sling against the body of the mother or sibling as they move about – and it is also a pleasure to many of us who enjoy rocking chairs, swings, and hammocks. Research on micro-rubato indicates that in traditional classical styles, a similar elliptical shape or wave motion seems to

---

58 Although this has been queried by Repp and others; see Epstein (1995) and Repp (1996).

59 Even the Windows 'busy' signal mimics this natural irregularity in the timing of a series of dots describing a circle.

operate at a hypermetric level, as we judge a performance as more musical when there is a very slight slowing of the beat at the end of each phrase, with a slightly longer slowing at the end of a section.[60]

Hypermeter is a useful term for hierarchical metric schemes which continue the familiar grouping of 3 or 4 beats in a bar (with the downbeat receiving more emphasis than the others) into a higher (larger-scale / longer) level, where 3 or 4 bars are grouped into phrases or sub-phrases, with the first downbeat of the phrase receiving more emphasis than the other downbeats. This structure can be continued upwards, with the organization of 3 or 4 (sub-)phrases being grouped into sections, as so on. The tendency is very prevalent in music which contains allusions to dance forms (e.g. Classical and mainstream pop) but is not so often integrated into analysis because, as we are much more tolerant of irregularities at the higher levels, composers frequently incorporate extensions or contractions into the scheme for musical reasons, and the basic hypermetric scheme may seem too obscured to serve as a useful reference. However, a work like Boccherini's famous *Minuet* provides a clear example of the subtle shaping of a piece when examined for its hypermetric structure.

The importance of regular pulses and metric-type structures in our processing of music is profound, as they can effectively constitute a type of reference clock for all the other elements of the music. At a primary level, sub-pulses help maintain the beat and propel a piece forward by their overt presence. Something that has regular pulses alone is generally not thought of as music but more as machine, unless those pulses are undergoing more complex rhythmic patternings, such as fast/slow alternations, notable speeding up or disintegrating, or complex superpositions.[61] The establishment of a periodic framework provides an easy way to compare the length of two or more phrases, for example, or to interpret the inner proportions of any sonic configurations. This is not so much due to a mental 'counting' of the various beats of a bar, or the successive bars of a phrase (although students typically may do that while learning how to perform a tricky passage), but an innate awareness (through latent entrainment) of where we are

---

60 This is a bit simplistic; a fuller description of the phenomenon can be found in Repp 1997 and 1998, for example, and Honing 2004. .

61 See for example the third movement of Ligeti's *Chamber Concerto* composed almost entirely from reiterated pulses on several instruments (Mountain 1993), or Ligeti's wonderful *Poème Symphonique For 100 Metronomes.*

at any given point in a repeating cycle - an awareness that is reinforced through every repetition that does not contradict it.

In addition, once the periodicities at these various levels has been established, we become much more sensitive to fluctuations in their audible regularities, especially when they are synchronized into a single regular flow. These fluctuations in tempo are often perceived as indicating an 'external force' on the ticking clocks, which can thus expertly model a shift in perspective such as we experience in our everyday world, when our sense of time is normally affected by a higher level of concentration or by a 'zooming out' to a more distant view of our surroundings. An iterated sub-pulse is thus particularly useful to help the listener track tempo fluctuations.

Another usage of the overt sub-pulse is well-exploited by diverse composers from J. S. Bach (unaccompanied violin and cello sonatas and partitas, Brandenburg Concerti, etc.) to Bartók and Shostakovich (string quartets) as a means of maintaining a steady framework for irregular groupings or meter. This becomes an efficient way to minimize information at one level to allow for deeper appreciation of less predictable groupings at a higher one, and can also serve as an elegant form of 'pivoting' from one metric scheme to another without unduly confusing the listener's tracking. I am personally convinced that some of these works demonstrate an 'additive' approach to rhythm, but I have met resistance from some musicologists and ethnomusicologists about the 'existence' of additive rhythms, although as I use them myself, I can guarantee that they are available as creative devices. Kunst (1950) clarifies how the combination of a narrow repertoire of traditional European classical music and issues of notation led to confusion about concepts of meter (from its poetic derivation), and the (wrongly) implied distinction between 'measure' with its strict sense of durational equality and the more fluid rhythmic patterns of stress of both poetry and music, and proposes that additive principles are the basis for 'synthetic' construction of music and opposed to the metric calculation of 'analytical measure.'[62]

The concept of additive rhythms in general is that one builds up from small units – like those of the pulse and sub-pulse levels – rather than working from a more top-down division of metre, as in poetry. In metric styles, one has a container, with predetermined properties, into which one arranges the sounds:

---

62 Kunst 1950, 9.

four phrases, each one four bars long, each bar holding three beats, each beat subdivided into 4 16th notes. This structure does not have to be constantly iterated – one bar can be filled with patterning at the sub-pulse and another may consist of a single chord and silence; also, once the meter is established, it is not uncommon to insert the occasional 'cross-rhythm' such as a duple figure in a triple-beat bar, and given the lower priority of the sub-pulse and ornamental level in establishing beats, such substitution of 3 for 4 or vice versa is quite common on the beat level. However, in additive rhythm, the design can be built up out of much shorter figures, like motives and sub-phrases, while the number of repetitions of any given pattern or series of figures will be driven by non-periodic design concerns. As a result, the phrases that emerge are much more organic in style.

There are in fact several problems in arguing for the existence of additive rhythms. One issue arose from ethnomusicologists studying African rhythmic structures who discovered that their earlier colleagues had assigned the term 'additive' to something which was in fact a much longer cycle of irregular units than the majority of the Western European canon, and could therefore be considered a complex type of meter. The second issue is that in some cases, what may look like an additive construction may have been the result of truncated or extended segments of metric forms (see for ex. Fig. 14), and it is true that some of these can be heard as such, thereby creating a sense of intensity. The third issue is that most composers in fact use something very like an 'additive' approach at the larger-scale level, adding one theme or movement after another, so it does not seem like a 'device'. However, Messiaen developed a very specific type of 'additive rhythm', apparently in a desire to incorporate features of Indian music, which he knew more from treatises than from concerts. In his case, he determined that any note could be expanded by one-half its original duration. The result was indeed quite a novel effect of freer non-metric organization, and is responsible for some of the attraction of his *Quartet for the End of Time*.

My own interest in music from different cultures and eras has led me to remain alert for additive structures in various styles of music, and because I have noticed it in numerous traditional songs in Europe, from Ireland to Portugal to Bulgaria, I do suspect that it was quite a common alternative to stricter meter in many regions. Additive rhythms appeal to me partly because they can seem more organic, while free of the implied connections of meter with human limb-movement repetitions. Such irregular forms seem to abound especially in 20th century music from eastern Europe – Khatchaturian, Shostakovich, Lutoslawski,

Ligeti, etc. – and I suspect that when we find similar styles in Bach instrumental works, it may be not simply a result of 'truncated metric phrases' but in fact an alternation between two familiar practices. Undeniably clear examples of modern practice include Terry Riley's *In C* and Rzewski's *Les Moutons de Panurge*; an earlier example is the structure of the opening theme of Lutoslawski's *Concerto for Orchestra*.[63]

❋ Higher levels: Phrases, sub-phrases, sections

Meter is very useful for audio comparison of similar phrases, but it does tend to infer limb movement. It is thus interesting to reflect on other audible body rhythms such as the inner irregularity of the breathing rate: at a slow rate, the respiration part of the cycle normally seems a bit longer than the inspiration, and can be consciously altered to some extent, but it may easily approach a more balanced rhythm at faster speed. Similarly, less regular structures may infer speaking (which unless stylized is more likely to heard in the absence of regular limb movement). Speaking, though generally universal in the broad sense, contributes much to the specific repertoire of associations for rhythm through our subconscious appreciation stemming from linguistic patterns with which we are most familiar. Some languages, for example, tend to incorporate more triple subdivisions which may become particularly audible in (and reinforced through) poetic contexts and song. I was informed while a student that what we recognized as Bartók's 'strong' and unusual rhythmic motifs were influenced by Hungarian stress patterns – although given his active work in ethnomusicology, one assumes that if so, some of the influence might have come via regional folk music which would itself have evolved in conjunction with local language characteristics. The expressive *Recitatives* of Bach, Handel, and others derive their extremely irregular rhythmic structures from the direct modelling or accompanying of vocal declamation – differing notably from the rhythmic poetry models of much other word-based music, and bearing only faint resemblance to normal conversation.

Although we are instinctively aware of periodicities (along with other more irregular configurations) at the quicker levels, our manner of apprehending regularities will shift to a much more cerebral level when they exceed a period of around 6 seconds. This apparent threshold is doubtless related in part to

---

63 Ex. 6.11 of my thesis (Mountain 1993) clarifies this.

the maximum duration of the 'short-term' memory, which is usually considered somewhere around 10 seconds at most,[64] as periodic events sounding 6 seconds apart will already fall outside that window by the third iteration. We can easily grasp a regularity at that level *if* the successive intervals are filled by recognizably parallel content. However, the ability to recognize that the content is parallel, at least in temporal proportions, may involve other factors like experience and familiarity, which will be reviewed below.

It is at the level of the phrase where many differences begin to emerge in terms of stylistic tendencies and the listener's aesthetic preferences and customs. The segmentation of Western pop music differs sharply from the prolonged lines of North Indian sitar improvisations, for example, and a listener may consider one or other as the 'default' organization and the other as more unexpected – which might be therefore welcome or repugnant depending on other features and the listener's willingness or reluctance to adjust their listening calipers.

24. General models of time in musical contexts

❋ Duration/succession

As mentioned earlier, musicians are accustomed to using the term 'duration' in the specific sense of the length of an individual note, especially as notated in a score - quarter notes, eighth notes, whole notes (or quavers, semiquavers, and semibreves) - but in discussions about time with non-musicians, duration is a key term used to delineate a view of a segment of time that is usually more in the order of an entire composition or at least a movement, or a track on a CD. In such cases, both musicians and non-musicians often define the duration in its clock-time measurement, although with liberal 'rounding up' to the nearest

---

[64] See Mountain 1993 for a discussion of different estimates; I have not yet noticed significant variations from the 2"-10" range current then; memory is still not very well understood. It has been suggested that a dedicated listener can expand that window in certain circumstances, which I strongly suspect to be true, but the 10- second limits works well as a general guide, if one remembers that it is a maximum and subject to considerable shrinkage in complex data situations.

minute or quarter-hour, which adequately accounts for permissible contractions and expansions of timings in different performances.[65] It is interesting to note that we have expectations of clock-time durations for individual songs/themes, movements, full pieces, and concert lengths according to convention of style: Indian concerts are generally much longer than Western classical, and rock concerts somewhere in between – just as pop songs used to be the standard length of a '45 record, and the so-called 'concept albums' by the Beatles and the Who then startled people by interlinking various short tracks into a longer piece more reminiscent of art music's scale.

Succession is often thought of as *opposed to* duration, in that it focusses on the link of one thing to the next thing occurring in time, rather than on a discrete unit of time during which many things may occur. Although musicians rarely speak about 'succession' per se, we tend to use this way of looking at the internal details of any musical passage. Traditionally, each note was understood as bearing some kind of relationship, as if causal, to the preceding and following ones. Many of our more temporally-based terms imply this view: *passing* tones, *leading* notes, harmonic *progressions*, etc. (see Appendix B). Similarly, a calm movement following an energetic one will appear to be related, in that one is a response, a reaction, or at least a contrast to the preceding one. These tendencies show the typical linear view that belongs to succession, and it remains a dominant listening mode for many people. Even in a situation such as a fugue, for example, where each line is independent although almost identical in profile and bearing its own internal connections, the different entries of the voices are understood as following one after another. This demonstrates that we can follow two levels of succession at two different rates: that of the note level and that of the phrase or theme level.

In the early 20th century, more composers began to play with forms in which different melodies co-exist, expanding the cleverly-intertwined independent lines of Mozart opera (where the visible presence of different singers on stage help the listener keep track) to more contemporary versions where such independent lines are as likely to collide and skid off into independent paths (such as in Bartók, Lutoslawski, Ligeti, and Reich). Interestingly, the ones which initially captured

---

65   Weber's concept of the JND of 8% tolerance seems to work well within musical contexts as well as in the outside world, although I would like to explore the possibilities of mapping musical complexities into the intensity values of Fechner's Law.

my interest were often modeled on complex physical environments from the world: Stravinsky's *Petruchka* was set in the context of a Shrovetide Fair; Varèse's *Amériques* was a portrayal of the chaos of the soundscape of his new home, complete with sirens; while Ives' work was influenced by various outside events such as his father's marching bands playing different tunes as they converged on the town square, and revealed in titles like *A New England Holiday Symphony*.

However, in some 20th-century Western music, there are pieces where notes and phrases seem to occur without any relationship to each other. The energy in one line does not seem to be echoed or contrasted by another sounding within the same duration of time. Experiments were often carried out deliberately by composers such as John Cage, Iannis Xenakis, and Horacio Vaggione, in order to probe the possibilities of such novel assemblages. The success of such pieces depends not only on the intuitive sense of the composer to be able to convince the listener of some interesting structures even in the absence of resemblance to traditional or natural forms, but also on the willingness of some listeners to concentrate on repeated listenings in order to find optimum perspectives for appreciation.

If we consider the apparently causal relationship between notes and phrases as analogous to the tracing of people's lives, affected by different events and each other, then these more modern pieces mentioned are analogous to a novel that delineates several biographies of unrelated people whose paths never cross. This is not much more typical of music than it is of novels – yet it is very similar to a modern view of life where we may have a dim awareness of many things evolving simultaneously but without obvious interaction, even into the projected near future.

❋ Linear & cyclic models

Music is most often heard as linear at a very local level. When one hears a melodic line or even a motif, for example, the 'line' is understood as such because the notes heard sequentially in time are meant to be mentally joined together as one 'unit', being emitted from a single event or source – even if played by the entire brass section. This effect is possible even in more complex contexts such as counterpoint, in which the listener may be able to track two or more 'lines' as intertwining, rather than merging into one. (This kind of effect depends on auditory cues such as timbral and registral similarity within each line). However, even a sonic mass that seems to stretch across the registral spectrum may promote a linear sense as long as the listener perceives that mass as a single entity – an illusion discussed in Ch. 27 under auditory imagery. This leads back to the idea of time as a continuum – the succession of things appearing to be causally connected. In a parallel way, the second phrase of a musical passage is understood as standing in a direct relationship to the first phrase – they are two sequential parts of the same thing (although we need to jump to a plane of slightly longer durations to view it this way).

However, in the textural, ornamental and timbral regions, some sounds which follow each other very quickly may appear 'fused together' into a unit simply by their proximity - just as the various phonemes of a word are usually understood as being components of that word, rather than as having causal relationships between their parts. The arrangement of the words themselves determines whether they form a sentence, a sound poem, or some other apparent order or random distribution; the subsequent phrases, in the case of prose and poetry, will often be the more important for determining causality. This analogy is subject to considerable flexibility in music, however, as the musical 'sonic objects' that might compare to a word are not always predefined, nor interpreted in the same ways by different listeners. In fact, ambiguity of interpretation is a common intentionally-used device in composition.

Various 20th-century music researchers who were familiar with psychology introduced concepts of Gestalt imagery, and subsequently auditory scene analysis and gesture, to explain how our innate tendency to group will promote various configurations as manifesting a perceived unity– meaning that as we recognize the unfolding of a familiar form, such as a descending scale, we begin expecting its completion.[66] The closer it gets to expected completion, the more assured we are that it will occur, and therefore the more surprising any deviation from the form.[67] This kind of processing, though occurring at a usually subconscious level and very quickly, provides much or most of our impression of how the music is 'unfolding' in time. The topic has received attention in tonal music contexts under

---

66   Key figures include Meyer, Langer, Bregman, McAdams, and Godøy – see Bibliography.

67   Of course, there is a larger-scale level of expectation which may expect a certain amount of deviation for stylistic reasons, which can be thwarted only by *not* deviating from the predicable.

the category of 'anticipation' and 'expectation', [68] while the electroacoustic world has contributed more abstract models such as those proposed by the MiM research group in Marseille. They identify 19 familiar and basic "Semiotic Temporal Units" (Unités Sémiotiques Temporelles) which they demonstrate can be observed as basic frameworks for various configurations of sonic material which, through our immediate comprehension of their nature, help us parse the music.[69]   Although some of these are most convincing when operating at a small time-scale, such as a few seconds, the less complex ones (endless trajectory, waves, propulsion, etc.) are easily expandable to a larger scale by applying global parameters like textural density, amplitude, and frequency range shifts according to their specific shape. Other groupings abound in the non-tonal musicology, beginning with Russolo's 1913 *Manifesto*, reaching enormous detail (and attention) in Schaeffer's 1966 charts. The problematic associations with the concept of an 'object', which was a misunderstanding of Schaeffer's initial analogy, spawned a variety of responses over the next several decades, and the surrounding discourse helped steer many away from the mistake faced by theorists in classical music by incorporating the sense of change into the 'primary' units of sound.[70]

We generally seem to look for linear connections in the small scale, and often in mid-range form as well, so it may seem surprising to realize the prominence of cyclic models in music. Probably one of the most important reasons for this is the (often under-acknowledged) influence of dance. Dances that are performed by amateurs – most folk dances and court dances, for example – require not only a recognizable beat for aligning the steps, but also a fairly simple series of rhythms which repeat, so that a series of dance steps can be repeated to different musical phrases.[71] Just as we can track two levels of succession in the fugue, we can easily track the linearity of one level while following another level of cyclic movement, as in a typical round dance form where each note in a phrase may seem to lead to the next, but each verse may cycle back to the beginning phrase,

---

68   For example, Narmour (1990), Huron (2006), and Huron & Margulis (2010).

69   See for example Dufour (2016); also Favory et al (2002) and Frey et al (2014).

70   Including for example the stimulating discussions by Smalley (1997) and the well-thought-out variations by Thoresen (2007) as well as Dufour (*ibid.*)

71   A cursory study of folk music from eastern and southern European countries will show that the component rhythmic patterns can be irregular, but will be more easily executed if their repetitions and alternations are simple.

while individual lines may be repeated two or three times before moving ahead again. Gigues (jigs), minuets, fandango, habanera - all have their characteristic metric frameworks. More skill-demanding dances can demand a much higher degree of complexity, but repetitive elements are still very common. Much of Baroque music in particular was derived from such styles, and even when it was intended for listening only, musical tension could be created by establishing such patterns and then deviating from them slightly; the same patterning holds true for many popular styles. Musical 'jokes' can be created and admired at the level of entrainment, by establishing a repetitive pattern and then inserting extra beats, dropping some, or changing the tempo. The alert, entraining listeners may smile at the knowledge that, had they been dancing, the steps would have become awkward or confused. This means, incidentally, that the less familiar we are with the original dance step, the less impact these deviations will have, and thus our appreciation of the music will be lessened.

Repetition had another major role in music which is now somewhat eroding: as music is so ephemeral, composers often found it necessary to repeat a musical idea more than once so that the listener would be able to commit it more accurately to memory.[72] With the move towards recording and easy replay, the degree of repetition has waned in some contemporary classical styles, although it is still clearly evident in pop music. In fact, the tendency of pieces in classical style to return to an initial section (as in ABA form) or refer to the beginning of the piece at the end (as in the classical recapitulation section) is a very familiar device, and present in many different genres of music. It is thus one of the most common allusions in music to cyclic time. Although an attentive listener may reflect on the difference in the 'feel' of a theme after much intervening material, this is no different from a human reflection on the recurring cycles of the seasons mentioned earlier. Good performers enjoy being able to add subtle variations to repeated material in order to influence this effect.

Many manifestations of linearity in large-scale form within the realm of art song and 'programme music' exist in the sense of the 'narrative' form that typifies fiction, and the music often also portrays a kind of story - Beethoven's *Pastoral Symphony* is a textbook example. Another clear example is presented by Zakir Hussain,[73] explaining how, within the North Indian musical tradition, a tabla player's

---

72   This may be thought of in terms of redundancy, in information theory terms (Ch. 12).

73   Hussain & Khan 1995.

choice of sounds can be an almost literal representation of a young boy's trip to market, with the embodiment of footsteps (and their hesitations) and association with mood. It would seem that opera would be a normal place for narrative structure too, but the sheer length of the work along with other dramaturgical considerations usually lead to more recurrence of themes and textures. But it is quite possible to have a narrative form in music without allusion to text or plot, as long as it appears that there is a cause-and-effect linear sequence. Even in much more abstract forms, the effects are found not only on the small scale, mentioned above, as one musical phrase appears to lead towards an answering one, but also on the medium scale as an angry or at least very active section wears itself out and is followed by a calmer one. A fascinating angle is presented by Katharine Norman (2004) who draws convincing similarities between the practice of tape music and oral storytelling.

The stunned reaction of many listeners to works by composers such as Webern, Stockhausen, and Xenakis was precisely because such cause-effect relationship seemed absent. (Sometimes because it *was* absent, and sometimes simply because the relationship was too complex – usually too cerebral – to be grasped by any but an *aficionado* with exceptional training, and preferably a score to study.)

One fairly codified example of narrative in music is exemplified by the *leitmotiv* – as used for example in Mozart and Richard Strauss. A leitmotiv allows us to keep track of a character's emotional life, allowing the discerning listener to sense that the various iterations of the same musical idea differ in their mood or character. This seems like a very basic idea but is difficult to explain in purely technical terms, as many of the differences are made not only by notated variants to amplitude, articulation, and rhythm, but also by minute alterations to the sound production: emphasizing particular component frequencies in a note's timbre, especially the initial attack of a few milliseconds; giving a certain amplitude profile to the musical phrase; and altering the notated durations by a few milliseconds less or more, depending on the effect desired. Therefore, the instrumental teacher does not usually explain such microscopic adjustments, but simply indicates them to the student by audio demonstration.[74] Such adjustments are gradually accumulated

---

74 In addition, academic musicians of the last century have been notoriously loathe to discuss emotional content, restricting their comments on composition and analysis to aspects more easily pinpointed in the score.

by the performer into a global adjustment scheme, as demonstrated by Manfred Clynes in his fascinating SuperConductor software.

Figure 5. The leitmotiv, tracing the character's state.

The leitmotiv, when used in a literal context in music – that is, tracing the life of a main character in a story – strongly reinforces the time-frame of that story. Such a time-frame is always longer than the time of performance by a significant magnitude: frequently, such stories will span at least several years, while the musical work will last only a few hours or less. Thus, the perception of changes in human behaviour that are transmitted by the musical device will help the listener maintain the illusion of time passing at human rather than concert scale.

On the other hand, the superficially-related 'theme & variations'[75] emphasizes the cyclic form, as the variations are frequently ordered by abstract musical characteristics like contrast of texture, density, and mode, and therefore defy an ordering according to a more linear evolution of mood typical of a narrative style (see Figure 6).

Cyclic patterns in music depend on the perception of repetition – but not all repetition in music is cyclic. In order for cycles to be implied, the full sequence needs to be recognizable (as in a song stanza) or, alternatively, some striking feature is noted to recur at more or less periodic intervals with intervening contrasting material. The repetition of a single note or gesture, however, will be heard more as a reiteration or a building up of tension rather than a cyclic event – because it is too short.[76] A rondo can serve as a good model of a cyclic form, because it tends to have an extended form with several distinct musical passages, one of which

---

75   If one thinks of a leitmotif's first or basic form as a theme, and successive occurrences as 'variations'.

76   Good descriptions of such devices can be found on the Laboratoire MiM website 2008.

keeps recurring. In this case – as suggested in Figure 7 – the intervening material might differ without changing the idea of eventual return to material A. If the intervening material is of significantly different durations, then the cyclic nature may become more ambiguous – does the A really represent a periodic event, and the intervening durations suggest a distortion of time, or are the intervening passages at a stable rate and the A part is simply a sporadic interruption?

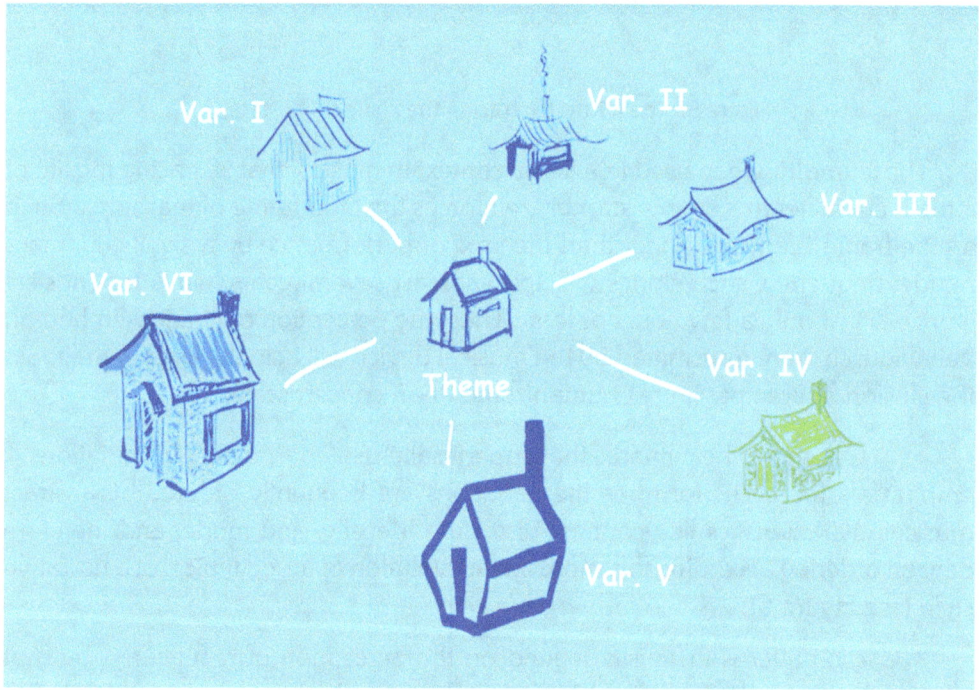

Figure 6. Theme & variations as non-linear form.

In traditional Western classical music, recurrence of an idea was usually dependent on a repetition of very similar note sequences that allowed the idea's identity to be recognized. This relies not only on the listener's memory, but also on his/her familiarity with the musical style, and by the contrast of material within the piece. Thus, in a late 20th-century or early 21st century work, if most of the material is atonal in nature, an occasional tonal fragment could represent a recurring idea even if the notes are quite different in order, as long as the impression of tonal material is there.[77] However, an atonal fragment may be too difficult to retain and recognize even if presented exactly later on - although a strong rhythmic configuration[78] will often substitute nicely as a memorable shape.

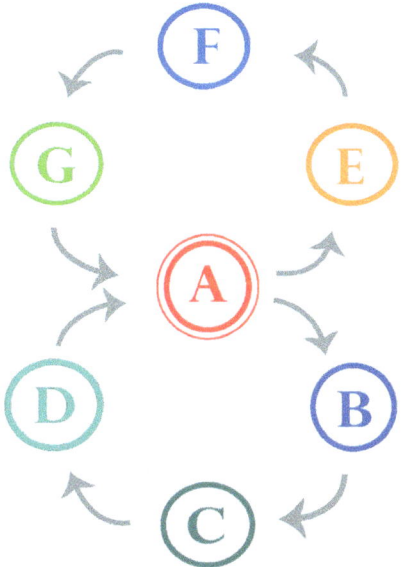

Figure 7. Rondo as cyclic form:- *AbcdAbcdA*... or variants such as *AbcdAefgAbcgA*.

Years ago an observation by Marvin Minsky[79] led to my understanding that the sense of 'permanence' which is easily created by the repetitive nature of an ostinato may be parallel to our way of seeing, whereby we scan an environment repeatedly in order to pick up increasing amounts of information while establishing a sense of what is permanent and what is more ephemeral -- and therefore, in many situations, potentially demanding of reaction from the viewer at least in terms of anticipating further activity. These strategies involve saccades (usually a

---

77 An excellent example can be found in Beatriz Ferreyra's electronic composition *La Siesta Blanca*, where tiny snippets of tango interrupt long passages of barely-fluctuating electronic organ sounds.

78 By strong I mean containing contrast - as opposed to the 'neutrality' of a steady progression of eighth notes, for example, approaching Schoenberg's concepts of liquidation and dissolution – see Heneghan 2019.

79 Minsky 1987, pp. 8-9 (and *passim*).

few quick scans & fixations per second) and the contrasting 'smooth pursuit' for following a target. As music often plays with our sense of scale, in which we hear familiar types of sonic configurations slowed down and sped up, it is plausible that this manner of building up an image of an audio environment may work at a larger scale as well. For example, a phrase is often followed by its repetition, or by another that starts off in the same way but ends differently. The listener can quickly compare the differences by mentally placing the profile of the second phrase on top of the first – something that has to happen as soon as the similarity is noticed or anticipated. In examining this analogy, I believe we treat much of the 'cyclic' aspects of phrase structures and motives, for example, as a product of changes over a background of reiterations.

❃ EXAMPLES OF THE RIVER METAPHOR IN MUSIC

Many pieces of music have a flow that even aurally can sound like water moving at a fairly constant rate, always containing some sense of motion, produced through local-level polyrhythmic structures which may seem to imitate babbling brooks, and integrated into longer passages with few or no cadential points to mark them: notable examples include Debussy's *La Mer*, Respighi's various *Fountains* and Smetana's *The Moldau*. Other works which maintain a similar sense of flow may achieve it through contrapuntal motion, as in Palestrina, when the cadence of one voice will be offset by the motion in others; or through much more fine-grained means such as employed by Ligeti, Reich, or Truax (e.g. *Riverrun*), where abstract textures are created through the use of similar-length notes and then are perceived to be slowly evolving through miniscule changes. Anne Southam wrote several entrancing works for dance that contain a similar effect at a slightly higher grouping level.

Traditional North Indian music (and Western works which are influenced by them) may also be appreciated for their very long melodic lines, continuously extended through elaboration of phrases and motives. Such works contrast with much of the Western classical and pop music that tends towards sectionalization, punctuated with more formal boundaries - whether full cadences or textural contrast (including silence). Listeners may have an aesthetic preference for one style or another, but if they are expecting sectionalization, long-flowing passages may seem surprising, and thereby elicit delight or frustration.

❋ Ebb & flow / growth & decay

The sense of flow discussed above is compatible with the idea of ebb and flow, which is also a typical water phenomenon, but one with an often gentle oscillation between two states of lesser and greater energy or dynamism. This is manifest in a broader context with the concept of growth and decay, which is commonly incorporated into musical terms, whether at the level of the melodic line, phrase, or theme; or on a larger scale affecting the musical form. Many themes, for example, have a general rise of tension and then relaxation, achieved usually through pitch contour, amplitude shaping, harmonic complexity, and local-level rhythmic activity. At larger levels, this model imparts sufficient character that it becomes a recognizable aspect of certain styles (and therefore avoided in subsequent ones that are trying to differentiate themselves from their predecessors). According to a commonly-held historical view, Debussy's music seemed 'odd' to many because it favoured successive waves of building up and dying away that was in contradiction to the more traditional Western building towards a single climax.[80] The most notable prior examples of such works were probably those of the post-Renaissance polyphonic works where the weaving of melodic lines was a direct inheritance from the plainchants of medieval times (see Timelessness, below). In much acousmatic music and similar styles, very slight but almost continuous changes of the sonic parameters can create the effect of observing a slowly-moving substance without necessarily implying a direction towards growing or dissolving.

❋ Movement & change; contrast; permanence

The effect of contrast in music contributes significantly to our perception of time passing; it tends to focus our attention on that aspect which manifests contrast, whether it be melodic form, harmonic flow, change in durational values, tempo, instrumentation, amplitude, etc. or perceived as a global change - indicating a 'new section alert' signal. A discussion of the specific ways in which contrast works in music is undertaken in Ch. 26. At a basic level, however, it is important to note the degrees of change that may be considered stylistically appropriate:

---

80 Personally, I was immediately attracted to Debussy's music while still a child, and wondered in retrospect whether my own ease with that formal structure was due to a previous extensive exposure to North Indian music.

traditional forms of well-behaved Western classical music would limit themselves to certain anticipated boundaries, whereas the 20th century introduced extreme examples where the composer might introduce a completely unexpected burst of sound into a more traditional or static texture, without necessarily providing any clues about its possible impact, if any, on the other sonic entity. This kind of effect may well shatter any time-tracking systems of the listener, in a parallel way to the interruption of one's daily routines by an unexpected event.

Permanence can be implied, conceptually, by any cyclic event in the music. However, ostinato figures in music can be seen to represent permanence - or at least an absence of change - at a much more recognizable, local level. An ostinato figure is a recognizable array of sounds – usually in a tonal or modal context - which follow each other in a constantly (obstinately) repeated short pattern. To merit the term of ostinato,[81] I calculate that the duration of the repeated unit needs to be quite short - perhaps less than 3 seconds? – so that it is graspable in its entirety, as our appreciation of a pattern of longer duration usually involves memory or at least processing, and more susceptible to distortion by other elements. Ostinato is a device employed frequently by several early 20th-century composers noted for writing complex musics (such as Stravinsky and Lutoslawski) presumably because it its ideal for adding a sense of rich texture of sound without overloading the listener with much new material for processing. In addition, by creating an effect of a permanent element in a soundscape, it can then be used to portray 'erosion' (by an outside force) through a levelling-off of its internal components, such as in the 'neutralization' of rhythmic and/or dynamic character. Alternatively, the simple manoeuver of causing an ostinato to fade away in volume can succinctly imply a receding into a distance or into the past – like a fading memory. Longer variations of the ostinato such as the passacaglia and chaconne figure in an intermediate scale between ostinato and cyclic music. Textures, in the 20th-century sense, have some elements in common with ostinati in that they may remain stable over a long period if one listens to the entire passage as a single 'field' with only surface fluctuations. They are discussed in more detail in Ch. 26.

❊ CONTEMPLATIVE TIME / TIMELESSNESS

As mentioned in Ch. 14, music designed for religious ceremonies often

---

81 Independent of the basso ostinato of a ground.

aims to promote a sense of timelessness in their listeners. Several 20th-century composers, inspired by the concept of space-time, have designed works which present apparently unrelated gestures outside of a causal sequence; this can produce similar results but the contemplative sense usually depends on a certain sparsity of texture not always present in such works. The piano piece "Wu" by the Czech-Canadian composer Rudolf Komorous is a wonderfully extreme example, where single notes are often presented so slowly that each seems an isolated event.

These musics accomplish an effect of timelessness by eliminating a perceptible rhythmic pulse; there is another body of music, however, which functions in a similar way by the opposite means: a rapidly reiterated static pulse. Examples of this are found in music of the Javanese gamelan and certain modes of African drumming and singing. This music has aptly been called "trance music" as it instills a sense of timelessness in the properly-conditioned listener by effectively hypnotizing him/her. It is most commonly found in conjunction with rituals where a semi-hypnotic state is desired. This reminds us that the function of music is quite specific in many cultures, and it is not always that of entertainment. Recent research has begun probing into the specific features that tend to promote a sense of timelessness in musical contexts.[82]

❋ Dream Time / Art Time

There are many works especially from the 20th and early 21st century that explore atypical models of time. In this currently 'miscellaneous' category we can include aleatoric or chance forms pioneered by such diverse characters as Stockhausen and Cage, and the 'spatial' forms of Webern where there appeared to be no causal connections between the short note groups. Because we are accustomed to a sense of temporal shaping being conveyed by the change from one state to another, the absence of such indications implicitly challenges that view of time: our temporal body markers are ready to measure durations and follow lines, but we find neither the lines to follow nor any sense of what durations are to be compared.

Multiple-strata works are those that seem to portray simultaneous but independent musical ideas, often with contrasting metric schemes and/or tempi - although not always clearly visible in a written score. (Some examples are noted

---

82   See for example Noble, Bonin & McAdams, 2020.

in Appendix D.) These can provide some of the most fascinating examples of temporal exploration, and are reminiscent of the categories of dream time as they defy normal entrainment-based listening. Other examples involve only one layer, but with such compression or expansion of familiar patterns that they will also provide a dream-like effect - as in Marais' work *Reveuse* [Dreamer] which hides a straightforward 4/4 dance rhythm by exaggerating its slow beat into the realm of the surreal (as demonstrated well by Gielmi & Pianca in the recording *Bagpipes from Hell*); or, at the other extreme, the impossibly fast melody in the strings at the beginning of the second movement of Lutoslawkski's *Concerto for Orchestra* or Mendelssohn's fairy music in the *Overture* to *Midsummer Night's Dream*.

25. INFLUENCES OF THE LISTENER'S PROFILE

Many factors within the music itself influence the perception of temporal design. As mentioned earlier, the training, temperament, and current attitude of the listener will influence the reception of all of these devices. However, once we understand the potential of different configurations, we can gauge how different listeners might react to them.

We can, for the sake of argument, assume that all the conditions of the transmission path of the musical performance are optimum: the composer was successful in notating her remarkable soundscapes and vivid characters with clarity, the performers gave an excellent and sympathetic interpretation, the venue was ideal for listening to the particular sounds and exempt from interruptions and extraneous noise, etc.

Then, we can continue by assuming that the listener is in fact able and willing to focus on listening - unencumbered by worries about other imminent events in his life, and eager to encounter a new performance. However, this assumption, although it may be valid at the onset, is always susceptible to derailment if the listener's capacities for appreciating the musical structure are not sufficient to the task at hand. Musical (and cultural) experience begins to move into the foreground, as someone with intimate knowledge of Beethoven will be in a privileged position to notice further nuances and links in a fresh performance of a similar genre, but might be quite unequipped to make sense of a Xenakis work, or appreciate the innovations of Hendrix. Perception of metric frameworks is also likely preconditioned by cultural music traditions, as shown by various studies;[83] the contamination of cultures (like the ubiquitousness of North American pop in the world at large) doubtless erodes some of the recognition of styles that used to happen more intuitively. Similarly, the predominant tuning in Western music nowadays is based on a 12-tone equal-tempered scale. The nuances of music which depends on more subtle tunings are therefore frequently overlooked by listeners, and often provoke anxiety from those trained for decades to treat all non-tempered intervals as 'out of tune.'

The degree of familiarity with the materials is thus a primary factor, but it is coupled also with the individual's aesthetics: some sounds and rhythms are simply found more appealing than others - whether or not they are familiar. These may be attractive (or repellent) for reasons of association, at conscious or subconscious levels - the patterning of sounds as reminiscent of the speech cadences of the mother tongue; the timbre reminding one of a sibling's efforts on a certain instrument; the chirping of a bird or the shrill whistle of a factory that figured large in the listener's childhood....

As discussed in Part III, one's personal 'experiential' sense of time is rarely in tight synchronization with clocks, but rather stretches and shrinks according to various factors such as the density and unexpectedness of events, the attention which we give them, our emotional state, and the temporal focus of our gaze. In order to achieve similar effects, composers and performers need to have a good sense of when and how much any given passage should appear to be stretched or shrunk in relationship with a clock-time (or body-clock-time) regularity in order to create the desired psychological effect in the listener - or at least 'in the music'. In the case of notated music, these modifications to the prevailing pace of unfolding then need to be expressed in terms that can be reproduced accurately by the performers, so they are usually indicated in terms of clock time. Frequently, this is achieved through the establishment and subsequent manipulation of a beat (described with reference to clock-time as necessary), as well as the careful placement of significant musical events - whether individual notes or changes in musical texture - on the piece's time-line. Other more subtle means involve increasing or decreasing the overall complexity, which will have a certain effect

---

83 For example, Ch. 9 of Dowling & Harwood 1986; however, there is little cross-referencing between Western research and the ancient and medieval treatises of Persian, Indian, and Arabic music theory.

on the listener's temporal focus and attention – working with the other elements like pitch, timbre, and amplitude that can emphasize any dramatic or otherwise noticeable quality of the various elements. The listener's musical experience & intelligence is almost as fundamental as the composer's skill when considering the perception of time. If the music is less familiar in its language or style than the composer expects, then the entire sense of pace may alter, as the listener can become overwhelmed by unexpected combinations and sequences, or by what seem to be chaotic arrays of sounds. The listener's degree of attention is likewise crucial, as a lack of total immersion in the sounds may result in a similar lack of grasping particular connections – rather like being distracted from understanding a lecture by watching activity out the window and missing a crucial element in the discourse. But more fundamental is the listener's training in comparison to the work's complexity, which will allow a reasonably appropriate 'parsing' of the sounds into the intended structures. Then, a willingness to invest energy into deciphering the musical messages will likely result in an appreciation of the work (if it deserves it) – and conversely, if it falls outside the listener's aesthetics, will lead to a sense of tedium. It should perhaps be pointed out here that many composers, myself included, are often in a 'plunder' mode, and become so fascinated by certain aspects of a particular timbre, sonic image, or abstract structure for future potential inspiration that it requires extra attention to focus on the currently-evolving performance.

It is also crucial to acknowledge that the act of listening does not always happen in a totally linear fashion. In fact, the linearity of one stratum of activity can actually deflect the listener's parsing to switch to a 'looser' view of temporal progression in order to complete the listening process which is in progress: this was demonstrated in laboratory conditions within a small-scale context in what was named 'click migration"; listeners focussing on a musical-type line actually 'displaced' the occurrence of a noise burst which interrupted that line, in order to maintain a coherent image of the line in question.[84]

---

84 See Kaminska & Meyer (1993) for some discussion about the phenomenon and its examination in both speech and music contexts.

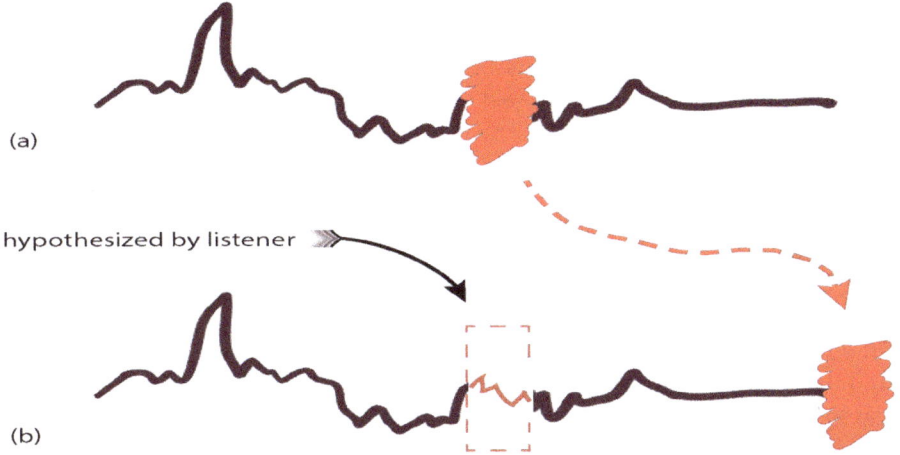

Figure 8. Click migration: (a) sonic signal (e.g. musical passage) interrupted by noise burst; (b) noise perceived as occurring later in order to preserve integrity of followed signal; obscured part of message reconstructed by listener.

There are also broader and more abstract parts to such non-linearity when we acknowledge the role of the individual listener's memory that may link parts of a musical experience to quite different and non-chronological occurrences, both within and outside a musical context. However, for the current discussion, we will assume that the transmission path of a given piece of music is of excellent quality, that the composer is skilled enough to notate her/his ideas appropriately, and that the listener is both sympathetic and musically-literate in the appropriate language, and attentive. We are then left with the musical structures themselves to analyze for their temporal impact.

Musical designs for affecting the sense of time will be discussed in the next chapter under 'temporal design', but the concept of complexity seems to me more accurately considered as a part of the transmission path, as it is really a question not so much of complexity *per se* but of the degree of predictability, as long as basic human perceptual limens are considered by the composer. In other words, it is sometimes as much a reflection on the listener's experience with decoding as it is on the design of the work. As such, it may shift as the distance between listener and source widens: chronologically, culturally, or aesthetically.

What is most unpredictable in such calculations is the listener's predisposition to listen to the work and to respond in the predicted manner, or at least to recognize the movements as those associated with the imagined moods. I believe that most composers work on the assumption that the listener (or at least, the valuable ones) will be attentive, and will possess the experience to hear the music as more than simply random sounds. The performer will then work to ensure that the composer's chronological presentation is respected as accurately as possible, and contribute enough skill and energy to keep the listener's attention, while the musicologists may work to help prepare the listener, through analysis and/or socio-cultural contextualization, to appreciate the piece in some depth.

Among the most vital tasks for the willing listener is that of setting all the mental 'trackers' and 'calipers' to focus on the most salient features of the piece. This seems to imply a dual alert for both repetition and change, with a hand on the 'zoom' knob to make adjustments as necessary; it also depends on the 'zoom' knob being adequately oiled, presumably through frequent use – but also hopefully facilitated by the music's density levels.

Repetition is often underscored by a metric scheme so that the listener (and performer) can maintain a sense of regularity which then facilitates comparisons between successive events. Such events do not have to be in immediate succession, but if there is any intervening material, the listener must be alert to the beginning of a second or third iteration so that they know to start the mental comparison with the first instance. For this reason, themes are often begun at a predictable point - such as after a short pause, and in line with a hypermetric scheme. In addition, themes are often designed to incorporate memorable contours – especially in their first few seconds - according to familiar syntax of the style.

When the music requires us to track various rates of temporal activity simultaneously, we will tend to focus in on a specific level (or nested set) when we detect higher activity rates: some form of movement or change in some parameter. If there seems little contrast or significant information being received on the fastest levels, then the listener may (subconsciously) elect to abandon active tracking to determine broader formal structures - which necessarily require more time waiting for information before deciding how it should be interpreted. This 'waiting' time thus encourages a shift to a longer tracking level, and may suggest a need to 'recalibrate' the entire array of trackers for subsequent material.

Change and contrast can of course happen at any level: change in pitch, timbre, harmonic structure, density of note attacks, etc. Just like the 'calipers' I suggest we use for measuring durations, I believe that listeners tend to set their trackers to prepare for the amount of change they expect in any given passage. If that is exceeded, they have to 're-calibrate' and in the process, might lose track of some important features. When we have a 'contrasting' section, it means that we perceive more change in one or more parameters than we were expecting, or had just been listening to, and therefore prepare ourselves for a new array of data. The 20th century saw such expansion in material, along with a severe reduction in repetition, that typical listeners of Western avant-garde music often brace themselves to be ready for anything at any time - especially in electroacoustic music, where the presence of isolated speakers on stage do nothing to prepare the listener for the kinds of timbres that might emerge.

Although listeners will usually not think about these issues consciously, they may still be aware at some level that their perception of time in a certain part of the piece is supposed to feel a certain way. For example, even if one does not feel particularly overwhelmed by the number of voices entering into a texture, one may appreciate that it is meant to represent a 'strikingly complex' part, and participate in that illusion. On the other hand, the listener who is particularly skilled at 'disengaging' the normal tracking mode may become very immersed in a given work, and be quite unable to give an accurate estimate of the clock-time duration of the piece. Oddly enough, this inaccuracy simply proves that the illusions were convincing (and can therefore serve as a mark of achievement for the composer).

❉ Capacities & Predisposition For Temporal Experiences

The listener's general sense of the experience of time in music may parallel or reflect their everyday experience of time as discussed in Ch. 10, as it involves similar factors. These include the tendencies and preferences of the listener to focus on shorter or longer durations of time; their perception of and tolerance for change; the capability of their memory and the ease of retrieval; and the impact of health, training, personality, culture, and clan. In particular, the relation of body to the music's rhythm is of paramount importance in the creating and perception of musical illusions. It seems that aesthetic preferences may thus be influenced by such things as the listener's knowledge of walking, running, hiking, skipping, chopping, sliding, etc. as well as their general mobility, and that those who limit their physical activities to driving and texting may lose out on many of the references. Conversely, those composers who are not physically as engaged with their physical world may well create music that will not provide sufficient associations for those of us who still hike and dance.

✻ Suspension of Time-Tracking

The suspension of time-tracking refers to the special adjustment made by many listeners who listen to a musical work in a focussed way (e.g. a concert). Although many people in modern society try to maintain a good awareness of the ticking of the clock during their normal activities, it seems that in the context of music we anticipate a different temporal experience. Listeners preparing to hear a piece of music will usually enter into a special mode where they deliberately suspend normal time-tracking activity. This happens naturally when the music is in the context of ritual, story-telling, or dance, for example; but a parallel shift seems quite clear for the concert-goer as well. The temporal organization of musical elements is generally out of proportion to our normal pace of life and things around us. Many things are presented in odd juxtapositions and at much faster rates of change - very much as though we are experiencing daily and yearly fluctuations of time in a microcosm. Although listeners will be subject to external factors that may influence their attention, an attentive person will tend to adjust to a particular time-perception mode that is open to different time-scales.

One of the benefits of attending a concert in a familiar venue is that we usually know approximately how long the concert will be: whether 'into the wee hours' or 'over by 10:00 pm at the latest'. Then we can mentally relax our own tracking of clock time for the (expected) duration of the concert, and abandon ourselves to the whims of the music creators and performers. Depending on the content, the adventure may seem like a roller-coaster ride of vastly-differentiated sonic textures, volume levels, timbres, etc., or a more sedate wandering through an ordered gallery of patterns and tunes. Usually, the concert-goer will have an expectation of which end of the spectrum will be presented; often, but not always, that expectation is met. In many ways, it seems that 'concert time' can be very similar to 'dream time'.

26. Temporal design & its reception

Even if one chooses to study a musical work 'in isolation' from its context and reception, there are different perspectives available. Usually, in academic contexts, the various musical elements are examined – through written scores – in terms of their local properties of pitch and rhythm, with amplitude (dynamics) and timbral treatment (instrumentation, range, articulation, etc.) playing a minor role due to the lack of detail conveyed in notation. Scores are often very precise about the clock-time speed of such configurations, although some deviation in overall tempi is considered the prerogative of the performers (especially if a conductor is involved, as time-keeping is one of their chief functions), and terms like *'rubato'* give this freedom explicitly. However, because scores evolved as instruction sheets, the performer only needs to know how fast each phrase, gesture, pattern, or other configuration is to be performed, and how long to wait until beginning the next one. Therefore, the overall organization of these elements is rarely viewed in its relationship to clock time[85] - although it could be, as there is almost always some indication of either duration or pulse expressed with reference to the clock.[86] As the beat is equated to a particular millisecond length (expressed as *x* beats per minute), all of these durations are theoretically measurable. An interested analyst can calculate the clock-time measurement of the overall structure and show the proportions mapped in minutes and seconds - a task often aided by sonogram- or amplitude-type visualizations of a recording.[87] Such information is not really

---

85 Except when it is necessary to coordinate with someone not playing from a score - such as a technician on a computer - or in a certain style of score notation popular in the mid-20th-century where blocks of sonic textures are coordinated (usually with the aid of a conductor with a stop-watch) with a running time-line notated on each system.

86 There are of course exceptions, such as in experimental mid-20th century works by composers like John Cage, Terry Riley, or Karlheinz Stockhausen, whose instructions give more freedom to the performer to choose the tempo, duration, or even the sequential order of performance of different passages. But they still often address the issue of relationship to 'external' time, if only by links to familiar body movements.

87 It needs to be mentioned that performers do sometimes make adjustments to the notated tempo, and so discrepancies then have to be critically studied to conclude whether the change in timings are there for legitimate reasons, such as in order to compensate for

helpful to the performer, however, who will simply learn how fast the fingers or arms or tongue or lungs have to move in order to produce the desired sounds at the prescribed tempo, and then embed that memory into the necessary motor or vocal sound production mechanisms, with audio feedback for confirmation.

Even the composer does not have to think very much in terms of seconds or minutes except in a very broad sense, as the custom in traditional-styled acoustic music is to think in terms of beats, bars, and phrases, or gestures, patterns, and sonic shapes. Often, in my experience, an idea will be conceived sonically complete with its temporal scale, and then - possibly after some experimentation with slightly faster and slower speeds - measured against a metronome, watch, or software equivalent before being finally notated in relation to clock-time. At that point, a performance that does not adhere fairly closely to the clock-time measurements risks losing its identity, as the impact of the various components have been calculated by the composer to occur with certain rhythms or in certain proportions – in other words, aligned with the human reference points of body rhythms and recognition of sonic signatures; therefore, as with most of the temporal things we try to convey to others, the (indirect) clock-based notations provide a robust reference point. Music performance training, however, still involves extensive amounts of oral tradition in that teachers often convey the precise timing of a passage simply by playing it and asking the student to approximate that aural model more closely.

❋ Contrast

Perception of contrast happens on both very subtle and very obvious levels. One of the most common examples at a subtle level is that of the changing timbre in a relatively familiar and short note: the change operates on component frequencies (harmonics) which have already been mentally 'fused' at a very early stage in the pitch perception, and it is only when those changes appear 'odd' - such as in a digitally-manipulated version of a sound produced by what first appeared to be a familiar acoustic sound source - that contrast between millisecond segments of the sound might attract conscious attention, although it may well convey expression

---

particularly resonant or overly-dry acoustic environments, or to stress a particular curve or feeling that seems in need of emphasis - or whether they are simply inaccuracies in score-reading, or an inability to perform the given sections at the indicated speed (which might also indicate the composer's lack of knowledge about the technical difficulties involved).

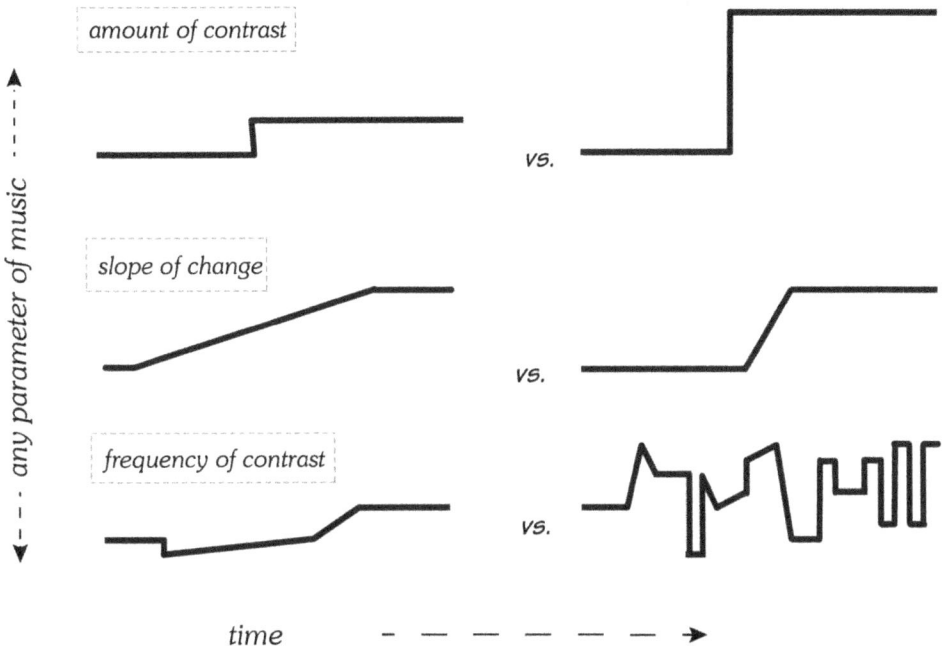

Figure 9. Variables of contrast

through association with vocal utterances, for example. A very different effect happens when one movement of a piece is followed by another, and the texture changes from a gentle murmuring on the woodwinds to a loud set of chords in the brass and an independent scurry of activity in the percussion (which had been hidden from the listener's view). Such a contrast may actually prompt the listener to turn to a companion with a look of exclamation. These various types of contrast should perhaps be differentiated, and the composer may well think of the contrast between sections *as* contrast, to be crafted to meet the requirements of the composer's design, whereas the contrast of frequencies at the level of timbre are usually a collaboration between the composer and the performer, according to directions (and their level of detail), through articulation symbols, dynamics, words, and/or diagrams in the score. The latter is not true in the case of the electroacoustics world, however, where both timbral and large-scale detail are often conceptualized together by the composer.

Contrast itself can be measured by its characteristics (as shown in Fig. 9): how much change is involved? how suddenly does the change occur? how unexpected is it? how frequently do these contrasts occur? etc. Such measurements can be extremely useful for the analyst or composer, and to some extent the performer may also benefit from a reflection on it, in case there are subtle links that might be emphasized, for example. However, the measurements may often be quite profile-specific, as the perception of contrast depends on the listener's decoding and chunking strategies.

In addition, we seem to differ on our calibre settings of the contrast 'boundaries'; not only according to aesthetic preference but also innate or acquired aptitudes or weaknesses in some of the sensory system. Therefore, some who have listened to high-decibel concerts may have little sensitivity to low amplitude levels, for example, and therefore miss contrast on those levels, whereas the same person could have very accurate discrimination for pitch if it is sufficiently loud. A good dancer is more likely to be sensitive to contrast at the limb-movement level, although a parallel sensitivity for recognizing non-human sound imagery might be important for a wider range of expression in abstract dance.

It should be noted that if there is a great deal of contrast in some parameter, changing from minimum to maximum and back with rapidity, the overall effect may be that of a lack of contrast, as the contrast itself becomes perceived as a "steady state". This impression can sometimes be altered by consciously tracking even faster rates, if they exhibit perceptible change. Ligeti's music with what he called "micro-polyphony" and Reich's early minimal works (such as *Six Pianos* or *Violin Phase*) provide excellent examples which reward that type of listening strategy.

❋ TEXTURES

I have found the term musical texture to provide a very useful concept for perception as well as composition (although its non-musical uses can be problematic in interdisciplinary discourse). It is described by Berry as follows:

> Texture is conceived as that element of musical structure shaped (determined, conditioned) by the voice or number of voices and other components projecting the musical materials in the sounding medium, and (when there are two or more components) by the interrelations

and interactions among them.[88]

Several prominent mid-20th-century composers including Stockhausen, Ligeti, and Xenakis were fascinated by perceptual issues, and as they saw the difficulties of perceiving large-scale structures within the current trends in dodecaphonic and serial music, each experimented with organizational schema that resulted in what may also be thought of as 'textures'. (These schema are also studied under the terms 'field music', 'stochastic music', and 'sound mass', although each has its own shades of meaning.) This idea of texture grew to denote a way of organizing musical elements, in contrast with the idea of a figure/ground relationship typical of melodic-harmonic music. When we hear a passage where there are several sounds combined, but no particular element is more prominent than the others, the result corresponds more closely to 'ground' alone. However, in the absence of a clear 'figure', the ground emerges in its place of prominence in the listener's attention, and so its characteristics are more in need of careful construction.[89]

Textures were often designed by determining the range limits of all the parameters, which permits the control and distinction of contrast between adjacent textures. For example, one passage could have mainly sustained notes at a central range of frequencies, with slow swells of amplitude, and a subsequent one could be differentiated by changing one or all of those characteristics. Figures 10 and 11 show two levels of detail from Ligeti's *Chamber Concerto* Mvt. III, which has very little pitch fluctuation (none in Fig. 11) and thus provides a nice illustration of varied rhythmic densities and shifting rhythmic dissonance.[90] Ligeti was particularly fond of creating textures that evolved very slowly from one state to another, at rates of perceptible change considerably outside the window of the 'now', provoking a rather interesting temporal focus relaxation.

---

88 Berry 1976, p. 191.

89 This usage was brought to my attention by the American composer Robert Erickson (1975), and although I found it highly appropriate, it did not surface in much musicological research until recently.

90 These sketches are adapted from Ch. 4 of my thesis (Mountain 1993).

A Musician's Guide to Time

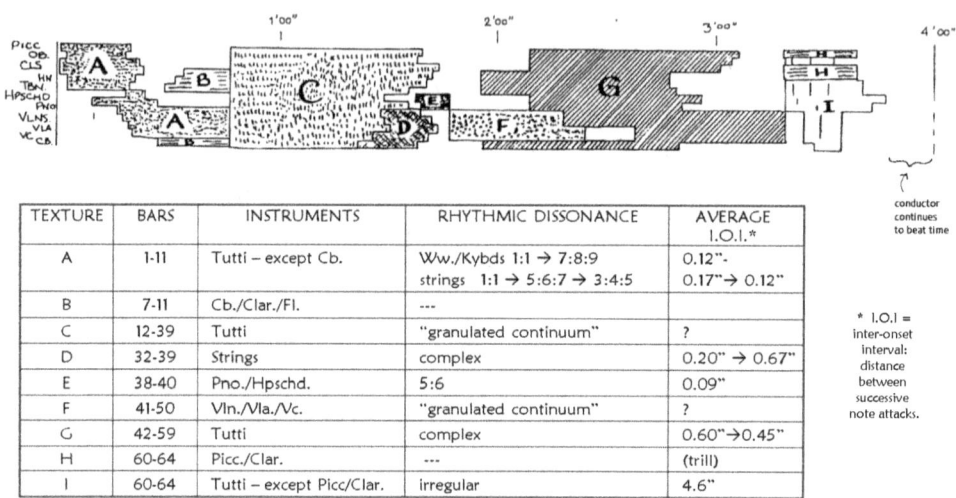

Figure 10. Ligeti's *Chamber Concerto Mvt. III* – sketch of overall textural design.

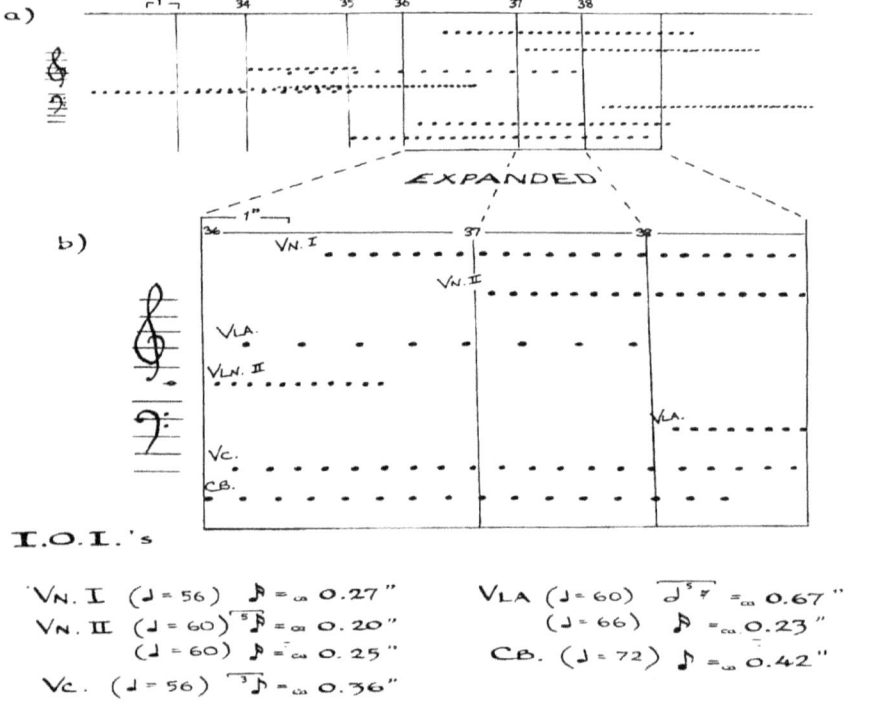

Figure 11. Ligeti's *Chamber Concerto Mvt. III*: 32-39 - Texture D, close-up view

Density can be considered a major feature of texture: it can refer both to the density of note attacks (or dramatic shifts of pitch, for example) per second, and to the range of the frequency band (where 'narrow' means that the sounds fall within a close range to each other). It is one of the most easily perceived attributes of sound in otherwise seemingly chaotic sonic passages (e.g. atonal &/or arhythmic), and therefore provides a kind of 'entry-level' discrimination of contrast. In fact, a useful strategy for music which seems to defy the listener's attempts at chunking into meaningful segments in such contexts is simply to listen to the 'whole' and wait for a change in the overall texture as an indication of at least one level of formal structure.

❊ LAYERS OF RHYTHMS

The most evident visual forms of timing, in a score, are the notes themselves, which are often easily read by a musician in terms of the main frequency (pitch) and their indicated duration. Even in simple contexts, though, an inexperienced analyst who is more influenced by the score than the ear may over-emphasize the difference between short durations followed by rests and equivalently-paced longer durations. This is especially true when the rhythm is not consonant[91] with the meter, as in Figure 12:

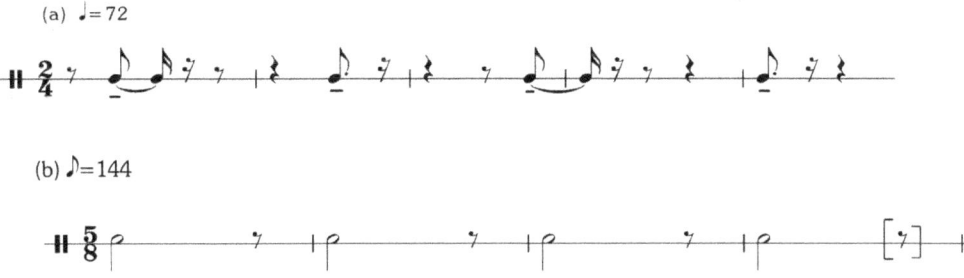

Figure 12. Same rhythmic structure, different notation.

In Fig. 12, (a) and (b) exhibit the same rhythmic pulse, although with a difference in held durations, and different metric notation which implies a

---

91 Consonance and dissonance on the rhythmic level is a very useful extension of the harmonic usage, discussed at length in Yeston (1976) and crucially refined by Krebs (1987). It refers to the alignment of two (or more) rhythms which will appear 'consonant' if they are related by simple harmonic ratios like 1:2, 1:3, 1:4, and dissonant when they are more complex such as 2:5, 4:7, etc.

A Musician's Guide to Time

downbeat-strength accent in (b) - but easily simulated by adding the accents to (a). Sometimes, for reasons of practicality (e.g. performer reading) the durational value specified may not precisely match the instrument's capacity: imagine that either is played by a wood-block or a gong, for example. Although it might initially seem odd to notate a periodic rhythm through notation that does not emphasize its periodicity, it is useful for temporary shifts of beat, for leading up to a future change of meter, and indispensable for notating one of two or more asynchronous rhythms.[92]

A closely-related issue occurs very frequently with audible accents that do not coincide with the beat or beat-grouping 'super-pulse'. Accents mean a perceptible emphasis on a particular sonority, achieved through dynamics (often notated by conventional markings such as '^', '<' or '-' over a note (as in Fig. 12a, above); through metric frameworks (i.e. landing on the first beat of a bar, and especially landing on the first beat of a first bar in an established 4-bar phrase); through a sudden shift in texture, timbre, or even an audible change in direction of a melodic line. Accents can often be emphasized or obscured by the performer, depending on their preferred interpretation. I believe that one reason so many solo violinists and cellists enjoy practicing J.S. Bach's unaccompanied *Sonatas & Partitas* is that they are full of patterns such as those composed of short sequential passages where a recognizable grouping of notes is immediately repeated more than once at different starting pitches. These sequences usually occur as initially consonant with the meter, but subsequently form their own 'temporary meters', which can be exaggerated by the performer or simply allowed to provide a gentle polyrhythm to the established metric scheme. Bartók's and Shostakovich's quartets provide numerous similar examples that can illustrate the same principle of clear segmentation in contrast with the notated meter.

Figure 13. Subtle cross-rhythms - from J.S. Bach's *Violin Sonata No. 1 - Presto*[93]

---

92   See Zukofsky, 2005 for similar and more complex examples.

93   It can easily be argued that my brackets should start one sixteenth-note to the right, but it does not change the shift to 2/8, which can be emphasized or not by the performer.

The ways in which notes are grouped together into gestures, chords, melodies, accompaniment patterns, textures, etc. is relatively clear in many cases. Basic phrase analysis, in which undergraduate music students learn to identify sub-phrases and motives in terms of their similarities and contrasts, can easily reveal something of the rhythm and timing of the section. The discerning student will realize that any deviation in a repeating pattern of phrases, such as in Figure 14, will inevitably involve a displacement of the fourth iteration of the pattern due to an internal varied repetition of one element (B).

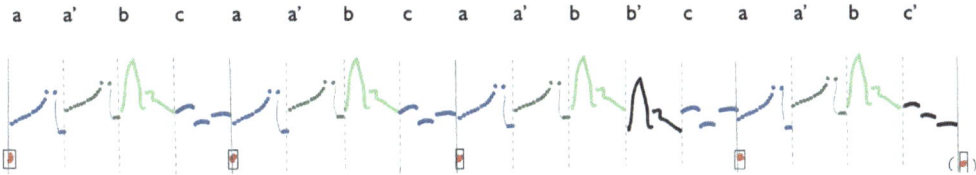

Figure 14. How an added unit upsets the periodicity of the next highest level.

When that pattern is at the level of the sub-pulse, the displacement will be more keenly felt, whereas at a larger level, such as that of the super-pulse, the displaced A will be only slightly sensed, and more likely so well followed in the causes for its displacement that it will not feel 'irregular'.

We often shift from a more direct body-tracking perception to one of following a story, in which the passage of time involved has to do as much with tracing details as it does with representing a time-frame in proportion. This is why the higher levels of grouping (i.e. that of longer-duration units) begin to be less evident without scrutiny, and larger-scale sections may require listening to a vividly-imagined or real performance, along with further analysis. Some theorists and analysts[94] work to investigate and highlight shifts of accented patterns, but the topic is still under-emphasized in many basic analysis courses, which means that performers are often less conscious of their potential role in emphasizing written meters over implied ones, or shaping a longer-term building or ebbing of energy. I suspect that the absence of large-scale temporal design notation helps explain why the emergence of detailed rhythmic theory in Western music has been so slow. Even irregular phrase lengths that are potentially powerful on a local level to the listener are not always obvious to the beginning score-reader – which is why I demanded of my music analysis students to examine the type of Bach and Shostakovich

---

94   Such as Gretchen Horlacher, see for ex. Horlacher 1995.

examples mentioned above. In addition, bars that consist of the same duration in clock-time seconds rarely occupy the same number of centimeters on the page, due to conventions of notation. In electroacoustic, jazz, and non-Western music where rhythms are particularly fluid and nuanced - such as Persian and Indian - there is often a total absence of notation, so that these musics are even less easily available to the score-dependent analyst. This is yet another reason why I believe music students (and their professors) would benefit from more awareness of the development of aural analysis tools and methods, as well as encouragement of new notational methods that can better express temporal designs.[95]

My own research was motivated by a desire to understand music that seemed to portray multiple events occurring simultaneously, usually through a combination of superpositions and juxtapositions. Although electroacoustic music often presents some of these 'events' as short, well-defined gestures, much of the orchestral music worked with multiple metric schema to produce more traditional extended passages, each with its own meter and rate of development. Such works often create a differentiation between layers through various parameters - pitch collection, frequency range of melodic material, amplitude contours, and textural parameters - but the rhythmic dissonances are particularly striking, as they encourage tracking of one layer at a time, since the brain (or more likely, the body) has difficulty in tracking multiple meters simultaneously. The composer may simply present the apparently chaotic results as a puzzle that will eventually reward the hard-working (repeat) listener, or may choose to lessen the major features of one layer while another is at a crucial point, just as 16th-century polyphonic composers would balance activity in one line with less movement in another.[96]

---

95 See for example the significant work in electroacoustics notations such as Couprie's *eAnalyse* and *iAnalyse*, the survey of newer notations provided by Hope (2020), and the comprehensive book by Vear (2019).

96 I developed an analytical method to help untangle such configurations in a score with the aid of auditory scene analysis guidelines; this is being prepared as a book entitled *Sorting out the Strata*.

27. Creation / perception of illusions in music

Music may be appreciated for presenting different ideas or events in temporal pacings that simulate the ways we experience time when *not* listening to music - albeit on a very different scale. In order to create such impressions, the composer takes advantage not only of the general factors that influence the sense of time passing - expectation, complexity of information, etc. - but also relies on additional factors that are special to the processes of listening to music or any other artform that involves sound. Depending on the clarity of the original intent and the performer's grasp of the appropriate pace and ability to imbue it convincingly into the music, the results may well be felt by the listener. The listener may not grasp the specifics of the composer's inspiration, or may react in an unanticipated way, but if the composer and listener are both experienced and skilled, the listener will usually appreciate something of the form: tension, release, contrast, etc.

One of these factors has to do with the personal attitude regarding awareness of temporal perception issues during listening. As mentioned, many listeners will suspend normal time-tracking activity while listening to music: we expect to be entertained by a familiar or novel assortment of activity levels. Although the listener will be subject to external factors that may influence the attention, an attentive person will tend to adjust to a particular time-perception mode that is open to different scales of presentation.

❋ Auditory imagery

A second factor is associated directly with the entire tradition of musical illusions. Research ranging from a study of the use of rhetoric in music to the incorporation of gesture and other basic shapes governing the pacing and contrast of elements indicate clearly that we have community-wide, if not universal, associations with certain configurations.[97] The crux of much

---

[97] See for ex. McCreless (2002), Godøy (2011), McAdams (.g. 1982), Dufour (2016).

of this research is that our knowledge of our natural environment (within which I include human) is carried as much by sound as by visual. Although our current educational system and other society shapers downplay the effect of sound, we clearly depend on it to provide information. Sounds indicate the behaviour of things - rain, wind, crying, hammering, approaching train, etc. Only in music do we have sound without its corresponding sound source. Of course, in most music, there are instruments producing the sound - but there is considerable evidence to suggest that we usually consider them to be the puppeteers of the play that is manifest through music. We can hear a particular line on the oboe as a plaintive cry, *glissandi* in the winds as representing turbulence, a slow pattern in the brass as underlining a royal ambience. We talk of melodies in terms of their inner character, which although often shaped by a specific instrument timbre, is rarely completely dependent on it. Music students learn to recognize melodic and harmonic configurations as independent from timbre (i.e. instrumentation, plus articulation and volume), and various composers' sketches confirm that a melody may well be notated before the specific instrumentation is determined. We hear a melody and accompaniment as two (related) things, and three melodies in counterpoint as three things, even though there may be 10-100 performers involved in each. We hear sounds emerging and fading away, even when none of the performers enter or leave the space. We hear heaviness and lightness, sorrow and playfulness. How?

Schaeffer, one of the key figures in musique concrète, was noted for his extensive explorations into new frameworks for discussing sounds that would be more relevant for composers wishing to work in the potentially abstract world of electroacoustic music. He coined the term 'objet sonore' as the units that might be constructed by the artist, but the static qualities associated with the term 'object' was problematic for many.[98] Therefore, I found the concept of 'auditory image' as articulated by McAdams very welcome, as it incorporates the notion of 'coherent behaviour' and presents the idea in auditory perception terms.[99] This metaphor seems quite compatible with other views such as those expressed by Kielian-Gilbert (1987) when talking about the importance of the recurrence patterns of gestures,

---

98   Kane (2014, Ch. 1) helps clarify how Schaeffer understood the time involved in the human perception of an object from different perspectives as being parallel to our perception of the sound over time.

99   McAdams, 1982, 1987 *passim*.

as one can interpret a gesture as a kind of 'utterance' of an animate thing, or the design aspect of a mechanical one, whose properties of recurrence are part of its identity.

By studying the cues that we use in the natural world to segregate sounds into distinct groups, we can reproduce similar cues if we take into account the limens of human auditory perception mechanisms. The 'auditory image' thus presents a robust metaphor for both the composer and the analyst, as it helps clarify to what extent the perceived 'image' or illusion can be segregated from adjacent material (adjacent in terms of temporal proximity), and can be used to create and recognize sonic 'shapes' of diverse character even without any direct reference to known sound sources.

The creation of illusions may be conscious on the part of the composer, or may be simply subsumed in the compositional process and style as learned by the study of past works and their accompanying commentary. When it is conscious, it may or may not impact the listener's reception; if a specific model is used - sloweddown bird calls, the sea, or a rugby match, for example - its proper identification is often not necessary to an appreciation by the listener. What *is* transmitted is the play of regularities, contrast, layers, patterns, etc. – which may or may not suggest distinct entities evolving in space. As both Stockhausen and Xenakis realized early in their investigations, certain natural sounds like rain can be understood as variations of a particular Gaussian-type distribution - which is easily transferable to the organization of notes (and other elements) in a musical work. The design of any given passage may evoke similar descriptions in many people in terms of mood associations (tragic, playful, etc.) or simply in abstract terms (stark, chaotic, intricate...). Although some attention has been given to the role of harmonies in such associations,[100] the specific temporal aspects of pacing, rhythmic patterning, etc. are significant contributors, as can be illustrated by changing the durations and tempo in a familiar passage while retaining the same pitch sequence.[101]

---

100   Of the type "major=happy, minor=sad", in the most crude matching of Western classical music; often more nuanced in older traditions.

101   It seems to me that this is what Schoenberg was doing in the earlier works: keeping phrasing, amplitude, and general pitch contour profiles from his familiar world of late 19th-century art songs, but applying a different set of rules to choosing the precise pitches. Thus, a standard 20th-century composer's strategy, to investigate which components signal what attributes.

❋ Cogs, oscillations, beats, clouds

A third factor in the perception of time within musical contexts is that much of the rhythmic information is articulated at a *very* quick pace, usually with some regularity and some irregularity in terms of clock time. A classic example can be found in the uneven contours of a melody against an established regular beat and metric structure; however, 'clouds' of sounds, sonic gestures, advancing and receding sonic textures, or abrupt bursts of noise interrupting extensive silences have become equally familiar to many of us. The way in which we track regularities at these fast rates appears to be quite distinct, as they link at a primal level to our bodies, as described in Ch. 22; this is not conditional on the presence of regularities, but simply to remark which receptor bands are most relevant to their tracking. Once we realize that our perception of things moving at the rate of the beat is different from those moving at the rate of the ornament, the bar or the section, for example, we can better appreciate the responses that any particular configuration is likely to produce - and how a composer might use that information in designing sonic works.

❋ Strategies

An interesting study could be made of the various strategies used by composers to influence the listener's sense of time. Although this is not the kind of subject normally expressed or reliably transmitted through words by pre-20th-century composers, we can infer that certain styles of music were designed specifically to induce particular sensations about the temporal world, according to their functions. For example, it is easy to understand that the long phrases and absence of clear metric structure in some of the liturgical music by Palestrina and contemporaries were intentionally designed to distance the listeners from the rhythms of the mundane world. Similarly, slow processional music from rituals could encourage an initial focussing of the listener's attention on a sacred time-frame, as it would be recognizably a form of 'walking speed', but slowed beyond the practical. It is easy enough to imagine that related uses were given to music in ancient times, when reading about the Celtic bardic tradition, for example, in which the composer/performer was expected to be able to induce the audience to weep, laugh, or drift off to sleep at will. In the 20th century, there were numerous experiments conducted in both acoustic and electroacoustic fields where the listener's attention would be shoved into different listening 'modes' and to very novel configurations: extremely slow (portions of Andriessen's *De Tijd*, for example); extremely fast (e.g. Ligeti's *Continuum*, Lutoslawski's *Concerto for Orchestra* [mvt III]); focus on microscopic details (Steve Reich's *Violin Phase*); or on multiple levels of activity (Stravinsky's *Petruchka* or *Rite of Spring*; Ives' *Symphony #4*).

Although this awareness and exploration of time and perception may be entirely subconscious on the part of the creator, it can on the contrary be paramount: several composers in the past century have enjoyed framing their reflections precisely in terms of time, in its full and seemingly elusive sense. Otherwise, these issues are often subsumed under the vague, if potent, word 'rhythm'. Attention to specific rates and body clocks is a fairly recent branch of study, and rhythmic aspects are usually relegated to clock-time descriptions by psychologists, but the term 'rhythm' is used in many different senses in music. However, it is always associated with temporal aspects. Often it is used simply to describe the patterning of the 'background' grid, or metric structure, which is thus closely related to the 'clock' model. More frequently, it refers to small cells that accentuate that grid. But in many circumstances, 'rhythm' refers to the patterns of tension and release, or perceived ebb & flow of events - at which point we have moved from clock-time to experiential time concerns.

Despite the existence of temporal illusions, composers (and performers) aim to create a temporal environment through physical sounds whose behaviour and flow is grasped in a similar way as during people's regular experience of time - or at least, using the same types of processing. For example, even if the listener senses that the flow of time is slowing down or becoming more chaotic, that will not likely interfere with the mildly-trained ability to recognize a tonic note for itself, at x cycles per second, rather than mistaking it for one a little sharper or flatter.

In order to probe more into this process of creating illusions, it therefore seems useful to clarify the distinction between clock time and experiential time in music. One deals with the practical matter of ensuring that the composer's ideas are accurately notated and transmitted, while the other is concerned with trying to create a specific series of effects on the listener's perception of elapsing time. However, it is also important to appreciate that our experience of time owes much to our own physical body clocks, which are not as tolerant of as extensive stretching and shrinking of clock time as our imaginations may be - so it becomes important to understand the physical implications of various specific rates of movement and pacing of events as measured in clock time.

Part of the problem is that we have been lacking easily-accessible frameworks for thinking about, creating, and analyzing music-visual interactions, with a few notable exceptions like those by Michel Chion, Marcelle Deschênes, Nicholas Cook, and Annabel Cohen - which is why we developed the *IMP-NESTAR* project.[102] This lacuna is slowly being addressed by researchers in various areas including moving image / film / cinema, multimedia, video art, visual music, cognition, etc. but remains stubbornly at the fringes of basic music and art training. The modern-day film industry has tried to establish connections between certain musical forms and emotional states – such as the dissonant screeching in *Jaws* – but for those of us who tend to listen to any soundtrack consciously, Western mainstream film music is so full of poorly-rendered 19th-century styles and self-referential clichés (like the equal-tempered keyboard rendering of simplistic pentatonic patterns to mean "oriental") that it is often a contributing reason for avoiding 'blockbuster' films.

On the other hand, the rich field of long association between the physical characteristics of many if not most of the musical illusions we hear has begun to be seriously considered by a few musicians and researchers, such as in gesture research (e.g. Godøy & Leman 2010) and electroacoustic musicology, such as revealed by Garro's comments:

> The electroacoustic language is intrinsically visual, even within its acousmatic paradigm. Visible morphologies acquire a sonorous dimension as soon as we uproot them from their cinematographic habitat and plunge them into the cauldron of a new alchemy.[103]

---

102   See Chion (1990), Mountain 2003c (on Deschênes), Cook (1998) and Cohen (1998); also Mountain 2003b, 2005, 2007a for some explanation and context for the *IMP-NESTAR* [Interactive Multimedia Playroom-Network of Exploratory Spaces for Temporal Arts Research] project.

103   Garro, 2012: 103.

28. Clock time and music performance

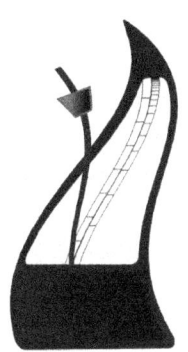

In music, 'clock time' is an intrinsic part of most composed music and its (re)production. Directions are given to the performer which can be translated with some degree of accuracy to minutes and seconds. Since the 17th century at least, the tempo was often indicated with reference to human activity (e.g. andante – 'walking pace') or mood (allegro – 'cheerful') but the rough equivalence to beats per minute was sufficiently understood to allow them to be indicated on the 19th-century metronome, devised to indicate a more precise beat-per-minute rate. In the 20th century, some composers indicated durations for sections or subsections in the notated score by the precise number of seconds (or minutes) allotted – as in the violin part of Figure 15.

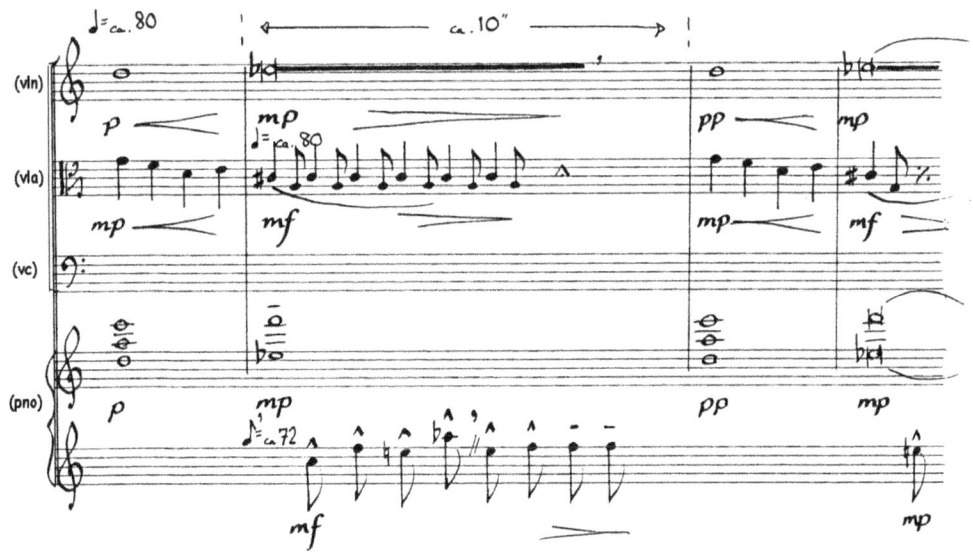

Figure 15. Excerpt from author's 1999 work *Ambar* with mixture of time notations

A Musician's Guide to Time

With the advent of electroacoustic music, clock time became even more prominent: composers working with computer-produced sound were initially obliged to calculate the exact duration of each frequency component in milliseconds as part of the input. Those who worked with recorded sounds were less constrained, but as soon as the sound was recorded, the recording itself provided the absolute measureable duration - and manipulations were often made in simple ratios of speeding up or slowing down the original sound by a factor of 2 or 4 (although pioneers like Dhomont and Lecaine created their own devices to allow for more variability). Tape music composers also appreciated the direct relationship between the length of tape and temporal duration, and could literally measure out five seconds of a sound by ruler. Nowadays, composers working with audio software may rely on millisecond measures just as designers work with (virtual) rulers and graph paper. Common visualizations of sounds being manipulated almost always incorporate clock time (directly or indirectly) as one of the two axes – as in Fig. 16.

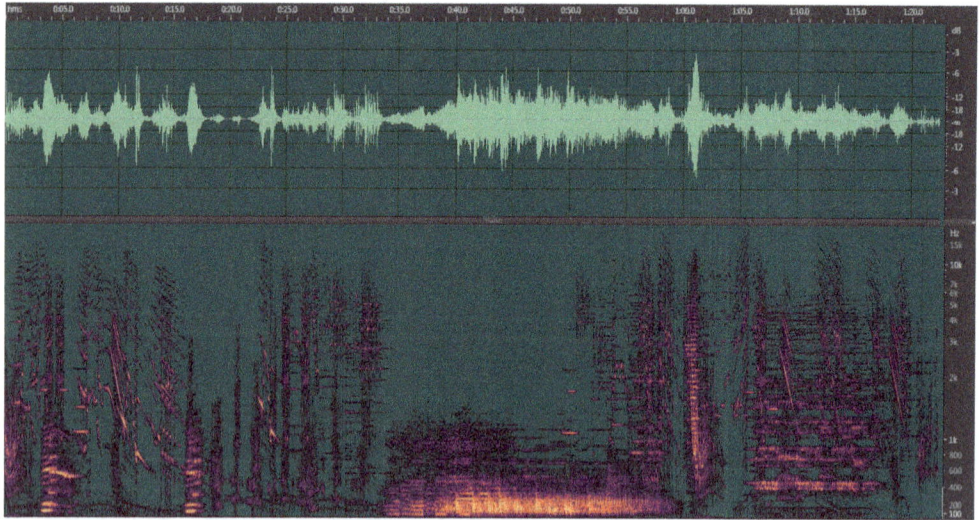

Figure 16. Amplitude graph and spectrogram of a musical passage; in both frames, the x-axis represents time; the y axis represents amplitude or frequency.[104]

---

104 This is from the author's 1999 electroacoustic work *Bits & Pieces,* composed with excerpts from previous acoustic works modified only by splicing, layering and extreme tempo fluctuations, hence the sweeping lines. The software used is *Adobe Audition*, a favourite programme of mine since it was *Cool Edit Pro*: not only are the zoom levels very adjustable, including the ratio of logarithmic to linear in the frequency display, the resolution of the

Of course, standard Western notation has been organized on a left-right time axis since it was first devised in the Middle Ages, just as our writing is read sequentially from left to right and top to bottom. However, there is little correspondence between the visual representation of the time-units to minutes and seconds; one line of music in a score may take 3 seconds or 30 to perform. This is interesting in the composer's early stages of composition if the composer imagines particular sonic 'shapes' along a time-axis: the sketch in Figure 17 represents a compositional idea which might work at 3 seconds or 30. My own experiments suggest that many sonic configurations are not easily recognizable when transformed into a different time-scale – although they may be noticed in an analysis and subsequently identified aurally as comparable in profile.

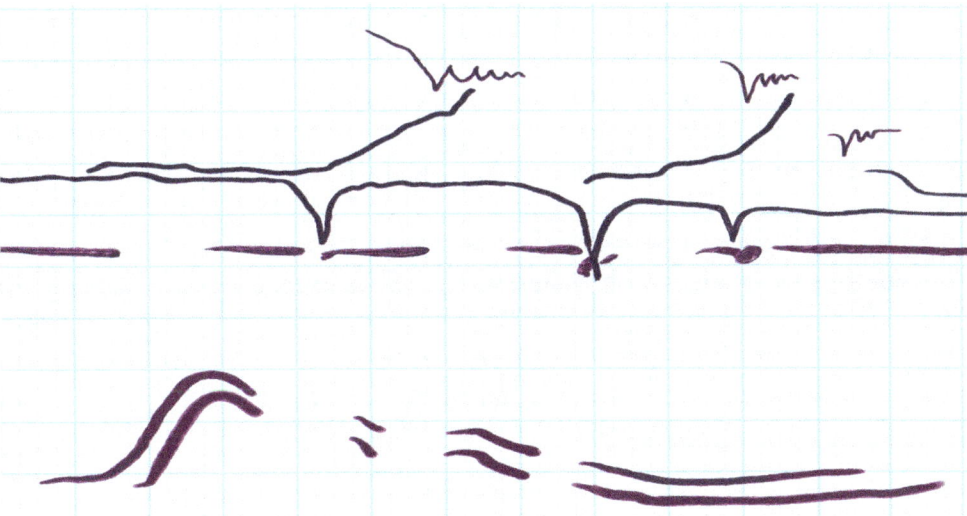

Figure 17. Compositional sketch written on graph where y-axis represents pitch/frequency and the x-axis represents time, but without reference to time scale or detail of pitch range.

The composer and the performers (if involved) will usually conceive of the work as a linear entity, at least in the final pre-performance stage on, regardless of how complex the metaphors of temporal passage within the compositional design. Again, this is for ease of coordination and even for the influence of performance. Theoretically, a composition in five sections could be practiced in a different

---

spectrogram, and the decibel sensitivity; but there are also various options for ruler units of (clock) time. This screenshot shows hours: minutes: seconds.

order than the final order of performance, but as it is in fact a physical activity when acoustic musicians are involved, one usually wants to practice the impact of one section on the subsequent one – to notice and compensate for fatigue, for example - or practice changes of position or sonic reverberation in relation to the instrument(s) or performing space. In addition, performers may also become aware of subtle links between different passages that will not necessarily emerge in the more random sequences of earlier rehearsals. On the other hand, a work which is conceived of as alternating between two or three different characters can be profitably rehearsed as independent (as pianists regularly do with segregating the different hands when they are associated with melody and accompaniment respectively).

On a compositional level, various composers have made specific reference to clocks in their writings and conversations. Ligeti's *Cello Concerto* opens with what seems a clear imitation of a ticking clock, while his wonderful *Poème Symphonique For 100 Metronomes* is a wry demonstration of the effect of multiple simultaneous beats – also explored instrumentally in the third movement of his *Chamber Concerto*.[105] The beat of any piece, when it approaches a clock rate (e.g. 58-62 beats per minute) or its double, may trigger the audio image of an analog clock for those listeners who have grown up with that familiar but disappearing household sound. On a deeper level, the beat or any other cyclic loop of musical pattern can represent this sense of 'mundane time' when exceptionally steady. Most importantly, such patterns can represent a stable grid against which an unevenly-moving melodic passage or gesture will be thrown into relief.

29. Different uses, different concerns

Depending on one's particular interaction with music, one may have quite different perspectives on time, as well as preferences for the metaphors used to deal with it. Compare for example the length of time involved in the performance of a piece, usually minutes, with the preparation of that performance (sometimes weeks and months), with the months or years which might have been involved for the creation of the piece, and with the time it

---

105   See Figures 10 & 11 (Ch. 26) and Mountain 1993, Ch. 4, for a fuller discussion.

takes (sometimes a century or more) for the analyst to produce a satisfactory analysis of it. We can also reflect on the time that elapses between the composition and the performance; and the performance and the hearing of it. For example, imagine listening, in 2015, to two recordings of a Schubert work written in 1819: one made in 1950 and one in 2010. It may be argued that the more recent recording is 'truer' to the original concept, as the performers and the recording engineers are more sensitive to such issues as period instruments, typical acoustic settings, etc. On the other hand, a recording from 1950 might have involved performers whose teachers' teachers' teachers were contemporaries of the composer, and therefore have a good innate sense of all those microscopic details which make it 'truer' in terms of aesthetics and stylistic coherence. Additionally, both media linkings and awareness of recording techniques may provide an aura of 'historical' for the older recording which might encourage a naïve listener to remember, at a subliminal level, that the piece itself comes from an older time period when things were experienced differently.

❋ Composers & Time

In one sense, the time of composition seems quite linear: one keeps working on a composition day after day, week after week, until it is done – except that sometimes, a piece is abandoned and picked up several years later. As time goes on, the piece is theoretically nearer to completion. Even if other activities get in the way, the mind may be working on little fragments of the process, which emerge into the conscious mind in the middle of other activities. However, beginning students are sometimes surprised to discover that the first notes written may well not be the first notes of the piece. That is, gestures, melodies, textures, and other components may be conceived independently of their final chronological position in the piece – and even if one might have decided that there should be a *Theme I* and a *Theme II*, and written them in sequence, it might seem fitting once one has arranged them that the whole piece would benefit from an introductory passage or even a separate movement. Even more difficult for a beginner is the concept that some material may have to be completely abandoned as marring the final product. So, although the process seems linear, in retrospect, as we like to imagine that we are starting at a good starting point to end up where we do, the connection between conception and finished piece is quite different. Similarly, the composer's attention may alternate between large-scale formal plans and foreground detail –

or start with either and then progress to the other. For example, I have composed several pieces by assembling a collection of little motives and short passages which I then combine and replicate in particular configurations to produce the desired amount of tension, complexity, shaping, etc. Other pieces have started from a very different angle, where I will imagine textures or fields of various vague characteristics – dense, strident, plaintive, murmuring, dissolving, etc. – and figure out their general overall durations and proportions to each other before choosing the specific notes.

However, even in the linearity of the process, the alert composer might notice that a section has been 'over-worked'; some part of it has lost the initial character that was treasured. Then, one has to 'back-track', perhaps working on a different composition or at least a different section, before returning to a 'previous' stage, trying to ignore the sounds that were formulated in the head. This is not unlike a 'rupture' in the linear time-sense.

Composers are probably the most likely of all music participants to think about time as a clear factor in what they are producing, to the extent that a piece may be based specifically on temporal phenomena, aiming to provoke very different impressions of duration in the listener. The consciousness of their thought processes may be obvious from their own talking and writing, or may be deduced through a careful study of their sketches.[106]

Composers of electroacoustic music often work with time in ways that differ substantially from those of acoustic music composers. Electroacoustic music is generally thought of as coming from a few distinct technologies: experiments with main-frame computers to produce sounds according to input of numerical data (frequency, amplitude, duration &/or position on a time-line); experiments with analog synthesizers which combined oscillators, amplifiers, filters, and resistors; or experiments with sounds recorded from the physical world onto tape or wire which would then be combined through splicings and re-recordings, with the potential of playback rates at any given stage of the compositional process of up to 4 or 5 times faster or slower than the original. The ability to isolate chunks of sound and place them in various configurations produces a strong effect of the 'manipulability' of time, especially once one realizes that a different sense of time can be achieved by swapping a few units, due to their inner properties. Further

---

106   A good example of such deduction is found in Besada & Pagán Cánovas (2020) looking at works of Gérard Grisey and Kaija Saariaho.

developments in computer software allowed for more global processing, like granulation (conceived by Xenakis and nicely exploited as well by Truax), which encourages larger-scale transformations by chosen increments. In recent decades, technological developments have greatly decreased latency,[107] so there has been a marked increase in the blending of these electroacoustic approaches with more traditional instrument production, as well as with fantastic experimentation in the area of gestural control, ranging from specially-designed instruments[108] to wearable sensors with which performers (e.g. dancers) can modulate sounds. A newer field (of which I am scarcely familiar) investigates the manipulation of sound with the same tools that manipulate moving images.

All of these modern technologies emphasized the profound changes that could be produced by changing temporal aspects: personally, I was enchanted by the possibilities of splicing tiny fragments of real-world sounds (like water, birds, and extraneous noises) into new sounds because the fragments were too small for recognition and were re-interpreted as providing unusual attack/sustain/decay contours of an unknown sound source.[109] My hunch is that the frequent lack of beat in much 'art' music from that world derives from extraordinary attention to detail at the 'timbral' and boundary levels, and I have proposed that composers working with significant organization at the timbral level may intuitively avoid the beat level that could distract the attention and overload the sensors (Mountain 2020).

---

107   Latency - the delay of a signal from one device to another, such as from a hand-held electronic instrument to the computer programme and then to the speaker. The difficulties for performers who had to deal with an audible delay while playing in a 'spatially-distributed' ensemble provided another indication of how fundamental this microscopic sense of time is to hearing and reacting - along with the practicalities of participants existing in sometimes widely different time-zones.

108   such as the wonderfully simple but highly programmable design of Joe Malloch's *T-Stick* and Michael Waiswicz's *Gloves*. The NIME (*New Interfaces for Musical Expression*) conferences provide wonderful examples of this area of creativity.

109   For practical reasons, my fragments would rarely be less than an inch long, but as I was using sounds recorded at 15 ips (inches per second), that could provide a duration of 66 ms; slowing down the original before splicing, or speeding up the spliced result, could compress that to 33 ms of the original sound. (As each re-taping could audibly reduce the quality, I would rarely do both.)

✹ Performers & Time

Performers know well that the time involved in learning a passage has nothing to do with the amount of time the performance will take: it is based more on mastering the necessary techniques – not only learning to execute the proper notes and rhythms with appropriate clarity, but also analyzing the work (at least in the sense of reflecting on and appraising the organization of its parts) in order to understand where to make those minute adjustments of timing, temperament, and dynamics that are normally left to the performer's discretion. With contemporary music, the performer is often required to play in ways which might be unfamiliar, so then they may have to invent their own 'études' in order to train their muscles and limbs for unusual motion sequences.

In many circumstances, the performer who chooses a new work to play, or agrees to play one for/with others, will mentally commit an appropriate amount of time which they intend to spend on learning it. Indeed, a first question before committing oneself is often not "Is it a really good piece?" but "How hard is it?" -- as that gives the performer a sense of the time involved in learning it. The answer, from a fellow performer, might be "a lot of black" (which implies many short notes to learn and to execute cleanly), or "lots of key signature changes" (which implies learning not only lots of notes but lots of counting schema) or "we just have mainly whole notes, the percussionists are the ones who have to work this time". When an ensemble is involved, the other very relevant question is "How many rehearsals?" which of course involves not only questions of the rehearsal's duration but also the travel which is usually involved, and the likelihood of all other activities having to be adjusted during the weeks affected.

A very typical aspect of rehearsing a passage involves playing it at different speeds – usually starting by slower speeds until the proportions and links between notes and phrases are smooth, but also then ensuring that the passage can be played faster than required, as a test of the skill and to impart confidence (in case the passage does become accidently 'sped up' in concert – a not unusual occurrence with amateurs). As a beginner violinist, I was taught the very useful trick of practicing evenly-spaced durations – such as a long pattern of eighth notes – in dotted rhythms (long-short, long-short, and then the reverse) to help the performer identify and compensate for natural tendencies toward irregularities caused by hand position, finger length and strength, bowing, etc. Performers also spend considerable time working on the inner shaping of notes – whether by altering the attack and the particular striker, for a percussionist, or by controlling the breathing and timbre for a singer or wind player, for example. These adjustments require a focus on extremely fine timelines of well under a second in length – adjustments that are generally made through a combination of physical alternating of parameters – such as bow pressure – and aural judging of the effect.

The importance of a 'dress rehearsal' in the particular performance venue is critical because such sound 'shaping' is also influenced by the acoustics of the space – which can subsequently be altered by the presence of a few hundred bodies at the concert. Attention is therefore required at the level of microseconds but also for the longer spans of the phrase or section. If the same piece is played numerous times, it is likely to produce a conscious reflection and comparison with previous performances on past days or years. The time during rehearsals in itself is a bit peculiar, as it incorporates several different attitudes towards temporal unfolding: usually, extreme precision at the level of milliseconds, but often recursive in numerous repeats of short durations, sometimes including a shift of tempo while learning the precise synchronization of often asynchronous-sounding passages, along with jumps forward and back in the temporally-ordered score, and interspersed with external references to other time-frames like those of the participants arranging a future rehearsal.

When the performer is working on the learning of a new piece, especially with no audio guides for models, the amount of allotted time may well seem insufficient to master the material as one begins to investigate it. The performer needs to be able to realize the audio instructions accurately enough to hear the potential relationships between all the varied musical materials, in order to gauge how the overall structure might be convincingly portrayed. In many cases, they are expected to internalize the music so that it can be played as though a given character is improvising (singing/speaking), thus producing a series of notes which emerge as a fluid phrase expressing a character's idea or emotion. This kind of internalization is difficult to do until the mechanics of producing the correct notes at the correct timings is mastered, so when the technical demands exceed the performer's predicted time-frames for learning them, the appropriate large-scale shaping and nuances of expression may suffer.

Of course, this sort of time calculation by performers is very much a learned skill, although experienced performers may be able to help others if they know each other well. But there are many variables – including the quality of the piece being learned: does it indeed have coherent interconnections? The performer's aesthetic reaction to small fragments of the music will also have an impact: if one needs to repeat a 15-second passage numerous times to ensure that the fingering becomes almost automatic, it is helpful when the notes form some kind of satisfying gesture or pattern.

❋ Improvisers & Time

The relationship with time for the improviser may be the most idiosyncratic, as the improviser combines the roles of composer and performer. However, those roles are combined in such a way that they might compress those of composer + performer or, as improvisers may always be alert to impromptu performances, even if only for themselves, their lives may be more fully immersed in practising their musical expression, giving them a special intensity of time experience. A crucial attribute of the improviser is the focus on sound in general, in which timbral concerns are not distinct from those of pitch and rhythm, and the music is not played with regard to the 'accuracy' of interpreting someone else's notational schema, but rather to the coherence of the overall effect. Of course, the best non-improvising performers will reach a similar state, wherein their learning of the notated piece will be sufficiently mastered that they can then move into a performance mode and imitate an improvising figure where tuning and timing appear naturally connected to the music.

One curious phenomenon is found in recordings of improvisations, an extremely common occurrence these days. In such cases, the listener should be aware that any familiarity that might result from having listened to the same recording before should theoretically be discarded from memory, as much of the excitement of the original depends on its component gestures and passages being conjured up 'on the spot' while any subsequent reiterations and transformations are thus 'time-stamped' and owe part of their identity to the time which has elapsed from the birth of the idea – the sparkle of wit from a lively conversation or engaging monologue.

❋ Recording & Time

Recording engineers work in a clear 'clock-time' environment these days:

not only do they 'view' the music they are recording through spectrograms and amplitude graphs which are measured and annotated in milliseconds, but when not in live venues, they are often working in high-demand facilities which have strict rules about the timing of bookings, so any but the richest are ultra-conscious about elapsing minutes and hours during recording sessions - sometimes in stark contrast to the musicians they are working for. On the other hand, they are the most complacent about the 'reality' of clock time, knowing that they can, if necessary, splice a few seconds from yesterday's recording into the old one from last week. Moreover, they are responsible for being able to record a musical event from a specific time and place, and repackage it for diffusion in very different venues and contexts. This modern technology that distances the listener from the performer can seem like a "fracturing" of time. However, arguably some contemporary composers are now writing for such a context (especially in pandemic conditions) whereby the live performance is simply another step in the path to the eventual digital version produced for the listener.

❋ Musicologists & Time

Musicologists are a diverse bunch who will have quite different attitudes towards time depending on their methodologies, perspectives, and subject focus. A musicologist may focus on works for flute & guitar, or folk music in northern Finland, or trends in 20th-century Europe, or the sonata-allegro form, or later works of Scriabin. That work may be undertaken mainly by scrutinizing written scores, or reading texts with occasional aural examples, or spending two years "in the field" making recordings and talking with practitioners. Therefore, they may deal with extreme compression and expansion of timescales – as in reading up on the historical accounts of the relevant time period in a few years, along with the investigation of two or three composers' lifetime endeavours, and then spending a subsequent year 'unpacking' a major work through an analysis of fifteen minutes of music.

Musicology is one field that I think is very ripe for thinking about time more overtly. Not only is there considerable need to redress the balance between talking about notes and talking about rhythm, in order to better reflect the impact on the listener, but also in the historical sense, as each composer and style has its own relationship to its own time period. Were they 'ahead of their time'? Were their artistic ideas socially acceptable in their community? Did they care? Were they trying to reflect their own environment in its current state, or trying to resuscitate ancient forms, or striving to capture something of the future, or the eternal?

Schenker is one of the leading figures in articulating the whole idea of different levels of time-frames – but this was certainly not clear to me for years when I was struggling to learn how to apply his schema to various analyses, although I did recognize eventually that his discernment of linear movement is quite compatible with guidelines of auditory scene analysis. I was therefore astonished when I finally discovered that, prior to his major contributions in analysis, he had been studying ornamentation and its symbolic representations. This instantly conveyed to me that he was testing the expansion of temporal scale by finding parallels on the large-scale for the 'ornamental' level – which would have simplified my understanding from the start. I have not kept abreast of any developments in Schenkerian scholarship, but trust that this is now more evident to curious students.[110]

❈ Listeners & Time

Although the main aspects of this category have been discussed at length in Chs. 24 and 25, it is important to stress that all the above categories – composers, performers, musicologists, recording engineers, etc. – are also listeners. The listening mode may be rather different – a recording engineer is trying to listen for details of microscopic timbre and relative amplitudes during work, but it is likely to spill over into their subsequent listening of a piece. Likewise, the composer may well listen very critically to other music in a similar way that they will listen to their own while in progress. The performer, however, has often lost out in the last century as fewer composers are writing music for the performer to enjoy as a participatory event, often treating them more as technicians required for the sonic material to be produced.

❈ Collaborators & Time

Many musicians work in collaboration with other artists, in the realms of dance, theatre, film, art installations, and various less-clearly-defined performance

---

110   although in retrospect I have found that the kernels of my objections were already mentioned by Forte in 1959.

acts. Their works are often not given much analytical attention because our music analytical methods are inherited from traditional contexts of concerts in recital halls, and although the emerging field of Performance Studies has given considerable attention to related issues, the theatre origins of the discipline with corresponding terms and frameworks have been sufficiently impenetrable to some musicians that there has been less attention given to the musical aspects. The nature of time in such collaborative works is thus not well surveyed, to my knowledge, but it seems logical to assume that each collaborator will bring their own attitudes and understandings of temporal frameworks which may or may not be consciously shared.

❋ Other researchers & Time

Like collaborators, researchers involved with music who come from non-music backgrounds such as art, history, literature, or neuroscience may tend to operate with the time sense which predominates in their own fields without being alerted to potential differences in both the 'feel' of musical time or the issues under discussion. Ironically, research into parts of the aural picture were initiated by psychologists who often had some casual knowledge of musical performance through a traditional 'classical' training and therefore framed many of their earlier studies within piano music of the 18th-19th Western European tradition, which was easy to recognize in notation, familiar to their colleagues, and easy to reproduce on a MIDI keyboard in the lab. As a result, their early experiments were constrained to a study of rhythmic and pitch features greater than the note itself, while often quantizing the component durations more than any trained performer would produce at an acoustic piano. The temporary rise in simplistic drum machines in music caused many musicians and other listeners to appreciate how detailed our attention must be: the drum machine, though completely accurate in its reproduction of the rhythms in a notated score, lacked the 'human' touch (quickly simulated by enterprising researchers through random fluctuations in the steadiness of the sub-beat range) - just as the MIDI keyboards were abhorred by many musicians for producing completely 'lifeless' – i.e. steady-state - notes. Increasingly, music cognition and related areas in neuroscience, information retrieval, etc. has become more multinational in its research base, so we are beginning to learn about linguistic differences that can affect speech perception, for example. Hopefully, in conjunction with the increasing number of musicologists moving in areas outside the Western European classical music canon, we will be able to arrive at more sophisticated understanding of the diversity of ways in which we can and do experience time in music, and eventually at more articulate ways to communicate our findings.

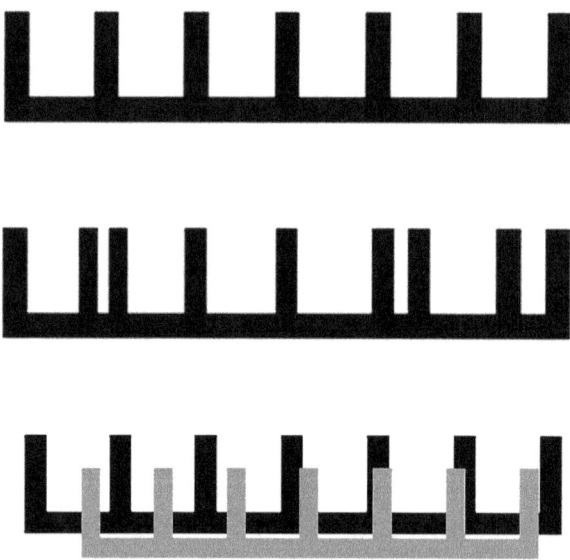

Section VI.

Concluding Thoughts

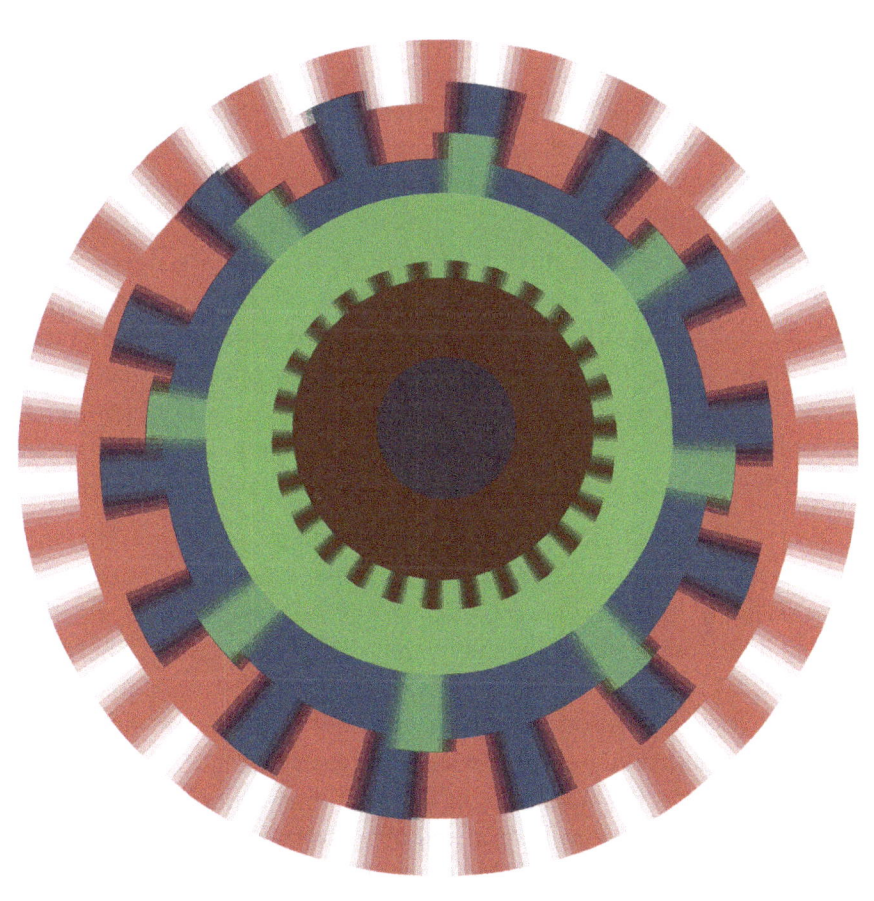

30. Time theft & our revenge

Many people seem to have little respect for other people's lifetime allotment of time, and will happily squander their colleagues' and neighbours' time with no sense of contrition. Wasting one's own time is presumably a prerogative of any individual who can afford to do so, but it seems that we would be a healthier society if people were held more accountable for their excessive usage of the time belonging to other members of the community. Of course, artists are often mistaking as wasting the time of those around them as they search the universe for stimulating ideas and ingenious connections, but familiarity with a range of artists will reveal the value of such play, which could well be transferred in small doses into other fields. Indeed, the value of high quality art is that the receiver benefits from experiencing a duration of time so rich in detail that it may help compensate for the more commonplace theft of time by others. On the other hand, all the artists I know have been plagued by friends and colleagues who frequently interrupt their working time with visits, phone calls, and other activities which clash with the artist's schedule because the mental state involved does not necessarily reveal itself in a studious position at the workstation or office. Some artists seem to take revenge by making artwork that does not seem worthy of the time it may take to decipher it, but those I admire usually create artworks that provide the listener/spectator with a wonderful set of magnifying glasses, which allow us to view previously undiscovered nooks and crannies of time, along with scaffolding and fieldglasses, so we can glimpse its larger-scale evolutionary behaviour.

It seems plausible to imagine that, especially having left my 'day job', that I do have some control over time in my own life, which has much to do with becoming skilled at focussing on details of things that reward such attention, and disengaging that close-up level for things that seem less worthy. This must be a prevalent feeling among music aficionados of all genres; for many ancient cultural traditions, the implementation of appropriate music for certain rituals, whether healing trances, battle preparation, worship, or feasts seems to assume that music can indeed help focus the attention on different time-frames and energy levels. Skeptics will claim that any such shrinking or stretching of time is simply illusory, and point to the clock as proof. However, I propose that we accept that the clock, although a very handy reference, is not much use for measuring time as we experience it.

On the other hand, I am increasingly convinced that music is a versatile medium for portraying how time appears in our lives. It can serve not only as a microscope or a telescope, but also as a working model of complex environments. The attraction of multi-strata musical passages, when their designs encourage such contemplation, is that they can provide illustrations of the complexity of our human temporal experience, where we are increasingly surrounded by different flows of events and behaviours. Any dedicated team of musicians – whether a composer + performer + recording engineer + marketer, or a group of friends singing songs from a shared cultural heritage – can easily learn how to 'manipulate' the experience of time. The sense of 'now' can be stretched into great lengths, whether by trance-like quick patterning or by fading correlation to limb movement; other styles, especially when transmitted with sincerity and focus by the performer, can encourage attention on miniscule details of sound, or their larger-scale aesthetic behaviours of emerging and fading away. Such demonstrations help contribute to a sense that time is flexible, at least within our experience of life. (In fact, it seems increasingly likely that time somehow oscillates in its behaviour, although for now it can suffice to assume that we are the ones who oscillate in our focussing and attention.) An extra feature of music is that we can become so intimate with a particular composition that we have access to a specific duration of time with its unique features, and although we may listen to different interior connections on each listening (even in the imagination), the phenomenon evokes for me a sense of a temporal patterning embedded in amber.

There is of course some aspect of great art music which excels in lifting us out of the mundane world into a metaphysical sphere, and this is probably not related to any musical devices for time manipulation but due instead to the presentation of something containing such exquisite shapes, colours, energies, transitions, etc. that the listener is 'transported' out of normal time altogether. A more intellectual listener might enter an equally atemporal state by appreciating the details of a well-crafted, multiple-level structural form, in the realm of abstract ideas. However, as such achievements are usually a slightly unpredictable result of the specific sounds, their combinations, and relative proportions, along with that of the listener's expectations and decoding, any highly-tuned sense of timing in the composer, performer, and listener will improve the likelihood of such a result. It must also be acknowledged, as various authors and artists have noted, that some forms will project fascinating structures in spite of the intentions of the composer.[111]

31. Gears, mosaics & waving tendrils

I have outlined some analogies and metaphors that have helped me think about time, and my recent attempts to flesh out an image of tendrils and gears with which we explore the waterways of time have been invigorating. In fact, as I began to appreciate how highly-tuned we are for interpreting incoming data, I found myself wondering if perhaps we humans are merely some kind of multimedia sensory units for alien beings who are depending on us for detailed information about sights, sounds, and temporal flows of our environment. Such imagery helps nourish the creative juices of artists like my friends and myself, but of course the danger is that analogies can sometimes preclude other insights, if they fall outside the intrinsic characters of those that amuse us. However, it seems that my speculations about our sensory system are not yet contradicted by current research in neuroscience and related fields, so the artistic juggling of analogies may help the occasional scientist grasp some insight more quickly.[112]

When I began probing our auditory system's capacity for listening to music, I began with the concept of periodicities, on the grounds that it would provide a clear set of properties, and encompass beat, sub-pulse, and all forms of meter (irregular meters, polymeters, hypermeter, etc.), in a way that would permit a comparative study of the specific periodic rate on its function and perception. Many modern 'textural' passages seemed to incorporate reiterations that seemed easily modelled by their internal rates, which could be approximated by periodic models. Additionally, as most Western music is notated (or at least able to be transcribed) in traditional formats, instructions to performers are generally written

---

111 See for example Pousseur's insightful article (1966) discussing Schoenberg, Webern, and the serialists in general.

112 In fact, just before publishing this, I came across a fascinating book called *Polyphonic Minds* which proposes links between mind and musical structures in ways which have much resonance for me, and calls on neuroscientists "to address and illuminate the fundamental polyphony that now seems a central and inescapable aspect of human personhood and the brain that embodies it" (Pesic 2017, p. 259).

as a series of instructions to initiate notes inside a quantized grid, such as a metric framework, thus indicating that periodicities are implied in our conceptualization and notation of such music. As we now know from music research, much of the periodicity we observe in such scores are not in fact as periodic as one might expect, but it seems that we can then appreciate the difference between the theoretically-equal gridlines and the distortions applied to them. It is this type of distortion which I think parallels our experiences of time in many instances.

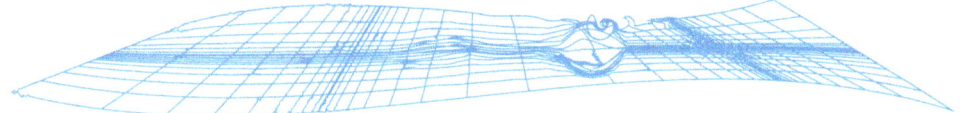

The model seems quite robust, and the limb-movement connection with the pulse and super-pulse levels is quite easy to grasp within these frameworks. However, in the electroacoustic world, periodicities and their quantizations play a much less critical role. Due in part to working with natural sounds and their dissection and reconstruction, and in part to the computer musicians who fed numbers into a computer for creating sounds – and subsequently filtered sounds into desirable 'shapes' – the periodicities that arise naturally from playing many acoustic instruments were not needed. This coincided with the movement (shared with the acoustic world too) to avoid the beat both as a hackneyed element of old styles and by its latent human body associations which might interfere with communicating more abstract designs. The only 'periodicities' that exist in some of these compositional styles are those of the frequencies themselves – and these are precisely the periodicities that we detect through the oscillations of tiny hairs in the ear.[113]

My reason for including 'tendrils' in as a supplement to our 'gears' is to stress that we seem to have radically different types of detection and processing for different aspects of a musical passage. I have not yet refined any clear idea of how the 'tendrils' absorb musical information, which makes me imagine that they probably absorb that which is more amorphous than what gears will pick up – prompting me to add a potential analogy of 'amoeba-like' to my list of ways to

---

113   This may have been a latent connection with my analogy of 'tendrils' – having seen a video online of a single hair follicle 'dancing' to music -- although I was thinking more consciously of river (and sea) creatures.

think of time. (Surely we could identify different 'blobs' of time in our respective lives, where time seemed to behave in quite coherent ways for a while, but radically different from the time-flows around it?)

I am relatively confident that the broad bands of sonic activity are in fact inseparable from different bands of our perceptual apparatus - but equally confident that we have some trainable ability to adjust our apparatus to a myriad of configurations. In my current model, therefore, I like to imagine that we have a finite number of channels for receiving all the different data that allow us to hear sounds and relationships between them, but that our various sensory processors are organized into arrays and types. I have further surmised that our individual aesthetic preferences and our preferred 'default' positions of these arrays must be intertwined.

❊ The gear shafts

Given that we seem to process different periodic events in different ways, it seems that we should be able, with the help of a few neuroscientists, to refine the analogy of 'banks of sensors' into specific groups.[114] Within a certain range, we seem to have at least some sensors which filter incoming data according to their specific periodic oscillations and iterations as well as the ways in which multiple data streams relate to each other. Since the periodic sensors (or gears, in my analogy) operate in different ways depending on the way the body and brain pick up the data, we can give these groups labels such as A, B, C, D, E, and F, where A deals exclusively with the identification of frequency, pitch, and timbre; B with pitch, timbre & sub-pulse; C with sub-pulse, pulse, and super-pulse; D is super-pulse, phrase, and section; E is phrase, section, piece; and F is larger-scale – memories, contexts, etc. The listener will normally be scanning all lower bands (A to D) at an appropriate periodic rate in a kind of 'idle' mode throughout the day and at night – though with a change of mode when asleep. When triggered by a sound or while preparing to listen to something (speech, wind, music…), the sensors are then shifted into a more 'alert' mode.

Depending on the projected source of the sound, certain arrays and subsets may then have an increased rate of periodic 'probing' and/or

---

114 Pesic discusses what seems to be a similar kind of configuration in brainwave processing oscillators (*ibid*. Ch. 15).

prioritized messaging to the central brain-sorting station (where for example there will be a search for complementary visual, olfactory, or other data). In such an array, A's sensor choices would be made at a pre-conscious level and thus influenceable mainly by indirect means such as a change in metabolism, whereas C's sensors are based on identification of those body clocks that govern limb movement, and E depends almost exclusively on the listener's mental processing applied to sorting out what A, B, C, and D have been picking up.

My hunch is that the sensors of one array might be supplemented by those of an adjacent one, even if they operate and communicate their messages by different means. Thus, sensors in band B are usually employed in helping A track pitch-related information such as timbre, but could be nudged over into helping C. Likewise, D is dependent on limb-governing body clocks in calculations, but is able to be over-ridden by conscious effort. In order to feel free to shift sensors from one group to an adjacent one, the listener needs to be confident that s/he won't miss vital information by the shifting, or at least that the effort will be worth a potential loss of data.

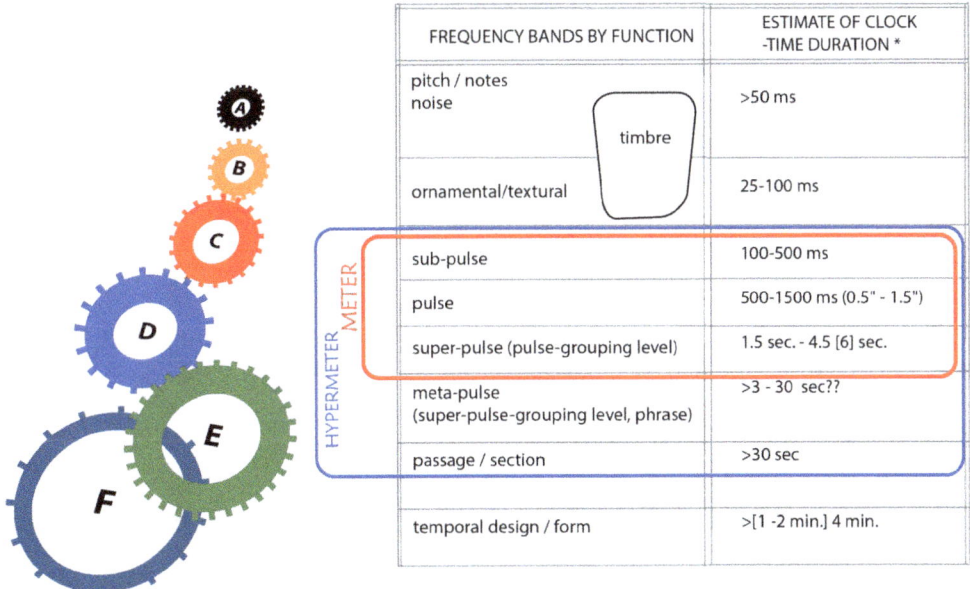

FREQUENCY BANDS BY FUNCTION	ESTIMATE OF CLOCK-TIME DURATION *
pitch / notes noise	>50 ms
timbre	
ornamental/textural	25-100 ms
sub-pulse	100-500 ms
pulse	500-1500 ms (0.5" - 1.5")
super-pulse (pulse-grouping level)	1.5 sec. - 4.5 [6] sec.
meta-pulse (super-pulse-grouping level, phrase)	>3 - 30 sec??
passage / section	>30 sec
temporal design / form	>[1 -2 min.] 4 min.

❈ QUANTIZATION

Much music, including a majority of the Western classical repertoire of instrumental music, seems to me to employ a type of quantization in both pitch and rhythm. As discussed in Ch. 23, the identification of pitch as a 'note' which implies a fixed and steady-state frequency is simply a convenience and rarely occurs in the realities of an acoustic performance. Nevertheless, the pitch organization does imply a convention that the melodies and textures are composed of discrete elements (often transferable to higher and lower octaves), while any timbral shaping is considered a different kind of component that does not adversely affect the recognition of pitch clarity. The apparent quantization of pitch is thus probably best understood as being part of the schema which allow the listener to process the variations of pitch and timbre into chunks corresponding to the number of available 'notes' in the relevant tonal or modal scale, in which any modifications of tuning or timbral variation, for example, will be understood as a nuance applied to the reference note.[115]

In a similar way, the building of pieces through the sounding of successive individual or grouped pitches seems to imply a quantization of time. There is in fact a bit less 'fuzziness' about short durations than about pitches, as a trained musician is quite capable of maintaining fairly accurate repetition of measured units if the pitch configurations are a reasonable fit for the instrument. The demonstrations of 'micro-rubato' which are normally applied to phrasing in classical music in order to clarify phrase structure are not of the same nature; in such cases, each note of a string of notes will be lengthened progressively according to a logarithmic-style curve, indicating that the curve is attached not to the note, as with a pitch's timbral shaping, but to a much longer line of notes. As such, the listener can quite easily untangle the slowing curve from the underlying patterning (which is why a faster patterning is more efficient for conveying the curve accurately).

I often think of music like the faster movements of Bach's *Brandenburg Concerti* or Bartok's *String Quartets* to be like mosaics, where the incessant eighth-note or 16th-note sub-pulse are like individual little blocks of stones, with

---

115   It plays a similar role for both the composer and performer, in providing simplified schema which can subsequently be modified for nuance.

which all kinds of designs can be delineated, and even curved lines approximated if they are large enough to survive the quantization. (This might seem similar to a pixellation of an image, but that implies a reduction or deterioration of a once-higher-resolution photo, whereas mosaic implies a deliberate construction with material that restricts one's choices for depicting organic designs.)

My passion for complex 20th-century works which seem to portray multiple layers of activity (such as certain works by Stravinsky, Messiaen, Ives, Ligeti, Xenakis, Bartók, Lutoslawski, and Reich) often incorporate this kind of 'mosaic' approach but with different results: either the mosaic blocks are maintained in the same proportion, but contribute simultaneously to different groupings (as in Figure 18); or there are two, three or four patterns each based on a mosaic design but utilizing slightly different sizes of block (Figure 19).

Figure 18. Mosaic style of conceptualizing pitch and rhythm, using a single common unit for three different coexisting configurations.

The stability provided by an increasingly-predictable size of block allows for the portrayal of much more complexity at other levels; therefore, my listening mode for such passages probably calibrates that 'block size' and tracks it easily so that other patterns can be attended to in more detail. However, in such an interpretation, any tracking of shifting details in the nature of the mosaic block unit itself seems to risk unfocussing attention from a broader level.

The periodicities of our body clocks are clearly connected to our music processing, so I expect that our tendency for 'quantization' is a corollary. My 'mosaic' sketches, which happen to resemble the system used in early piano rolls (and subsequently migrated into some sound software) are easily compatible with the analogy of gears related to finger-tapping and arm-pounding rhythms.

A recent shift in my listening to more vocal and vocal-inspired music has caused me to reflect that I am, at least temporarily, shifting my 'default' settings to a greater focus on the timbral/ornamental levels after decades of immersion in more of these 'mosaic' styles. On the other hand, when I listen to electroacoustic music, I generally seem to anticipate a 'sensor setting' that is configured as optimum for natural environmental sounds, as that is the most likely to remain open to multiple interpretation levels without any expectation of reference to human movement, speech, breathing, etc. These reflections are leading me to suspect even more strongly that our aesthetic preferences and current listening habits will tend to reinforce particular settings of our musical 'sensors' into certain configurations.

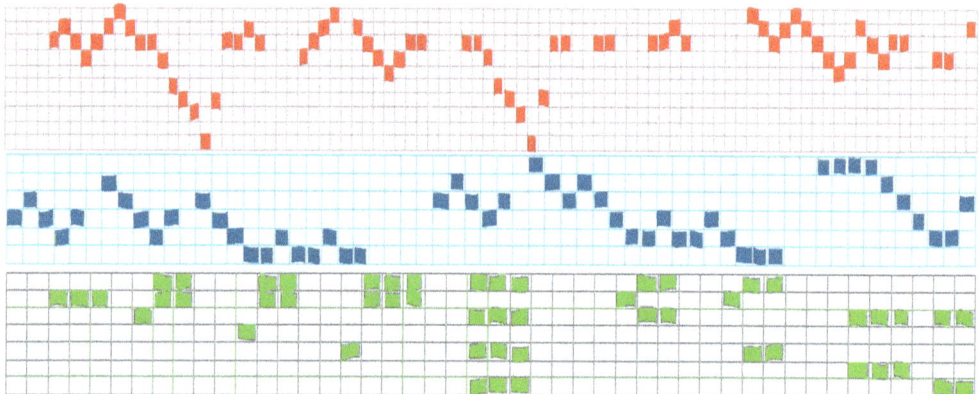

Figure 19. Mosaic style applied in a more complex scenario with different layers of music moving to different basic units of duration. (The three strata are best imagined as being somewhat superimposed in pitch space as well.)

I have not yet managed to produce drawings of my beings and sensors (as they would need to be animated at least) but have been assembling a list of features that I imagine being incorporated – see Appendix B.

32. Temporal focus & Further Speculations

My original impetus for all of this research was an attempt to figure out what happens perceptually to allow me to discern the coexistence of two, three or even four 'layers' of musical activity within the same passage – as I wanted to create my own designs borrowing from models provided by Stravinsky, Ives, Lutoslawski, and others without importing other details of their specific musical language. As I had initially recognized such structures as a kind of 'textural polyphony', my fortunate discovery of Bregman's research into auditory scene analysis provided considerable insight into how the rules of traditional counterpoint (which were themselves developed with an intuitive knowledge of human perception) could be expanded into more generic guidelines of segregation and fusion, while also incorporating information about our sensory capacities at the level of detail. However, the cerebral strategies that enable such illusions to be created and received are still a bit vague, as neurological research has not yet transferred its attention to such complex artificial situations. Moreover, verifying who hears what in any given musical context is not only difficult but also somewhat unproductive, so I am trying to follow my partner's advice and simply design compositions that will provide me with some intriguing structures for further perusal.

Unlike non-art contexts, which subject us to sounds from multiple sources, our objective in a musically chaotic environment is markedly different; we are not necessarily driven to isolate the 'important' element from the noise, but instead wish to examine their individual characters and interactions. Ambiguities in art are often deliberate features rather than roadblocks to communication. However, it seems probable that such complex processing will take advantage of our innate mechanisms for scanning and sorting sonic input.

One of the most compelling aspects of my image of arrays of gears and tendrils is that of the hierarchies in time-scales or time-streams.[116] I have thought about 'zoom' levels for years, but realized only belatedly that we are almost always tracking multiple time-streams (that is, if we are focussed on the ornamental

---

116   It is also a hindrance to visual depictions....

textures in Scarlatti, we are still tracking the bar and phrase at some level). This is what led me to imagine that we probably tend to formulate 'default' or 'preferred' settings of an array of focal levels. Moreover, I have noticed in different conference presentations and papers how important it can be to identify the 'optimum' zoom level on a spectrograph or amplitude graph for showing relevant information about the piece's structure (as well as the importance of the x:y proportion in some cases), and I wonder if similar zoom levels hold some correspondence with our own listening strategies.

A topic that is starting to attract me these days is to speculate to what extent such a model of arrays of time sensors may in fact operate in our lives beyond music, and beyond the time-frame of music. While extrapolating from music to life in general, and expanding the range of time-sensors from micro-seconds to centuries, I find that I can identify my own tendencies to focus more on certain time-scales than others, but also that my configurations shift depending on the particular topic of my attention: thus, day-to-day for a current composition-in-progress, but perhaps decade-to-decade for analytical thoughts.

It seems that we conceive of "Time" most often as a neutral path, measurable to almost infinite gradations, upon which we are positioned *now*, and which stretches back from an almost infinitely distant *past* and leads into an unknown *future*. Usually we find it easier to deal with a sub-section of that path, such as one which starts somewhere before our grandparents and extends into the future of our grandchildren. That particular time-segment has more prominent markers as far back as our memories will allow (such as our own youth) – and extending to what we might imagine as a probable time of death. Then there are the more immediately-tangible sub-sub-sections, which might stretch back to the beginning of this year, or this month, or even this week - and extending a proportionate distance forward into the future. It seems natural to assume that paying attention to the sequence of events in a week-long view of time implies a much finer level of detail - minutes and hours become primary units rather than years and decades, or centuries and eras. Being able to reflect at one level and then another likewise implies a flexibility of temporal focus. The issue is complicated by the fact that as time moves on, our perspectives and environments naturally change, and our experiences, against which we compare and gauge new activities, multiply. What was once seen as being fairly linear shifts over time start to appear more complex.

However, another common stance of thinking about time involves the observing of change in the behaviour of things, people, phenomena, civilizations - and as such is not necessarily quite so linear in conception if one includes several phenomena in one's glance. Such observations and anticipations of change may be indeed be focussed on a single thing, but frequently involve tracking the motion or growth/decay of various things moving at different rates. In such cases, the interaction of those rates may become themselves a point of focus or at least a relevant ingredient. When observing change, the attention may be mostly on the way in which the thing moves in relationship to its past motion only: evolving more quickly now, more slowly, suddenly changing its nature, etc. The particular rates of change may be consciously tracked against clocks and calendars; on the other hand, they may be appreciated at a more intuitive level - against memories of past occurrences or our own body clocks.

❊ Timing

A "good sense of timing" is sometimes regarded as the intuitive gift that will differentiate the great composer from the dilettante. But it seems more likely that such a "sense" is present in all humans to some degree, although some are more dependent on the benefits and rewards of sharpening that sense. A farmer who can sense when it is just the right time to plant and harvest has an appropriately good sense of timing for their livelihood; a trapeze artist requires an exquisite sense of timing to fly through the air and catch onto a swinging bar; a biologist may have an excellent sense of how quickly an organism might reproduce - yet none of these necessarily translate to being attuned to clocks for punctuality at a scheduled meeting. Music can likewise be relatively free of the realm of clock time that binds most scientific research in some aspects, but as we usually incorporate clock-time 'translations' for musical composition, performance, and analysis, we are in an ideal place for studying the shifting relationships between clock time, body time, and our perception of time in different contexts. My own self-training as a composer - recommended also to my undergraduate students - involved many hours of practice working with specific short clock-time durations (20 seconds, 2 minutes, 5 minutes, 30 minutes) to improve the ability to estimate clock-time durations accurately in different (musical and non-musical) contexts, to imagine the myriad of ways in which I could organize musical information within those durations, and to experiment with models for compositional form which stretch or shrink typical densities of other durations, in the form of mapping. On the other hand, my long-term sense of time, such as underestimating the time it would take to put this book together, might be seen as in need of tuning....

❋ Suggestions for future directions

The current state of my observations leads me to the conclusion that it is more helpful, when trying to envisage what time is, to develop an ease in swinging from one perspective to another; that is, to avoid total dependence on a more linear view of time as a constant clock-aligned ribbon on which we are positioned, and substitute it frequently with other ideas such as a breathing globe, a constellation of points, an interweaving of streams, a growing tree, etc. in order to remain open to more insights. Perhaps time is itself an oscillating energy; certainly it can be manipulated to some level. Cultures and trends can help speed up and slow down the rates of change in our environments, which can impact the sense of temporal experience for all the community, and affect how they deal with time in their own lives.

For the purposes of the musician, although all such ideas can provide the necessary stimulus to the imagination, it seems most relevant to discover how time may be perceived by those around us, and to appreciate the myriad of ways in which composers, performers, and listeners can stretch the experience of temporal phenomena through musical design. Although I have not described in detail how to create specific types of illlusion, any inquisitive composer who keeps all the influences in mind can begin to identify places in their favourite models which seem to do so, and subsequently identify the techniques utilized. Of the various techniques which a more cerebral sonic designer might employ, I would identify some of the main features as relating to (a) the flow of densities of information, (b) the specific rates of the most salient activity, (c) the variety of possible ways of listening, and (d) the attractiveness of the specific sonic materials – pitch, rhythm, timbre, etc. In such a list, both (a) and (d) are highly dependent on the specific community for whom the composer is designing her pieces, as the density of information is derived in large part from the familiarity or novelty of the musical structures, and the attractiveness is also dependent on the listener's aesthetics as well as the performer's grasp and the composer's skills and clarity of design. On the other hand, an awareness of the possible listening strategies might well prompt a composer to provide sonic material that can be heard as connecting in different ways, depending on one's focus – while also leading to the realization that unexpected links might be noticed by a listener from a different community or world-view.

In music analysis, I believe that it would be useful to incorporate more discussion of time as it seems to be portrayed in a given piece of music. Rhythm studies in general are still relatively new, and although some analysts are quite willing to describe temporal density, temporal flows, active and more static passages, etc. the discussion has not generally percolated down into basic analysis courses – whereas my experience shows that even secondary school students can learn to perceive and articulate these features in any music they listen to. Broader personal impressions are often shunned as being unscientific, so academia remains ignorant of how much concurrence can exist between different listeners' opinions on the same performance of a piece. However, many exercises can be designed to heighten awareness of the issues involved, such as comparing three or four different performances of the same work and the impact on the perception of rhythm, duration, pace, density, elegance, etc.; also similar studies of various music/image relationships to highlight latent qualities.

A more complex issue arises when one compares temporal designs from different cultures and eras. It is more than a figure of speech to talk of the acceleration of time in the present day versus (for example) the apparently stable societies of ancient Egypt and China. Urban life is generally more chaotic and hectic than small-town or rural life. As a result, the unwitting listener may well be frustrated by an unexpected temporal organization. City dwellers may think that a slow-moving piece will help relax them at the end of a busy day, but if it is too slow-moving, their not-yet-abandoned state of alert for dealing with disparate things may find that some pieces do not have enough information to keep them focussed. Conversely, someone who craves the high energy and multiple activities of an urban environment might be unprepared for the amount of attention and processing required to absorb a dense and seemingly chaotic piece. However, as we become better at describing music for ourselves, and then for our friends and close colleagues, we could be better prepared for choosing a particular piece or style to match our own temporal mood. To accept that we have different listening modes, and that different styles benefit from different modes, seems to me a useful premise for further exploration.

Most stimulating for me, as an artist, is the idea that I can continue to explore time and our perception of it through the careful or whimsical design of sonic material. Although a young artist may occasionally despair that everything has already been tried out and nothing new left to be invented, I have been more frequently startled to realize how many different configurations have not yet been clearly presented – at least not with the dialect or nuances I prefer. And, like familiar walks in the countryside which can been revisited in reality or imagination to recapture the same sense of time, each different path has its own character, so the walks might be in similar environments, explored at a similar pace, by the same person, and yet each is differentiated and cannot fully substitute for the other.

    The collective memories of all one's musical experiences, just like one's collective wanderings, will shape not only expectations but also preferences. Repeated listenings may well reveal new connections or, sometimes, lose their freshness and ability to convey a sense of adventure.[117] Oddly enough, some recordings of improvisations seem to suffer less from this fading than recordings of composed and performed music: this might be due to the unusually high degree of involvement by the improviser which communicates its real spontaneity – including the tracing of the performer's shift of mode, for example – and thus communicates coherence on large- as well as small-scale because it is embodied within the performance. However, there are many wonderful performers of previously-composed music, in both the contemporary and older music worlds, who can convey the impression that they are improvising the music on the spot – breathing life into the apparently more rigid frameworks of notated metric music at both micro- and macro-levels. Then there are other equally-wonderful performers, especially of 20th and 21st-century music, who can reproduce the sonic designs of the composers so well that the human (re)producers of the sounds seem to disappear, allowing for full concentration on the abstract structures being erected in virtual space.

    In conclusion, there seems to be an infinite variety of ways to modulate a temporal experience in sound, and to listen to those modulations. I hope that any creative person who has managed to follow my meanders through this book will be inspired to imagine some new ones, while those who indulge us by listening to our designs will find some new temporal pathways through the sonic landscapes they already know.

---

117   Orlov was bold enough to sketch a nice diagram of this second possibility in his 1979 article.

APPENDIX A

Sketches for a resource tool

I remember the enormous help of Jonathan Kramer's 1985 bibliography when I embarked on my doctoral research on rhythm and perception -- but also the frustration that I could not easily find a comparable list of music compositions and artworks that present clear examples of temporal aspects like "large-scale polyrhythm" or "interweaving textures". This is essentially a problem of 'tagging', as the music information retrieval people know, but it is also a problem of who will identify those characteristics, and how universally suitable they might prove to be.

Over the years, I have been building my own lists of composers, artists, musicologists, and others who have provided me with the greatest stimulation for thinking about and experimenting with the temporal aspects of music. I know that others have been compiling similar lists, as they work on analyses, prepare classes and conference talks, or simply listen attentively to music. Such lists are sometimes written down (as graduate students were once encouraged to do on 3" x 5" cards) but are more typically collected into a mental set of familiar names and titles to be shared with others if and when one has the opportunity (which itself implies a robust memory retrieval ability).

Although any style of anthology could presumably be helpful for exploration of temporal devices in music, the most useful solution I can imagine is the establishment of (presumably online) resources -- though preferably with downloadable, customizable, offline, printable versions for those days in the future when easy and stable internet access becomes elusive, or one simply doesn't want to turn on the machine. I have proposed a similar project – "A Template for a Tool Kit for Music Analysis" - in my companion book *Conversational Musicology*; it could be easily tweaked to incorporate temporal organization of musical works and commentaries on them. There are also increasing numbers of databases involving music classification in use and under development, so an alternative is to ensure that some of these will also facilitate the type of search that we might find useful.

My idea is to establish or customize a database that could be searched by some general categories of temporal manipulation as well as by the standard ones: name, title, role (performer, teacher, musicologist, acoustic researcher, etc.), era, culture, genre, instrumentation, etc. These temporal manipulation categories would ideally be tagged by the type of treatment – in both musical terms referring to function (e.g. timbre, ornamentation, note, motive, phrase, section, form) and in terms of their clock-time measurements (milliseconds, seconds, minutes, hours) as well as the type of illustration: multiple layers, tempo manipulation, stretching / shrinking, performance freedom / flexibility, unusual constraints, etc. For written work, it would also be helpful to indicate not only the field or discipline but the style and level of detail: casual conversation (which are often the most insightful), academic treatise, etc. Meanwhile, any study focussed on a particular region, genre, instrument, culture, compositional technique, etc. will easily provide useful perspectives for further investigation, while other cognate areas such as performing arts also should be linked (examples in Appendix B).

Electroacoustic music has so many relevant aspects and participants in the area of temporal exploration that it is worth considering as a separate category, especially as some techniques, terminology, strategies, frameworks and contexts developed within the field have not yet been properly transferred into other areas of music. Its practitioners' familiarity with new technology and search for pertinent information about dealing with it has allowed it a privileged position for exchanging information with other fields outside music – although sometimes to the detriment of intra-music discourse. Subfields and cognate disciplines are listed in Appendix C.

For this kind of project to work, I have already discussed (2021) how a single database in itself would be always inadequate in terms not only of completeness and remaining up-to-date, but in suitability of input and retrieval methods, etc. - although having versions designed by different individuals could be an improvement. Additionally, as we are facing problems in academia, and perhaps music in general, of information overload, we cannot expect the gathering of massive amounts of data to be useful without some filters and recommendations. To some extent, I believe that instead of trying to create the impossible 'definitive' database which takes into account all possible connections and shades of meaning, we might benefit from having the ability to add the inputter's name and type of expertise to any entries or comments within them, so that I might look over the recommendations of an admired researcher, for example, and add my own endorsement to those I agree with.

More fancifully, perhaps, I have also proposed (2021) that we establish a network of "conversational musicologists" who could provide guides to the explorer who wishes to wade into adjacent research fields. Despite its apparently playful and unscientific sound, the concept is a deliberate attempt to capture something of the breadth of thought of the music research communities of the past, and the open-ended conversations that allow hunches to be examined for their potential rather than their detailed fit to every situation. It also seems more fruitful in the long run to acknowledge the particular biases of different individuals, which can be gathered from their favourite repertoires and modes of exploration, as one can then gravitate towards those who seem to be sharing the same passions and languages for expression.

Different key ideas in research involving sound and time are already beginning to permeate quite diverse fields, as research accessibility improves and geographical proximity diminishes as a primary concern. So even an imaginary construction of such a resource network can be rewarding for some – and a few special journal issues and conference themes are always helpful.

I have put together a list of some sketches and the first few entries for my own contributions to this as-yet-imaginary database, and include them below as Appendices B and C (with their own caveats) as well as the Bibliography.

APPENDIX B

Topics, perspectives, keywords

N.B. These are incomplete, personal sketches for structuring a resource – critical revision highly recommended…

- **Disciplines / areas relating to perception of time in temporal art or in sound:**

  - MUSIC SUBDISCIPLINES / AREAS OF INQUIRY
  - performance techniques; pedagogy; theory; analysis; conducting; organology; tuning & temperament; percussion; etc.;
  - musicology – historical, theoretical, analytical;
  - styles: jazz; Baroque; Carnatic; Javanese; art song; etc.
  - electroacoustics - computer music, musique concrète, tape music, electronic music and instruments, mixed media; soundscape compositions; etc.

  - EXTENDED MUSIC-RELATED AREAS
  - opera
  - multimedia works (and commentaries on them) where the temporal flow of sound is reinforced, contradicted, woven, or transformed when experienced with other elements: dance, film, performance art, installations, video, etc.
  - also, as a special category, those in which technology allows for direct or artistically-designed correlations between sound and movement, through sensors, digital synchronization, etc.
  - sound effects, digital processing, etc.

- music information categorization & retrieval

  - OTHER ART FORMS
- theatre, and the still-emerging Performance Studies area
- novels which contain fascinating and highly relevant comments about time and music: these are difficult to discover but easy to spot, so one could imagine the benefits of a "Quotations" section of the resource dedicated exclusively to such pairings. Also, resources relating to literature and story-telling in which the temporal elements of different styles are discussed.
- poetry – whose terminologies and sensibilities used to permeate music discourse, but without updating to reflect changing conventions in both realms
- visual arts – especially those which deliberately involve time elements, such as earth art, kinetic sculpture, etc.

  - OTHER DISCIPLINES WITH RELATED INTERESTS
- communication: verbal, non-verbal, multimodal; language; gesture; song; dance; etc.
- linguistics – syntax, sound production, etc.
- acoustics; auditory perception & sound behaviour
- acoustic ecology; sound pollution;
- speech – perception; production; cross-cultural vs. language-specific traits; anthropological origins; etc.
- neuroscience: body clocks, brainwaves, memory, sensory processing, etc.
- health: impact on audition of memory, aging, diseases (e.g. Parkinson's); amusia, etc.
- psychology / psychomusicology / perception & cognition / auditory / temporal / attention
- cultural / cross-cultural studies; human geography; etc.
- religious traditions; mythologies incorporating or regarding sound
- philosophy – time, phenomenology, aesthetics, etc.

- communication theory; sonification
- [music] classification and information retrieval

■ A RANGE OF POSSIBLE PERSPECTIVES / CONTEXTS FOR EXPLORATION

- dance forms with respective moves, tempi, and music: belly dance, flamenco, tango, hip-hop, waltz, jig, folk dances from any given region: etc.
- chanting from religious traditions: e.g. Indian Vedic
- children's rhythm games, such as those commonly found in different regions of Africa, whereby individuals play their own pattern to interlock with those of the others.
- Indonesian gamelan tradition, which is clearly oriented to time-based schema.
- minstrels / troubadours / bards / griots, etc. from various cultures
- literary works / historical documents with detailed descriptions of (real or imagined) sounds, soundscapes, ritual use of music, programmatic information, etc.

■ WORDS & CONCEPTS DESCRIBING TEMPORAL ASPECTS OF MUSIC

N.B. There are numerous conflicts of metaphors, arising in part from terminology borrowed from diverse other contexts without full attention; also; anthropomorphizing of musical passages ('it swept up to a climax before dissolving); and volition attributed to the composer, the performer, the instrument, or the sounds themselves. Qualities of temporal design that imply a concept of the whole piece or section as a single unit is significantly different from one in which movement, change, or other aspects of temporal evolution are prominent. These can create 'traps' for less alert students, non-musicians and especially those whose association with music is closely connected with its visual notation, in promoting latent associations with more static objects. This caveat applies to most terms from the 'Spatial' category, and extends to related terms like proportions, large-scale form; and formal structure, as well as the term "colour".

- **SPATIAL**
- structural levels, large-scale form, formal design, etc. – imply a kind of 3D architectural or design model which seems compatible with many composers' thinking about an entire piece as a whole;
- acoustic spaces – real, enhanced, artificial, or mixture; live or recorded;
- volume [amplitude] – referring to loudness, (ironically also qualified by 'up-down' rather than 'small-large' or 'far-near');
- physical models as basis for compositional design – 'blocks' or 'clouds' of sound; dense, soft, hard, fibrous, porous, latticework – they may be conceived of as static, or may shift into temporal (see below); also object [objet sonore - see discussion Ch. 27]
- texture – especially when used in the 20th-century sense; smooth, hard, rough, ornamented, etc. – can be thought of as 2-dimensional or surface of 3-D model – may be conceived of as an unchanging property

- **SPATIAL + MOTION**
- environments – especially in the context of installations, soundscape composition; etc. but also metaphorically – c.f. Bartók's 'night music'.
- physical models and textures which are conceived of as being fluid, building up, dissolving, decaying, transforming, etc.
- animate models – especially in multimedia contexts (Bharatya Natyam, Fantasia, Peter and the Wolf) where the music seems to be linked to volition of a specific character

- **AMBIGUOUS**
- pitch space – up-down of melodic lines; implies a two-dimensional space, but usually treated as the y-axis to the x-axis representing [clock] time, although accessible in the 'outside time' category.
- linear similarly can imply 2-D except it is almost always used in forward-motion analogies in music
- motives / cells: often described with attention to inner 'character' but then treated as 'units', comparable to a note on the next higher level

- ornament / pattern – can imply abstract, physical, or moving things
- neighbour tones [auxiliary] and 'appoggiatura' [leaning note] do not imply temporal direction

  - ### FORWARD MOTION

- melodies: often described as 'linear'; forward-moving flow upwards, rising, ascending "against gravity" causing more tension;
- passing tones, leading tones
- sequence
- 'unfolding' implies Schenkerian terminology, and is temporal but at a rate dependent on the musical passage under analysis
- harmonies: progression; cadences.
- spectromorphology – incorporates concept of evolution of timbre over time
- causal: tension / release, antecedent / consequent, etc.

  - ### PACE & MEASUREMENTS

- tempo
- timing
- pacing
- rhythm
- measure [bar]
- all the terms for tempo markings: e.g. *moderato, andante,* etc.

  - ### MODIFICATIONS OF PACE

- all the terms for local tempo modifications: *accelerando, ritardando, ritenuto; fermata;* etc.
- rubato / micro-rubato – used in both local and global discussions

- **DESCRIPTIONS OF RHYTHMIC FEATURES**
- beat; pulse
- meter / metric organization / metric design
- additive rhythm / 'divisive rhythm' (rarely used except in contrast with 'additive')
- irregular meter
- repeats / da capo / recapitulation, etc.
- heterophony
- polyrhythm / polymeter
- designated forms: sonata form, rondo, through-composed, narrative, etc.
- dance forms – implied specific movements
- poetic meters and related terminology; e.g. strophic
- retrograde!

- **MIXED METAPHOR!**
- attack-decay envelope – 'behaviour' might have been a better term; in the analog studio, those of us students who liked things to make sense struggled with the admittedly letter-envelope drawing of the ADSR [attack-decay-sustain-release] confusing our understanding of the word "decay" by applying it as a term for that part of the amplitude envelope being concerned with the initial 'attack' rather than the end of any given sound one was creating.
- movement (as in Mvt. III: Adagio) – generally used to describe a unit, which was often in the same pace throughout in Western Classical period, but for centuries would have been more appropriately named "chapter" or "section".

- **OTHER TERMS REFERRING TO TEMPORAL FEATURES**
- duration – used at different levels of music (notes, movements)
- dramaturgy – borrowed from theatre

- time-scale
- structural levels – foreground-middle ground- background (from Schenker) which correspond to small, medium, and large-scale timeframes
- time compression / expansion
- polychrony
- synchrony
- aleatoric / chance music / indeterminacy
- moment form (Stockhausen)
- inter-onset interval (psychology / acoustics – distance between the attack of two successive notes
- memory

Temporal measuring

- **CLOCK-TIME (DERIVED FROM IMITATION OF PLANETARY MOVEMENTS AS OBSERVED FROM EARTH):**

- years: sun / constellation rotation / asteroid showers etc.
- seasons: solar effect on some aspects of natural environment
- days: sun visibility hours roughly calculable by tracking degree of visibility & heat from sun (waxing/waning); more accurately tracked by sundial.
- months: solar year subdivision to approximate moon cycle (29.5 days) - also observable through ocean tidal cycles
- weeks: approximating quarter cycle of moon

- **BODY CYCLES:**

- circadian – day/night corresponding to sleep : active (usually 1:3) (Note that some evidence of humans in circumstances without natural light or other reference may tend to adopt a "day"-length that varies from 24 hours.
- feeding cycles – usually 3-5 times per day – affects body metabolism / movement

- FAMILIAR NON-HUMAN AUDIBLE RHYTHMS:

• natural: wind, rain, babbling brook, waves on beach, birdsong, falling or sliding object, etc.

• human-made: motors, machines, trains, planes, cars, sirens, foghorns, ticking clocks, etc.; also simple tools which extend human limb movement (such as hammers).

N.B. Some of these rhythms appear as reiterations of a single or similar sound, whereas others are perceived as an 'envelope' of sound growing and fading (as with wind during a storm, planes passing overhead, etc.) The combination of various rhythms may form recognizable patterns (as in a complex machine where three sounds governed by three different gears exhibit a regular periodic synchronization) or may appear unrelated to each other.

- MEDIUM- TO LARGE-SCALE TIME-FRAMES:

deduced by observing the daily / monthly / seasonal / yearly cycles of earth/
   moon/sun; confirmed by observing familiar life-cycles such as plants / pets
   / people / events; tracking with time-keepers (calendars / watches / diaries /
   etc.)

- SMALL-SCALE / DETAILED VIEW OF TIME:

identified through familiar activities / events; also learned durations: time
   required to brush teeth, boil water, eat breakfast, arrive at bus stop, etc.;
   confirmed by comparison with body movements or directly retained in
   temporal memory

▪ TEMPORAL MEASURING IN MUSIC:

Several different measurement styles are used in music and music research to refer to clock time. Tempo markings are often expressed in metronome marking style (M.M.), indicating beats per minute (bpm). Frequencies are usually expressed in Hertz (Hz), indicating 'beats' per second; while auditory & neuroscience research findings are usually expressed in milliseconds (ms.).

Thus:

60 bpm = 1 Hz;   72 bpm = 1.2 Hz;   40 bpm = 0.67 Hz

15 bpm = 0.25 Hz = 4000 ms = whole note at M.M. ♩ = 60

I have not noticed clear links between brainwave frequencies and music, but there are undoubtedly some, known for example to shamanic trance practices, so I list the estimates below for reference.

Delta 0.5-3.5 Hz

0.5 Hz. = 30 bpm: ♩ at ♩ = 60; 𝅝 at ♩ = 120, ♩. at ♩ = 90
3.5 = 210 bpm = 285.7 ms ≈ ♪ at ♩ = 53; ♪ at ♩ = 106

Theta 4-7 Hz

4 Hz = 240 bpm = 250 ms = ♪ at ♩= 60; ♪ at ♩= 120
7 Hz = 420 bpm = 143 ms = ♪ at ♩= 104

Alpha 8-12 Hz *(short-term memory, emotional arousal)*

8 Hz = 480 bpm = 125 ms = ♪ at ♩= 120
12 Hz = 720 bpm = 83 ms = ♪ at ♩ = 90

Beta 13-30 Hz

13 Hz = 77 ms = ♪ at ♩ = 96

Gamma >30 Hz *(motor function)*

30 Hz = 1800 bpm = 33 ms 𝅘𝅥𝅲 at ♩= 112

Likewise, as the effect of electromagnetic frequencies attract more attention (and become more ubiquitous), there may be new relevant research, as the ultra-low to extremely-low-frequency radiowave bands intersect with auditory rates.

*P.S.   It seems curious that the double quotation mark (")
is used as a 'short-hand' indicator of both inches and seconds,
and the single quotation mark (') for feet and minutes.*

- **OTHER FACTORS INVOLVED IN TIME MEASURING:**

- focus region – narrow/wide; past-present-future
- focus intensity – peripheral glance / full
- concentration – slight / full
- adjustable multiple lenses (perhaps the magic 7 +/- 2 groups?)
- proportion /harmonic relation of foci to each other [logarithmic? fractal?]
- rate & manner of fluctuation
- aesthetic preferences
- health: temporary and permanent predispositions to particular rates, motor movement, auditory system functioning, memory, etc. and individual compensations for any condition which might impair intended reception.

APPENDIX C

SOME CLASSIC & INNOVATIVE TREATMENTS OF TIME IN MUSIC

I include here some preliminary notes for adding to my imagined database as described in Appendix A. It gives a current 'screenshot' of a few of the musicians, musicologists, research areas, techniques and styles which have drawn my attention for their articulate and often unexpected treatments of time, and stimulated my own thoughts & compositional approaches. I have hesitated to include it, as of course this is not only a personal but a very incomplete and fleeting personal list; almost all music I like attracts me for its temporal design and/or timbral shaping and/or tunings, and the names that come to mind are those which are most recent or prominent in my memory, sometimes because they are ones I have often referred to in classes in analysis and perception. This link with my coursework has created another twist in that my list has few of the names of mainstream Western classical music repertoire as well as many of the electroacoustics world, in order to avoid cross-course redundancy – in other words, my lists were compiled somewhere between "supplementary" and "boundary indicators" as I tended to be skeptical of analytical discourse which appeared to address 'universals' but could not adequately incorporate the following types of examples. However, with the exponential increase of researchers and tools to discover their respective fields of interest, it is relatively easy to discover analyses in both mainstream classical and electroacoustic music, that address issues directly relevant to temporal design, so any student in need of a project could devise a tool to extract many relevant articles from current and past journals.

For some of the works alluded to, I could pinpoint exactly the few seconds which epitomize their treatment of a certain temporal aspect – as I would expect to include for my database – but to avoid increasingly arbitrary selections, these notes are best considered simply as a suggestion of the type, diversity, and [lack of] information which a contributor might wish to incorporate into any useful anthology or database of time & music artworks and analysis. A database would enable one to search according to the particular time-scales (or level of greatest activity) under scrutiny, but as composers often work with several time-scales simultaneously, it was not feasible to do the same here. For similar reasons, I did not distinguish in my list between composers and performers, since several of them combine at least two of those profiles. However, those whom I know only as research authors are included only in my bibliography (even if they are not directly mentioned in the text). This is on the basis of their influence on my own thinking - or at least my sense that they were sufficiently influential that others should be aware of them; also, most of them have been directly referenced in previous writings of mine.

ALIZADEH, HOSSEIN – artful fusion of traditional Persian with elements of Western style and contemporary outlook in his large ensemble works (like *Ney Nava*) and film music (*From Eons Ago*); his solo setar improvisations are also remarkable, and show the flexibility of tempo inherent in Persian music roots.

ANDERSON, LAURIE – a wide range of interest from timbral experimentation with technology on violin and voice, as well as later works where the form was directly influenced by story-telling.

ANDRIESSEN, LOUIS – *De Tijd* [Time], etc. - a composer who thought consciously about time and timelessness and its portrayal.

BACEWICZ, GRAZYNA – although she was renowned for both violin and piano performance, it is her compositions that attracted me for their particular sounds and rhythms, often energetic and additive.

BACH, J. S. – especially works like the *Sonatas & Partitas* for solo violin and solo cello: fascinating examples of dance music forms which are elongated and truncated from their original hypermetric models or built on additive designs, as well as clear interweaving of distinct lines in the 'single-voice polyphony' technique.

BARTÓK, BELA – *Music for Strings, Percussion & Celesta* incorporates the Golden Mean into the temporal design of its first movement (perhaps inaudibly, as he himself ponders); various works such as his *String Quartets* have numerous examples of steady sub-pulse regularity over long passages while the grouping pulse becomes shorter, providing tension; also his frequent incorporation of irregular meters. *The Sonata for Two Pianos and Percussion* and several examples of 'night music' seem to draw on both the aural and the psychological aspects of a nocturnal country soundscape as impetus for rhythmic organization and timbral shading.

BEETHOVEN, LUDWIG VAN – known in part for his integration of more expressive timings into musical forms which had been traditionally more sectionalized in the Baroque era. His *Symphony No. 6* provides a classic example of a narrative form incorporating a series of natural events: sunny day, storm, clearing, evening party. As with most such notable figures in the Western musical canon, many aspects of his rhythmic designs, from motivic variation to shifts in his chronological output, are discussed in various analytical texts, although not always indexed as such.

BOCCHERINI, LUIGI – his delightful *Minuet* presents an excellent example of hypermeter with subtle shifts in phrase lengths - which is maybe why it became such a classic a century later.

BOULEZ, PIERRE – his writings and music abound with temporal exploration, while his ability to bring many 20th-century works to attention is due to his related skills in conducting, with an impeccable sense of timing and intonation.

BRAHMS, JOHANNES – Ever since early childhood I appreciated the extreme tempo fluctuations of his *Hungarian Dance #5*, although they were probably inherited from the Hungarian dance styles which influenced him, and music scholars now believe that the tunes were probably from his contemporaries Béla Kéler or Ede Reményi – thus reminiscent of Liszt's models in several ways.

BRYARS, GAVIN – for ex. *The Sinking of the Titanic* which is notable not only for its evocative sounds of a submerging quartet but also in the dual sense of conjuring up an historical event and submitting the work itself to updating as different information is discovered.

CADIZ, RODRIGO – impressive talent in evocative sound-image pairing.

CAGE, JOHN – tremendous impact of musical experiments of many types such as a composition that involves random tuning on local radios among its sounds; also provocative scores and books that blur the distinctions between their traditional modes.

CALON, CHRISTIAN – e.g. his opera *Ulysses* that beautifully juxtaposes voice and electronic music and imbues a dynamic energy not always found in electroacoustic works.

CARILLO, JULIÁN – composer, theorist and designer of microtonal pianos in various configurations, from third-tones to 16th-tones. Many works composed for these pianos deserve more attention by analysts and historians as well as listeners.

CARTER, ELLIOTT – noted in part for his development of the concepts of rhythmic modulation. Personally, I found his intellectual reasonings much more articulate than much of his music – but I blame some of that on the quality of the recordings I heard, for example in the *Double Concerto for Harpsichord and Piano*.

CHRISTIE, WILLIAM – a harpsichordist who excels in delineating multiple layers through rhythmic clarity.

COLE, NAT "KING" – although known more for his vocals, his piano technique enabled him to improvise long passages at breakneck speed.

COWELL, HENRY – esp. his book *New Musical Resources* in which he deplores the lack of training in Western academia for the study of polyrhythms, which he rightly argues should be as important as pitch interval recognition. His 'elastic' music technique, which was developed to provide adaptability for Martha Graham's choreography while he was working remotely, involved flexibility of the number of repeats of certain cells and short passages.

CRAWFORD SEEGER, RUTH – e.g. *Quartet 1931;* avant-garde concerns including precise rhythmic notations of dynamics and varied sub-pulse divisions to produce 'rhythmic fluidity' as well as thinking about durations of silence between entries in terms of their proportions- see Tick 2000.

CRUMB, GEORGE – Ancient *Voices of Children, Makrokosmos,* etc. He is reputed to have worked out his very free rhythmic placement of gestures and textures by intuition rather than system; timbral choices are also fundamental to the design.

DAVIS, MILES – an exuberant and well-known jazz pioneer whose experiments often involved rhythmic play at various levels.

DEBUSSY, CLAUDE – interest in and expressive articulation of non-Western temporal organization reflected in most pieces, see for ex. *La Mer, La Cathédrale Engloutie,* various *Préludes,* etc.

DESCHÊNES, MARCELLE – important for her reflections and creative work on sound-image connections and experiments with variable time-flows.

DHOMONT, FRANCIS – electroacoustic pioneer with a stunning ability to sustain the listener's interest over long durations with numerous ingredients and degrees of complexity through skilful balance of familiar and new, density and space, attesting to a keen sense of timing for the design of the macro- and not just the micro-level - for example *Forêt Profonde*.

DIAWARA, FATOUMATA – extremely talented Malian singer whose innovative timbral shaping is beyond the reach of many trained Western singers.

ECKHARDT-GRAMATTÉ, SOPHIE-CARMEN – *Caprices for Solo Violin* seem an excellent evocation of non-dramatic improvisation and irregular flow of time

ENO, BRIAN – numerous relevant explorations including his development of 'ambient music' and drone music that challenged normal listening modes.

EVANS, BILL – jazz pianist whose sense of timing allows him to build long coherent passages without metric confines, such as in *Conversations with Myself*.

FERREYRA, BEATRIZ – imaginative and diverse treatments of time in her electroacoustic works.

LES FILLES DE ILLIGHADAD – apart from the hypnotic qualities of the Tuareg music which has charmed me for decades, these singers also show fantastic timbral shaping in their music; the slightly imprecise rhythm of clapping that goes well with the gentle attack of the water drum timbral envelope; the ululations are precious examples of an ancient style of vocal utterances.

GILBERT, KENNETH – harpsichordist with very fine sense of timing.

GRISEY, GÉRARD. A pioneer in the development of music exploring not only timbral shaping but also the creation of coherent non-harmonic sounds.

HADADI, PEJMAN – fabulous improvising drummer from Persian tradition who can create an astonishing variety of rhythmic complexity through careful attention to timbral as well as rhythmic shaping, enjoying the blurry region.

HASSELL, JON – *String Quartet, Fourth World Possible Musics,* etc. have some of the clearest illustrations of different layers of music moving in complex but comfortable relationships; different listenings provide different perspectives.

HENRY, PIERRE – e.g. *Variations pour une porte et un soupir.*

HINDEMITH, PAUL - I was startled when I attempted to graft a (tonally-based) Schenkerian analysis method onto an apparently atonal *Sonata for Violin & Piano,* and discovered that the piece seemed to be constructed from two tonal parts 'slid' out of synchrony.

HODGES, JOHNNY – both timbral shaping and expressive use of vibrato make him a good example of big band era sax playing.

HONEGGER, ARTHUR – mapping of the motion of a rugby match into musical form – but irritated Xenakis for not continuing to expand into new directions....

IVES, CHARLES – especially fascinating for his articulate portrayal of coexisting but contrasting musical 'layers' such as in his *'Concord' Piano Sonata #2, 4th of July, Symphony #4, A New England Holiday Symphony*, etc. *Concord Sonata* is a wonderful illustration of the importance of appropriate parsing to perceive the form: the piece contains numerous fragments of American popular folk songs and hymns which, if unknown to the listener, will further obscure the collage elements which are already 'submerged' in the overall textures.

JOÃO, MARIA – a master of 'scat singing' in a free style which demonstrate the variety of sonic characters which a skilled vocalist can produce.

JOHNSTON, BEN – esp. temperament e.g. *String Quartet #4* with its microtonal version of *Amazing Grace*.

JOPLIN, JANIS – her energy and disregard for conventional singing style allowed her to experiment with timbre and tempo well-attuned to early electronic modifications.

KALHOR, KAYHAN – not only for the typical Persian musician's sense of timing and timbre, but also for his ability to play lines on his kamancheh at such speed that they fuse into new shapes.

KAVACOS, LEONIDAS – violinist whose rendition of *Paganini Caprices* (a combination of tuning and expressive micro-adjustments to tempo and accent) makes him a favourite in our household.

KOMOROUS, RUDOLF – *Untitled 2 for Trumpet, Wu*, etc.

KRAFTWERK – pioneers in incorporating mechanical rhythms into pop styles ['robot-pop'], such as *RadioActivity* and *Autobahn*.

LANDY, LEIGH – electroacoustic composer and musicologist familiar with dance and non-Western styles who has been indispensable in the field for his work in facilitating relevant research, through organisation of the international Electroacoustic *Music Studies* group (with Daniel Teruggi and Marc Battier) and their annual conference, editing of the wide-ranging journal *Organised Sound*, development of terminology databases *(EARS)*, spearheading different research projects, etc.

LANSKY, PAUL – his *"Idle Chatter"* pieces caused some stir within the more academic of the electroacoustic crowd due to their irresistible charm being generated by a blatant rhythmic pulse which had been studiously avoided for decades by those wishing to focus attention on the more spectral qualities of sound.

LECAINE, HUGH – pioneer in musique concrète, including the development of devices to permit temporal manipulation of tape recordings, beautifully illustrated in *Dripsody*, based on a drop of water.

LEE, PEGGY – her timbral voice shading is completely integrated into the overall profile of slow-tempo songs like *Black Coffee*.

LIGETI, GYÖRGY – a pioneer in exploring the timbral-textural region in works like *Continuum, Piano Études, Cello Concerto*, etc.; also very articulate in his writings.

LOCKWOOD, ANNEA – articulate composer and researcher with diverse approaches to sound & rhythm (in the larger sense), especially those of nature.

LUTOSLAWSKI, WITOLD – *Jeux Vénitiens, Concerto for Orchestra, String Quartet* – notable for presenting different layers moving at different paces, even to the extent of his refusing to give the *Quartet* a coordinated score.

MAHLER, GUSTAV – strikingly novel treatments of time in having very sparse textures within orchestral works at the close of the lush sounds of the Romantic era.

MALLOCH, JOSEPH – researcher in musical interfaces whose simple *T-Stick* design has inspired and facilitated many musicians and dancers to use gestural control of sounds.

MARAIS, MARIN – a favourite composer in part because of the rich timbres of the viols revealed through often sustained sonorities and simple harmonies.

McLAREN, NORMAN - pioneer who is known not only for wonderful animations produced at the Canadian National Film Board but for his early production of sounds by scratching directly on the film – thus sharing the tape music composers' direct links between physical distance and speed of rotation of the tape with the duration of the sounds.

MENDELSSOHN, FELIX - *Midsummer Night's Dream* – the fairies' dance exploits an excessively fast-moving melody. His popular *Violin Concerto*, scorned by some musicologists for a lack of harmonic complexity, lends itself to a non-tempered tuning to emphasize the overtone structures that appear in arpeggiated form.

MESSIAEN, OLIVIER - Chronochromie, Turangalîla, Quatuor pour le fin du temps; Mode de valeurs et d'intensités; etc. all merit considerable study as the rich field of a composer who thought about time as a principle element of music.

MIDORI – violinist whose rendition of Paganini's *Caprices* imbued them with what seemed an entirely appropriate dynamic energy and shaping.

MINGUS, CHARLES – *Pithecanthropus Erectus* provides a wonderful example of a 'suspended' impetus.

MONAHAN, GORDON - *Speaker Swinging, Tape Pulling* are both artworks focussing the spectator's attention on temporal elements of sound and their potential relation to physical action.

MORRICONE, ENNIO – soundtracks for Sergio Leone films in which audio cues are prominent for conveying time-jumps among other features.

MOSOLOV, ALEXANDER – e.g. *Iron Foundry* (1927) and *String Quartet 1* (1926) with incorporation of repetitive rhythms to represent factories and other aspects of the modern world.

MURAILLE, TRISTAN – pioneer in 'spectral' music.

NANCARROW, CONLON - *Studies for Player Piano* provide a wonderful array of temporal design at various hierarchical levels, as well as comically highlighting our knowledge of speeds that lie inside and outside human piano-playing capacities.

NAZERI, SHARAM – expressive singing of Rumi poetry in particular demonstrates his fantastic timbral control.

OLIVEROS, PAULINE – highly influential American musician whose 'Deep Listening' project helped train many in different levels of temporal experience with and without sound.

PAGÁN, JUAN – Madrid composer (& poet) with a wonderfully ideosyncratic style; the first piece I heard in the 1980s attracted me with its novel intertwining linear qualities.

PAGANINI, NICCOLÒ - *Caprices for Solo Violin* provide a nice repertory of rhythmic treatments at the level of the sub-pulse and higher.

PALACIO-QUINTIN, CLÉO – composer-performer-improviser who designed a 'hyper-flute' to extend her range of timbral possibilities in such a way that they could be incorporated easily into her performances; notable for combining engineering inventiveness with musicality and 'good timing'.

PALESTRINA, GIOVANNI PIERLUIGI DA – renowned for his polyphonic style that excels at keeping a sense of motion without a prominent beat.

RAMAMURTHY, VITTAL – notable Carnatic violinist whose flexibility in timing and tuning combined with a fantastic dexterity enables individual notes to merge into lines that create complex timbral shapes and colours.

REICH, STEVE – expert in exploring the timbral-textural boundary in works like *Violin Phase, Music for 18 Musicians, New York Counterpoint*, etc.

RENOUARD-LARIVIÈRE, RÉGIS – *Futaie* – dramatic use of short sounds and silence near opening.

RESPIGHI, OTTORINO. Both the *Pines of Rome* and *Fountains of Rome* have attractive long passages poetically and temporally modelled on wind and rain.

RILEY, TERRY – *In C* and other pioneer work in minimalism.

RISSET, JEAN-CLAUDE - One of the rare modern researchers who excelled in both scientific and creative exploration; his musical experiments were usually quite consciously organized and often dealt with the limens of the human perceptual system and the possibilities of computer music to create impossible scenarios like the ever-climbing glissandi, or the presentation of one voice singing within two acoustic spaces, or the organization of a compositional passage with moving from one complex sonority to another by timbral steps. His interactive piano piece *Duet for One Pianist* provides a particularly fascinating array of temporal study, and becomes quite delightful if one is present to watch, as the computer plays the same piano as the pianist, in a kind of counterpoint.

RUSSOLO, LUIGI – his manifesto *The Art of Noises* and the machine for producing noises for artistic use, the *Intonarumori*.

SAARIAHO, KAIJA – Diverse musical output with considerable attention to innovations in temporal organization – also synaesthete.

SATIE, ERIK – repetition and simple harmonies cast much of his work into a startling contrast with late 19th-century; his "musique d'ameublement" or furniture music could contain infinite repeats of small sections – an anticipation of Cowell's 'elastic' music.

SAVALL, JORDI – major influence on the resuscitation of early European viol music and larger ensembles, due in large part to his extraordinary sensitivity to the instrument timbres and appropriate pacing of the large and small scale details of the compositions.

SCARLATTI, DOMENICO – especially harpsichord sonatas that provide a scintillating array of textures.

SCHAEFFER, PIERRE – pioneer in musique concrète and thinking about the natures of sounds and our perception of them.

SCHAFER, R. MURRAY – apart from a generally good 'sense of timing', his creative work challenged stereotypes in musical forms, in particular, extremely long performances and at unusual times (e.g. daybreak in *Princess of the Stars*); he paid careful attention to sounds of nature (and tried to avoid urban ones) and also helped influence the subsequent soundscape compositional styles and related artworks.

SHAJARIAN, MOHAMMED REZA – vocal technique & compositional styles fusing Iranian / European; also modification of traditional instruments for timbral effect.

SHEPP, ARCHIE – amazing timbral shading as well as lively rhythmic organization.

SHOSTAKOVICH, DMITRI - much additive rhythm at phrase level that helps give his music some of its intense energy,

SMETANA, BEDŘICH – *Moldau* as portrayal of both micro- and macro-qualities of the flowing river.

SOUTHAM, ANNE - music inspired by and often for dance, with unusual blends of almost static forms composed of active textures.

STOCKHAUSEN, KARLHEINZ - moment form, multiple strata, field music, etc., well-articulated in his musical works such as *Klavierstücke, Zeitmasse* (and writings – see Bibliography).

STRAUSS, RICHARD – *Ein Heldenleben*, etc. – very flexible juxtapositions of short passages in different tempi.

STRAVINSKY, IGOR - *Petruchka, Rite of Spring, L'Histoire du Soldat*, etc. - constructivist attitude towards time, many new ideas about temporal forms; also notable ideas expressed in the lecture series *Poetics of Music*.

THORESEN, LASSE – both in tunings and timbral as well as a variety of large-scale forms controlled through intuitive pacing of elements; in addition, an articulate researcher.

TRAORÉ, ROKIA – a Malian musician whose timbral expertise is revealed not only in her singing but also in her imaginative instrumental performance.

TRUAX, BARRY –notable in part for his pioneering work in granulation and its evocation of real-world sounds from computer – e.g. *Wave Edge*; also mixed media works.

UUTAI, OLENA – singer from Yakutia who gives a hint of the extent of realism of natural and animal sounds that can be conveyed by the human voice -- and which shamanic practices doubtless incorporated.

VAGGIONE, HORACIO – conscious attention to temporal aspects of music in writings and composition.

VAL DEL OMAR, JOSÉ – film-maker / inventor / photographer.

VARÈSE, EDGARD - *Amériques* provides a wonderful display of different coexisting 'layers' of music; he was also a pioneer in exploring the 'blurry' region of pitch/rhythm.

VAUGHAN, SARAH – free experimenting with timbral variety.

VIVALDI, ANTONIO – the classic *Four Seasons,* apart from providing an early example of freely 'mapping' the year's season into one work, gives a great variety of textural passages that evoke particular characters.

WAISWICZ, MICHAEL - inventor of new musical instruments such as his Gloves that allowed for tremendous expressive potential through intuitive movements and simple triggers.

WEBERN, ANTON - works compared to a Calder mobile, moving parts but no evolution; listener corresponding to a viewer with a shifting view-plane.

WESTERKAMP, HILDEGARD – pioneer in soundscape music, ranging from works like *Cricket Voice* to *Gently Penetrating beneath the sounding surfaces of another place.* She is a master at retaining key aspects of real-life sounds despite extensive temporal manipulation, thereby capturing something of the experience of human perception along with the recognizability of some sound sources.

WILSON, ALAN "BLIND OWL" – lead singer for the group *Canned Heat* whose popularity was due to some extent on his impeccable non-tempered tuning e.g. *On the Road Again* – he learned many songs aurally through recordings and doubtless refined his pitch discrimination through trombone lessons in his teens.

XENAKIS, IANNIS - A highly influential composer for those who want to explore time in music. As his influences were drawn principally from the physical and natural world (seen from the perspectives of mathematician & architect), he provided novel insights such as a sonic representation of Brownian motion and audible snippets of burning charcoal (*Concret PH*), while *Pleiades* is a wonderful example of carefully-designed temporal textures arranged in hierarchical layers.

YAHAGHI, PARVIZ - Prominent violinist in the Persian tradition who incorporated unique subtle embellishments to his playing through electronic enhancement, more or less in keeping with the aesthetic of traditional styles but transposed into a smaller time-scale than typical.

YOUNG, GAYLE – temporal interests span soundscapes, composition and instrument-building; she has also been long involved in 'tracking' the changing times of new music in her journal *MusicWorks*.

ZEHETMAIR, THOMAS – violinist whose renditions of *Bach Unaccompanied Violin Sonatas & Partitas* are so expressive of the nuances of rhythm (i.e. nice distinction between clearly-articulated pulse, linear accents, and expressive micro-rubato) that they became a favourite Sunday concert item for us during a decade or so.

APPENDIX D

N.B. *I differentiate between figures and illustrations in a slightly arbitrary way: in general, the illustrations are poetic and often self-evident comments on the subject of the chapter or section, whereas the figures give slightly more concrete examples in terms of diagrams and charts.*

LIST OF FIGURES

Figure no. & description	*Ch:pg*
Fig. 1. Time axis of music represented by graph paper.	21:60
Fig. 2. Body rhythms, musical functions, clock-time alignment.	22:68
Fig. 3. Activity bands and musical functions [adapted from thesis – Mountain 1993].	23:72
Fig. 4. Vibrato slowing to alternating notes.	23:77
Fig. 5. The *leitmotiv*, tracing the character's state [drawing developed for Mountain 2010-*ISST* presentation].	24:91
Fig. 6. Theme & variations as non-linear form [drawing developed for Mountain 2010-*ISST* presentation].	24:92
Fig. 7. Rondo as cyclic form	24:93
Fig. 8. Click migration	25:101
Fig. 9. Variables of contrast [first designed while teaching secondary school music in the UK, later integrated into presentations (Mountain 2003-*ESCOM*) and publication (Mountain 2003 - *Organised Sound*)]	26:107
Fig. 10. Ligeti's *Chamber Concerto Mvt. III* – sketch of overall textural design [from thesis – Ch. 4, Mountain 1993].	26:110
Fig. 11. Ligeti's *Chamber Concerto, Mvt. III*: 32-39 - Texture D, with 'close-up' view [from thesis – Mountain 1993]	26:110
Fig. 12. Same rhythmic structure, different notation.	26:111

Fig. 13. Cross-rhythms from J.S. Bach's *Violin Sonata No. 1 - Presto*	26:112
Fig. 14. Added unit upsets the periodicity of the next highest level.	26:113
Fig. 15. Excerpt from author's work *Ambar* [1999] with mixture of time notations.	28:121
Fig. 16. [Computer-generated] Amplitude graph and spectrogram of the author's 1999 electroacoustic vignette *Bits & Pieces*.	28:122
Fig. 17. Compositional sketch written on graph paper [from the author's collection of compositional 'doodles'].	28:123
Fig. 18. Mosaic depiction of imaginary passage with 3 layers all built on the same unit duration	31:143
Fig. 19. Mosaic depiction of imaginary passage with 3 layers each built on different unit duration	31:144

Notes on Illustrations

Illustration description	*Ch:pg*
1. A sketch of a favourite design for music: short units of discrete sets of events interpolated with longer and much less active durations; possibly with layering of similar structures. Designed for 2008 presentation at *EMS-08*.	front matter: i
2. Gears image and runner – see Chs. 22-23 and 31 for context	Sec I:1
3. Figure with sistrum and rattle	4:15
4. Distorted clock, cyclic representation of calendars & seasons	Sec II:16
5. Apparently straight arrow towards future leads into spiral	8:24
6. River with diver, watcher, canoe and motor boat – teasing out the river metaphor – [redrawn from sketch presented at ESCOM- 2003 talk *The Breathing of Time in(to) Music*].	8:25
7. Four figures proceeding towards future on different tracks and different speeds, one with intent to meander across tracks. [This illustration is from several years back, and lacks the detail of my current imaginings of the same analogy.]	8:27
8. Trees - examining as potential metaphor for time	9:31

9. Sketch of time analogy using 3-D diagram of the layering and distortions of time: clock time on the x axis, psychological time on the y axis, and past-present-future (represented as layers with occasional holes and hills implying perforations) on the z axis – [drawing from many years ago (2002?), incorporated into ISST talk (Mountain 2010)]	Sec III:32
10. Two dancers (leg movement complemented with arms); two drummers: one with sticks (arm movement) and one tapping (finger movement).	13:41
11. Two linear figures composed of dots, representing perception of two different melodies or layers of music, differentiated by colour and patterns of size as well as temporal arrangement (green has gradual gradations in size, and gradual shifts in proximity).	Sec IV:46
12. Representation of three layers of coexisting musical passages that do not seem to influence each other; differentiated mainly by colour and some coherence in flow type.	18:50
13. Representation of layers with more complexity: one figure with variations of colour and fragmented form; a second of a different style tracing a single gesture; and a final figure that may be related to the first in some features. This is taken from a sketch of the author's for a passage about 30" long. The blurriness of the lines represents a more electroacoustic approach where pitch is not likely to be quantized.	20:53
14. Excerpt from a 2017 score by the author (*Iberian Trails*) with a magnifying glass showing a spectrogram to represent the study of microscopic detail in sound.	Sec V:54
15. Image of a distorted metronome to represent the divergence between strict clock-time measurement and the natural 'rubato' that permeates most music.	28:121
16. Components of icons designed to illustrate my talk on marketing of computer music at the ICMC 2004, as options for the rhythmic section of my proposals for graphic symbols to indicate basic musical features to help in classification like CD covers – in this case, metric, irregular, or polyrhythmic rhythmic profiles. See Mountain 2004 for context.	29:134

17. Four spinning gears, to represent the adjusting of our calipers according to the shifting periodic elements of music and to hint at my 'gears' analogy described in Chs. 13, 23, and 31.	Sec VI: 135
18. The listener's image of time, an echo of (d) in Fig. 2.	31:139
19. An echo of Fig. 3, with the addition of gears to illustrate.	31:141
20. An excerpt from the author's 1995 piano work *Sondas Sonoras*, distorted to suggest the impression of uneven time flow and changing focus of the viewer/listener.	App B: 163
21. A gestural trajectory where dots simulate musical events in the super-pulse range, similar to the runners' logarithmic slowing pace that seems to match a good decelerando – see Ch. 13.	App. C: 165
22. Variation of Illustration 11, rendered much more complex visually by removing the colour segregation of the two lines, thus creating possibilities of other parsings – a familiar compositional device in 20th-century music.	App. D: 181

BIBLIOGRAPHY

Arnheim, Rudolf. 1971: *Entropy and Art*. Berkeley: University of California Press.

Becker, Judith. 1979. Time and Tune in Java. In *The Imagination of Reality: Essays in Southeast Asian Coherence Systems* (eds. A. L. Becker and A.A. Yengoyan). Norwood, New Jersey: 197–210.

Benjamin, W. 1984. A Theory of Musical Meter. *Music Perception* 1: 355-413.

Berry, Wallace. 1985. Metric and Rhythmic Articulation in Music. *Music Theory Spectrum* 7: 7-33.

Besada, José L. & Cristóbal Pagán Cánovas. 2020. Timelines in Spectral Composition: A Cognitive Approach to Musical Creativity. In *Organised Sound*, 25/2: 145-155.

Bielawski, L. 1981. The Zones of Time in Music and Human Activity. In *The Study of Time IV* (eds. J. T. Fraser and N. Lawrence). New York: Springer Verlag, 173–9.

Boulez, Pierre. 1987. Timbre and Composition - timbre and language. *Contemporary Music Review* 2: 161-171.

Brower, Candace. 1993. Memory and the Perception of Rhythm. In *Music Theory Spectrum* 15/1:19-35.

Bregman, Albert. 1990. *Auditory Scene Analysis: The Perceptual Organization of Sound*. Cambridge, Ma.: The MIT Press.

____. 1993. Auditory Scene Analysis: Hearing in Complex Environments. In *Thinking in Sound: The Cognitive Psychology of Human Audition*. Stephen McAdams and Emmanuel Bigand (eds.), Oxford: Oxford

University Press: 10-36.

Bregman, Albert, and Pierre Ahad. 1996. *Demonstrations of Auditory Scene Analysis: The Perceptual Organization of Sound.* Cambridge, Mass., MIT Press (audio CD + booklet).

Brower, Candace. 1993. Memory and the Perception of Rhythm. *Music Theory Spectrum* 15/1: 19-35.

Budón, Osvaldo. 2000. Composing with Objects, Networks, and Time Scales: An Interview with Horacio Vaggione. *Computer Music Journal*, 24:3: 9-22.

Buhusi, C.V., and W.H. Meck. 2009. Relativity Theory and Time Perception: Single or Multiple Clocks? *PLoS ONE* 4(7): e6268.

Butler, David. *The Musician's Guide to Perception and Cognition.* New York: Schirmer.

Chion, Michel. 1990. *L'audio-vision. Son et image au cinéma.* Paris: Editions Nathan.

Clarke, Eric C. 1987. Levels of Structure in the Organization of Musical Time, *Contemporary Music Review* 2/1: 211-238.

Clynes, Manfred, and Janice Walker. 1982. Neurobiologic Functions of Rhythm, Time and Pulse in Music. *In Music, Mind, and Brain* (ed. M. Clynes): 171-216. New York: Plenum Press.

Cogan, Robert, and Pozzi Escot. 1976. *Sonic Design.* Englewood Cliffs, N. J.: Prentice-Hall.

Cohen, Annabel. 1998. The Functions of Music in Multimedia: A Cognitive Approach. *Proceedings of the Fifth International Conference on Music Perception and Cognition*, 13-20.

Cohn, Richard. 2021. How Music Theorists Model Time. *Journal of Music Theory* 65 (1): 11–16.

Cook, Nicholas. 1998. *Analysing Musical Multimedia.* Oxford: Clarendon Press.

Cowell, Henry. *New Musical Resources.* 1969 [1930]. New York: Something Else Press (originally published by Knopf).

Csikszentmihalyi, Mihaly. 1975. *Beyond Boredom and Anxiety: Experiencing Flow in Work and Play.* San Francisco: Jossey-Bass.

Dahan, Kevin. A temporal framework for electroacoustic music exploration. *Organised Sound* 26/2: 248-258.

Deutsch, Diana. 1977. Memory and Attention in Music. In *Music and the Brain* (eds. Critchley & Henson): 95-129. London: Heinemann.

Doob, Leonard W. *Patterning of Time.* New Haven: Yale University Press, 1971.

Dowling, W. Jay, and Dane L. Harwood. 1986. *Music Cognition.* New York: Academic Press.

Dowling, W. Jay, Kitty Mei-tak Lung, and Susan Herrbold. 1987. Aiming attention in pitch and time in the perception of interleaved melodies. *Perception & Psychophysics* 41/6. 642-656.

Dufour, Frank. 2016. A Study of Sound Objects and Structures. *Interference Journal* - Issue 5: Writing About/Through Sound: pp. 58-71.

Epstein, David. 1981. On Musical Continuity. *The Study of Time 4:* 180-197.

_____. 1995. *Shaping Time: Music, the Brain, and Performance.* New York: Schirmer.

Epstein, Paul. 1986. Pattern Structure and Process in Steve Reich's Piano Phase. *Musical Quarterly* 72/4: 494-503.

Erickson, Robert. 1963. Time-Relations. *The Journal of Music Theory* 7/2: 174-92.

_____. 1975. *Sound structure in music.* Berkeley: University of California Press.

Favory, J., Formosa, M., Frémiot, M., Gobin, P., Malbosc, P., Mandelbrojt, J. and Prod'homme, L. 2002. *Les Unités Sémiotiques Temporelles. Nouvelles clés pour l'écoute.* Marseille: Laboratoire Musique et Informatique de Marseille. CD-ROM.

Forte, Allen. 1959. Schenker's Conception of Musical Structure. *Journal of Music Theory* 3/1, pp. 1-30.

Fraisse, Paul. 1963. *The Psychology of Time.* New York: Harper.

_____. 1982. Rhythm and tempo. In D. Deutsch (ed.), *The psychology of music* New York: Academic Press: 149–180.

Fraser, J. T. 1982. *The Genesis and Evolution of Time: A Critique of Interpretations in Physics.* Amherst: University of Massachusetts Press.

_____. The Art of the Audible 'Now'. *Music Theory Spectrum*, vol. 7 (1985):181-184.

Frey, Aline, Xavier Hautbois, Philippe Bootz, and Charles Tijus. 2014. An experimental validation of Temporal Semiotic Units and Parameterized Time Motifs. *Musicae Scientiae* 18(1) 98 –123.

Friberg, Anders and Johan Sundberg. 1999. Does music performance allude to locomotion? A model of final ritardandi derived from measurements of stopping runners. *Journal of the Acoustical Society of America*, 105, 1469-1484.

Garro, Diego. 2012. From Sonic Art to Visual Music: Divergences, convergences, intersections. *Organised Sound* 17(2): 103–113.

Gilmore, Sean A. and Frank A. Russo. 2021. Neural and behavioral evidence for vibrotactile beat perception and bimodal enhancement. *Journal of Cognitive Neuroscience*, Vol. 33(4): 635-650

Godøy, Rolf Inge. 2006. Gestural-Sonorous Objects: Embodied

extensions of Schaeffer's conceptual apparatus. *Organised Sound* 11(2): 149–157.

_____. 2003. Motor-Mimetic Music Cognition. *Leonardo* 36: 317 - 319.

_____. 2011. Sound-action awareness in music. In Music *and Consciousness: Philosophical, Psychological, and Cultural Perspectives* (eds. David Clarke and Eric Clarke). Oxford: Oxford University Press.

Godøy, R. I. & M. Leman. 2010. *Musical Gestures: Sound, Movement, and Meaning.* New York and Abington, UK: Routledge.

Görgün, İpek. 2020. Exploring Temporality in Horacio Vaggione's Compositional Thought. *Organised Sound*, 25(2), 168-178.

Hasty, Christopher. 1981. Rhythm in Post-Tonal Music: Preliminary Questions of Duration and Motion. *Journal of Music Theory* 25: 183- 216.

_____. 1986. On the Problem of Succession and Continuity in Twentieth-Century Music. *Music Theory Spectrum* 8: 58-74.

Hautbois, Xavier. Temporal Semiotic Units (TSUs): a very short introduction. Posted on the website of the *Laboratoire Musique et Informatique de Marseille [MiM]*: http://www.labo-mim.org/site/index.php?2013/03/29/225-temporal-semiotic-units-tsus-a-very-short-introduction.

Heneghan, Áine. 2019. Liquidation and Its Origins. *Journal of Music Theory* 63/1: 71-100.

Honing, Henkjan. 2005. Is there a perception-based alternative to kinematic models of tempo rubato? *Music Perception* 23/1 (Sept): 79-85.

_____. 1993. Issues on the representation of time and structure in music. *Contemporary Music Review* 9: 221-238.

Hope, Cat. 2020. The Future is Graphic: Animated notation for contemporary practice. *Organised Sound* 25(2), 187-197.

Horlacher, Gretchen. 1995. Metric Irregularities in Les Noces: the problem of periodicity. In *Journal of Music Theory* 39/2: 285-309.

Hukin, R. W. & C. J. Darwin. 1995. Comparison of the effect of onset asynchrony on auditory grouping in pitch matching and vowel identification. *Perception & Psychophysics* 57 (2):191-196.

Huron, David. 2006. *Sweet anticipation: Music and the psychology of expectation*. Cambridge, MA: MIT Press.

Huron, David & Margulis, Elizabeth Hellmuth. 2010. Music, Expectancy, and Thrills. In *Handbook of Music and Emotion: Theory, Research, Applications* (eds. P.N. Juslin & J.A. Sloboda): 575-604. New York: Oxford University Press.

Hussain, Zakir and Sultan Khan. 1995. *Tabla & Sarangi Virtuoso*. Audio CD. Stuttgart, Germany: Chhanda Dhara SNCD 70495.

Jacobs, Nathan S., Timothy A. Allen, Natalie Nguyen, and Norbert J. Fortin. 2013. Critical Role of the Hippocampus in Memory for Elapsed Time. *The Journal of Neuroscience* 33(34):13888–13893.

Johnson, Julian. 2015. *Out of time: music and the making of modernity*. Oxford: University of Oxford Press.

Johnson, Mark. 1999. Something in the Way She Moves: Musical Motion and Musical Space. Keynote presentation at the *Conference on Musical Imagery*, Oslo, Norway.

Kaminska, Zofia & Peter Mayer. 1993. Transformation, migration and restoration: Shades of Illusion in the Perception of Music. *Contemporary Music Review* 9 (1-2): 151-161.

Kane, Brian. 2014. *Sound Unseen: Acousmatic Sound in Theory and Practice*. Oxford: Oxford University Press.

Kielian-Gilbert, Marianne. 1987. The Rhythms of Form: Correspondence and Analogy in Stravinsky's Designs. In *Music Theory Spectrum* 9: 42-66.

Kramer, Jonathan D. 1985a. Studies of Time and Music: a bibliography. *Music Theory Spectrum* 7: 72-106.

_____. 1985b. Temporal Linearity and Nonlinearity in Music. *The Study of Time* 5: 126-137.

_____. 1988. *The Time of Music*. New York: Schirmer Books.

Krebs, Harald. 1987. Some Extensions of the Concepts of Metrical Consonance and Dissonance. In *Journal of Music Theory* 31/1: 99-120.

_____. Review [of Schachter and Rothstein]. In *Music Theory Spectrum*, Volume 14, Issue 1, Spring 1992, Pages 82–87.

Kunst, Jaap. 1950. Metre, Rhythm, Multi-part Music. *Ethnomusicologica* Vol. I: 1-47.

Kuppuswamy, Gowri and M. Hariharan, eds. 1979. *Readings on Music and Dance*. Delhi: B. R. Publishing Corporation.

Laboratoire Musique et Informatique de Marseille. 2008. *Liste des 19 Unités Sémiotiques Temporelles*. http://www.labo-mim.org/site/index.php?2008/08/22/44-liste-des-19-ust.

Langer, Suzanne. 1942. *Philosophy in a New Key: A Study in the Symbolism of Reason, Rite, and Art*. Cambridge: Harvard University Press.

Larson, Steve. 2012. *Musical Forces: Motion, Metaphor, and Meaning in Music*. Bloomington: Indiana University Press.

Lauzon, A. P., Russo, F. A., & Harris, L. R. 2020. The influence of rhythm on detection of auditory and vibrotactile asynchrony. *Experimental Brain Research*, 238(4), 825–832.

Lerdahl, Fred, and Ray Jackendoff. 1984. An Overview of Hierarchical Structure in Music. *Music Perception* 1: 229-252.

Ligeti, György. 1958. Metamorphoses of Musical Form. *Die Reihe* [trans. Cornelius Cardew]: 5-19.

Lochhead, Judith. 1986. Temporal structure in recent music. In *Journal of Musicological Research* 6: 49-93.

London, Justin. 2004. *Hearing in Time: Psychological Aspects of Musical Meter*. Oxford: Oxford University Press.

Mann, Maud. Abolish Harmoniums! *The Modern Review* 11:496-500. [ed. Kedar Nath Chatterji, Calcutta]

McAdams, Stephen. 1982. Spectral Fusion and the Creation of Auditory Images. In M. Clynes (Ed.): *Music, Mind, and Brain*. New York: Plenum Press: 279-298.

_____. 1987. Music: A science of the mind? *Contemporary Music Review* 2: 1-61.

McAdams, Stephen and Carolyn Drake. Auditory Perception and Cognition. In *Steven's Handbook of Experimental Psychology Vol. I: Sensation and Perception* (eds. S. Yantis and H. Pashler): 397-452. New York: Wiley,

McCreless, P. 2002. Music and rhetoric. In *The Cambridge History of Western Music Theory* (ed. T. Christensen): 845-879. Cambridge: Cambridge University Press.

Merriam, Alan P. 1981. African Musical Rhythm and Concepts of Time-reckoning. In *Music East and West: Essays in Honor of Waller Kaufman* (ed. T. Noblitt). New York, NY: Pendragon Press.

Meyer, Leonard. 1956. *Emotion and Meaning in Music*. Chicago: University of Chicago Press.

_____. 1967. *Music, the Arts, and Ideas: Patterns and Predictions in Twentieth-Century Culture*. Chicago: University of Chicago Press.

Michon, J. A. 1975. Time Experience and Memory Processes. In: *The Study of Time* II (eds. J. T. Fraser and N. Lawrence), Berlin: Springer.

Miller, G. A. 1956. The magical number seven, plus or minus two: Some limits on our capacity for processing information. *Psychological Review* 63 (2): 81–97.

Miller, L. 2000. Relating Music and Concert Dance: Henry Cowell's Search for Equality. Presented at the conference *Toronto 2000: Musical Intersections*.

Minsky, Marvin. 1982. Music, Mind, and Meaning. *In Music, Mind, and Brain* (ed. Manfred Clynes): 1-19. New York: Plenum Press, 1982).

Mountain, Harry. 1981. *The Development of Contemporary Earth Art.* essay available at <www.SculptCity.com>.

Mountain, Rosemary. 1989. Factors that Influence our Perception of Time in Music. *Proceeding, CEC conference >convergence<*, Banff Centre for the Arts, Canada.

_____. 1993. *An Investigation of Periodicity in Music, with reference to three 20th-century compositions: Bartok's* Music for Strings, Percussion and Celesta, *Lutoslawski's* Concerto for Orchestra, *and Ligeti's* Chamber Concerto. Ann Arbor, Mich: UMI - PhD dissertation (U. Victoria, Canada).

_____. 1998. Composition: my laboratory for auditory perception research. Presented at the *Symposium of Musical Cognition and Behavior Relevance for Music Composing*. University of Rome - La Sapienza (ECONA / ESCOM); published in *General Psychology*, 99/3, Edizioni Scientifiche, Rome, 1999: 241-254.

_____. 2001a. SuperPulse: Clarifications, Refinements, Implications. *Society* for *Music Perception and Cognition conference*, Kingston, Canada.

_____. 2001b. The Training of Time-Smiths. *Proceedings of the VII International Symposium on Systematic and Comparative Musicology / III International Conference on Cognitive Musicology* (Jyväskyla, Finland).

_____. 2003a. The Breathing of Time in(to) Music. *Proceedings of the 5th triennial conference of ESCOM (European Society for Cognitive Studies in Music)* Hannover. Eds. R. Kopiez, A. C. Lehmann, I. Wolther & C. Wolf: 670-673.

_____. 2003b. Flexible Frameworks: The Multimedia Thesaurus. *Proceedings of the 5th triennial conference of European Society for Cognitive Studies in Music* (eds. R. Kopiez, A. C. Lehmann, I. Wolther & C. Wolf): 212-214. Hannover. ESCOM.

_____. 2003c. Creating and Contributing. The Expansive Spirit of Marcelle Deschênes, *MusicWorks* 86: 14-21.

_____. 2004. Marketing Strategies for Electroacoustics and Computer Music. *Organised Sound* 9 (3): 305–313.

_____. 2005. Tool / Game / Environment: The Interactive Multimedia Thesaurus & Playroom. *Proceedings of the Electroacoustic Music Studies conference EMS-05 - Sound in multimedia contexts* (Montréal).

_____. 2007a. Playful Tools, Serious Questions. *Canadian Acoustics* vol. 35 no. 3: 54-55.

_____. 2007b. Review of *Hearing in Time* by Justin London. *Music Perception*, 24/4.

_____. 2008. Sorting sounds: testing tools and strategies. Presented at the *Electroacoustic Music Studies EMS-08* conference, Paris-GRM: June.

_____. 2009. Auditory Scene Analysis & Electroacoustics. Presented at *EMS-09, Electroacoustic Music Studies* conference, Buenos Aires, Argentina.

_____. 2010. A Musician's Guide to Time. Presented at the triennial conference of the *International Society for the Study of Time*, Monte Verde, and Costa Rica.

_____. 2013. Traces of Time: Reflections of a Musician. Presented at the triennial conference of the *International Society for the Study of Time*, Chania, Greece.

_____. 2020. Elaborating analogies of time perception. *Organised Sound* 25/2.

_____. 2021. *Conversational Musicology.* Self-published e-book: <https://books2read.com/u/mgzdRx>

_____. 2022. Music: a versatile interface for explorations in art & science. [Issue ed. A. Hugill] *Interdisciplinary Science Reviews.*

Narmour, Eugene. 1990. *The Analysis and Cognition of Basic Melodic Structures: The Implication-Realization Model.* Chicago, IL: University of Chicago Press.

Noble, Jason, Tanor Bonin, and Stephen McAdams. 2020. Experiences of Time and Timelessness in Electroacoustic Music. *Organised Sound,* 25/2: 232-247.

Norman, Katharine. 1994. Telling tales. *Contemporary Music Review* 10/:2: 103-109.

Orlov, Henry F. The Temporal Dimensions of Musical Experience. *Musical Quarterly,* v.65 (1979): 368-378.

Ornstein, Robert. 1969. *On the Experience of Time.* Harmondsworth, England: Penguin.

Pesic, Peter. 2017. *Polyphonic Minds: Music of the Hemispheres.* Cambridge: The MIT Press.

Phillips, D. 2002. Central Auditory System and Central Auditory Processing Disorders: Some Conceptual Issues. *Seminars in Hearing* 23(4): 251–61.

Pogoriloski, Andrei. 1994. *Energies of Musical Time. Essential Studies of Pulsatory Functionalism.* Bucharest, Romania: Ararat Press.

Pousseur, Henri. 1966. The Question of Order in New Music. *Perspectives of New Music* 5: 93-111.

Proust, Marcel. 1913-1927. *Remembrance of Things Past* [Transl. C.K. Scott Moncrieff of *À la recherche du temps perdu.*] New York: Random House, 1934. Two vols. [compiled from original seven].

Rammsayer, Thomas, and Eckart Altenmüller. 2006. Temporal information processing in musicians and nonmusicians. *Music Perception* 24/1: 37–48.

Repp, Bruno H. 1989. Expressive Microstructure in Music: A Preliminary Perceptual Assessment of Four Composers' 'Pulses'. *Music Perception* 6/3: 243-274.

_____. 1998. Musical Motion in Perception and Performance. In *Timing of behavior: neural, psychological, and computational perspectives* (eds. D. A. Rosenbaum & C.E. Collyer): 125-144. Cambridge, MA: MIT Press.

_____. 1990. Patterns of expressive timing in performances of a Beethoven minuet by nineteen famous pianists. *The Journal of the Acoustical Society of America* 88/2: 622-641.

_____. 1996. (Book Review) "Shaping Time: Music, the Brain, and Performance" by David Epstein. *Music Perception* 13/4: 591-604.

_____. 2000. The timing implications of musical structures. In *Musicology and Sister Disciplines: Past Present and Future. Proceedings of the 16th International Congress of the International Musicological Society* [London 1997] (ed. David Greer) Oxford: Oxford University Press.

Reynolds, Roger. 1975. *Mind Models*. New York: Praeger.

_____. 1987. A perspective on form and experience. *Contemporary Music Review* 2/1: 277-308.

Roads, Curtis. 2002. *Microsound*. Cambridge, MA: MIT Press.

Rochberg, George. 1975. The Structure of Time in Music: Traditional and Contemporary Ramifications and Consequences. *The Study of Time* 2: 136-49.

Rossetti, Danilo, Micael Antunes & Jônatas Manzolli. 2020. Compositional Procedures in Electronic Music and the Emergence of Time Continuum. *Organised Sound*, 25(2), 156-167.

Rothstein, William. 1989. *Phrase Rhythm in Tonal Music*. New York: Schirmer Books, 1989.

Rowell, Lewis. 1979. The Subconscious Language of Musical Time. *Music Theory Spectrum* 1: 96-106.

_____. 1981. The Creation of Audible Time. *The Study of Time* 4: 198-210.

Russolo, Luigi. 1967 [1913]. *The Art of Noises* [Translated by Robert Filliou]. Something Else Press. [Originally a manifesto sent to friend, published in 1916 as *L'arte dei rumori* by Edizioni Futuriste di "Poesia", Milan, Italy.]

Sachs, Curt. 1953. *Rhythm and Tempo: A Study in Music History*. New York: W. W. Norton.

Sallis, John. 1971. Time, Subjectivity, and the Phenomenology of Perception, *The Modern Schoolman* 48: 343-357.

Santarcangelo, Vincenzo & Riccardo Wanke. 2020. The Early Stage of Perception of Contemporary Art Music: A matter of time. *Organised Sound*, 25(2), 130-141.

Schachter, Carl. 1976. Rhythm and Linear Analysis: A Preliminary Study. *The Music Forum* 4 (1976): 281-334.

_____. 1980. Rhythm and Linear Analysis: Durational Reduction. *The Music Forum* 5: 297-232.

_____. 1987. Rhythm and Linear Analysis: Aspects of Meter. *The Music Forum* 6: 1–60.

Schaeffer, Pierre. 1966. *Traité des objets musicaux*. Paris, France: Le Seuil.

Shaffer, L. H. 1982. Rhythm and Timing in Skill. *Psychological Review* 89/2: 109-122.

Smalley, D. 1997. Spectromorphology: explaining sound-shapes.

Organised Sound 2, 107-126.

Stockhausen, Karlheinz. 1957. ...how time passes... [trans. Cornelius Cardew]. *Die Reihe 3*: 10–40.

_____. 1959. Structure and Experiential Time, [trans. Leo Black]. *Die Reihe* 2: 64-74.

Tenney, James. 1988. *Meta + Hodos and META Meta + Hodos: A Phenomenology of 20th Century Musical Materials and an Approach to the Study of Form*, 2nd rev. edn. Lebanon, NH: Frog Peak Music.

Tenney, James and Larry Polansky. 1980. Temporal Gestalt Perception in Music. *Journal of Music Theory* 24: 205-41.

Thomson, Phil. 2004. Atoms and errors: towards a history and aesthetics of microsound. *Organised Sound* 9(2): 207–218.

Thoresen, Lasse. 2007. Spectromorphological Analysis of Sound Objects: An adaptation of Pierre Schaeffer's Typomorphology. *Organised Sound* 12/2: 129-141.

Tick, Judith. 2000. *Ruth Crawford Seeger: a Composer's Search for American Music*. E-book, New York: Oxford University Press.

Vear, Craig. 2019. *The Digital Score: Musicianship, Creativity and Innovation*. New York: Routledge.

Westerkamp, Hildegard. 2019. The Disruptive Nature of Listening: Today, Yesterday, Tomorrow. In *Sound, Media, and Ecology* (eds. M. Droumeva, R. Jordan) Switzerland: Palgrave MacMillan, pp. 45-63.

Winckel, Fritz. 1957. The ear – a time-measuring instrument (A Review on New Hearing Theories). *Gravesaner Blätter* III no. IX.

_____. 1967 [1960]. *Music, Sound, and Sensation: A Modern Exposition*. Translated by Thomas Binkley from original 1960 ed. in German. Don Mills, Canada: Dover.

Wojtczak, Magdalena, Anahita H. Mehta, and Andrew J. Oxenham. 2017. Rhythm judgments reveal a frequency asymmetry in the perception and neural coding of sound synchrony. *Proceedings of the National Academy of Science of the USA*, vol. 114 no. 5: 1201–1206.

Woodrow, H. 1951. *The Perception of Time*. Handbook of Experimental Psychology (ed. S.S. Stevens) Wiley, New York.

Xenakis, Iannis. 1970. Towards a Metamusic. *Tempo,* no. 93: 2-18.

____. 1971. *Formalized Music: Thought and Mathematics in Composition*. Bloomington: Indiana Univ. Press.

____. 1989. Concerning Time. *Perspectives of New Music* 27/1: 84-92.

Yeston, Maury. *The Stratification of Musical Rhythm*. New Haven: Yale University Press, 1976.

Zuckerkandl, Victor. 1956. *Sound and Symbol: Music and the External World*. New York: Pantheon Books.

Zukofsky, Paul. 2005. *Purloined Rhythms*. On his website: http://www.musicalobservations.com.

- **ABOUT THE AUTHOR:**

Rosemary Mountain is a composer with decades of experience in research and music training especially in university contexts. She is particularly known for developing more robust frameworks for discussing and teaching music across stylistic and cultural boundaries as well as across disciplines and media. Her own creative output is in acoustic and electroacoustic genres, and her research expertise spans musicology, perception & cognition, multimedia, pedagogy, and classification.

Her formal training in music included a B.Mus. Honours (music theory & composition), University of Western Ontario (London, Canada); M.Mus. (music composition) and Ph.D. (interdisciplinary: music/perception/philosophy), University of Victoria (B.C., Canada); she also took various studies in art (sculpture) mainly at the Nova Scotia College of Art & Design (Halifax, Canada). Most of her university teaching experience was gained at the University of Aveiro (Portugal) and Concordia University (Montreal, Canada), where she developed and delivered a variety of courses in music composition, electroacoustics, analysis, 20th-century music history, music in multimedia contexts, Persian & Indian musical traditions, etc.

She began learning classical Western piano and violin at a very early age, but an equally early exposure to Indian and other non-Western and non-classical musics led to a continual search for more variety of sounds – part of the incentive to enter the musique concrète world. She has recently been experimenting with the flexible tunings and expressive potential of santur and kamancheh, as well as collecting bells and sounds of nature for her electroacoustic works, and returning to more intensive focus on acoustic compositions.

questions & comments: rosemary.mountain@concordia.ca

author's website: < https://armchair-researcher.com >

Conversational Musicology:

a composer's perspective

© 2021 Rosemary Mountain

A smaller 'companion' book with four parts: [1] a wry look at problems hindering music research and proposed strategies to address them, (such as senior 'guides' to help interpret cross-disciplinary research); [2] a survey of various perspectives on music (composer, performer, listener, choreographer, etc.) [3] a discussion of the resulting nuances in terms and concepts depending on perspective and style; and (4) a suggestion of areas (from sound pollution to multimedia) which merit more attention in music training. The author refers to the book as "a collection of footnotes for future books" and as her own "scholarly GPS" - her term for the identification of background influences and filters to provide context for readers.

Rosemary Mountain also has several publications in journals and books from diverse areas in music and cognate research. See website for details.

https://armchair-researcher.com

www.ingramcontent.com/pod-product-compliance
Lightning Source LLC
Chambersburg PA
CBHW060313240426
43661CB00059B/2753